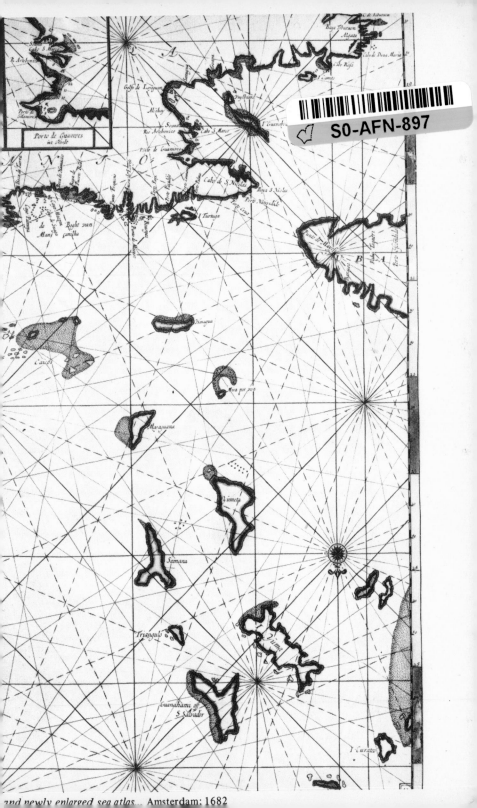

and newly enlarged sea atlas... Amsterdam: 1682

Sir Henry Morgan (1635–1688) *Exquemeling.*

ON THE SPANISH MAIN

OR, SOME ENGLISH FORAYS ON THE
ISTHMUS OF DARIEN. WITH A DESCRIP-
TION OF THE BUCCANEERS AND A
SHORT ACCOUNT OF OLD-TIME
SHIPS AND SAILORS

BY

JOHN MASEFIELD

Naval Institute Press
1972

© Conway Maritime Press Ltd
7 Nelson Road, Greenwich, London SE10

First Published 1906
New Edition 1972
In the United States of America

NAVAL INSTITUTE PRESS
Library of Congress Catalog Card no. 72 86339
ISBN 0 87021 857 3

Printed in Great Britain by
Latimer Trend Ltd., Whitstable, Kent

CONTENTS

CHAPTER I

vii

CONTENTS

CONTENTS

LIST OF ILLUSTRATIONS

ON THE SPANISH MAIN

CHAPTER I

DRAKE'S VOYAGE TO THE WEST INDIES

His quarrel with the Spaniards — His preliminary raids — His
landfall—The secret harbour

FRANCIS DRAKE, the first Englishman to make
himself "redoubtable to the Spaniards" on the
Spanish Main, was born near Tavistock about the year
1545. He was sent to sea, as a lad, aboard a Channel
coaster engaged in trade with the eastern counties,
France and Zeeland. When he was eighteen years of
age he joined his cousin, John Hawkins, then a great
and wealthy merchant, engaged in the slave trade. Four
years later he sailed with Hawkins on a memorable
trading voyage to the Spanish Main. On this occasion
he commanded a small vessel of fifty tons.

The voyage was unfortunate from the beginning, for
the Spaniards had orders from their King to refuse to
trade with any foreigners. Before the English could get
rid of their freight the ships of their squadron were
severely battered by a hurricane, so that they were forced
to put into San Juan d'Ulloa, the port of Vera Cruz,
to refit. While they lay there a Spanish fleet arrived,
carrying a vast quantity of gold and silver for tranship-
ment to Spain. It was not to Hawkins' advantage to
allow this Spanish force to enter the haven, for he feared
that they would treat him as a pirate if they had an

opportunity to do so.   However, the Spaniards came to terms with him, an agreement was signed by both parties, and the Spanish ships were allowed into the port.   The next day the Spaniards treacherously attacked the English squadron, sank one of the ships at her moorings, killed many of the men, captured a number more, and drove the survivors to sea in Drake's ship the *Judith*, and a larger ship called the *Minion*.   It was this treacherous attack (and, perhaps, some earlier treachery not recorded) which made Drake an implacable enemy of the Spaniards for the next twenty-eight years.

After the disaster at San Juan d'Ulloa, Drake endeavoured to obtain some recompense for the losses he had sustained.   But "finding that no recompence could be recovered out of Spain by any of his own means, or by her Majesties letters ; he used such helpes as he might by two severall Voyages into the West Indies."   In the first of these two voyages, in 1570, he had two ships, the *Dragon* and the *Swan*.   In the second, in 1571, he sailed in the *Swan* without company.   The *Swan* was a small vessel of only five and twenty tons, but she was a "lucky" ship, and an incomparable sailer.   We know little of these two voyages, though a Spanish letter (quoted by Mr Corbett) tells us of a Spanish ship he took ; and Thomas Moone, Drake's coxswain, speaks of them as having been "rich and gainfull."   Probably Drake employed a good deal of his time in preparing for a future raid, for when he ventured out in earnest in 1572 he showed himself singularly well acquainted with the town he attacked. The account from which we take our information expressly states that this is what he did.   He went, it says, "to gaine such intelligences as might further him to get some amends for his losse.   And having, in those two Voyages, gotten such certaine notice of the persons and places aymed at, as he thought requisite ; and thereupon with good deliberation, resolved on a third Voyage, he accordingly prepared his Ships and Company . . . as now followes further to be declared."

There can be little doubt that the two tentative voyages were highly profitable, for Drake was able to fit out his third expedition with a care and completeness almost unknown at that time. The ships were "richly furnished, with victuals and apparel for a whole year: and no lesse heedfully provided of all manner of Munition, Artillery, Artificers, stuffe and tooles, that were requisite for such a Man-of-war in such an attempt." He himself, as Admiral of the expedition, commanded the larger ship, the *Pascha* of Plymouth, of seventy tons. His younger brother, John Drake, sailed as captain of the *Swan*. In all there were seventy-three men and boys in the expedition; and we read that they were mostly young men—"the eldest . . . fifty, all the rest under thirty." They were all volunteers—a fact that shows that Drake had gained a reputation for luck in these adventures. Forty-seven of the seventy-three sailed aboard the *Pascha*; while the *Swan* carried the remaining twenty-six, probably with some inconvenience. Carefully stowed away in the holds of the two vessels were "three dainty Pinnases, made in Plimouth, taken asunder all in pieces, to be set up as occasion served." This instance of Drake's forethought makes it very clear that the expedition had been planned with extreme care. The comfort of the men had been studied: witness the supply of "apparell." There was a doctor aboard, though he does not seem to have been "a great proficient" in his art; and the expedition was so unusually healthy that we feel convinced that Drake had some specific for the scurvy.

"On Whitsunday Eve, being the 24 of May, 1572," the two ships "set sayl from out of the Sound of Plimouth," with intent to land at Nombre de Dios (Name of God) a town on the northern coast of the Isthmus of Darien, at that time "the granary of the West Indies, wherein the golden harvest brought from Peru and Mexico to Panama was hoarded up till it could be conveyed into Spain." The wind was steady from the north-east the day they sailed, so that the watchers from the shore must soon have lost sight of them. No doubt the boats of all the ships in the Sound came off to give the adventurers a parting cheer, or, should they need it, a tow to sea. No doubt the two ships were very gay with colours and noisy with the firing of farewells. Then at last, as the sails began to draw, and the water began to bubble from the bows, the trumpeters sounded "A loath to depart," the anchor came to the cathead, and the boats splashed back to Plymouth, their crews jolly with the parting glasses.

The wind that swept the two ships out of port continued steady at north-east, "and gave us a very good passage," taking them within sight of Porto Santo, one of the Madeiras, within twelve days of their leaving Plymouth. The wind continued fair when they stood to the westward, after sighting the Canaries, so that neither ship so much as shortened sail "untill 25 dayes after," when the men in the painted tops descried the high land of Guadaloupe. They stood to the south of Guadaloupe, as though to pass between that island and Dominica, but seeing some Indians busily fishing off a rocky island to the south of Dominica they determined to recruit there before proceeding farther. This island was probably Marygalante, a pleasant island full of trees, a sort of summer fishing ground for the Dominican Indians. There is good anchorage off many parts of it; and Drake anchored to the south, sending the men ashore to live in tents for their refreshment. They also watered their ships while lying at anchor "out of one of those goodly

rivers which fall down off the mountain." Running water
was always looked upon as less wholesome than spring
water; and, perhaps, they burnt a bag of biscuit on the
beach, and put the charcoal in the casks to destroy any
possible infection. They saw no Indians on the island,
though they came across "certain poore cottages built with
Palmito boughs and branches," in which they supposed
the Indians lodged when engaged upon their fishery.
Having filled the casks, and stowed them aboard again,
the ships weighed anchor, and sailed away south towards
the mainland. On the fifth day, keeping well to seaward,
thirty miles from the shore, to avoid discovery, they made
the high land of Santa Martha on "the Terra Firma."
Having made the landfall they sailed westward into the
Gulf of Darien, and in six days more (during two of
which the ships were becalmed) they came to a secret
anchorage which Drake had discovered in his former
voyage. He had named it Port Pheasant, "by reason of
the great store of those goodly fowls which he and his
Company did then dayly kill and feed on in that place."
"It was a fine round Bay, of very safe harbour for all
winds, lying between two high points, not past half a
cable's length (or a hundred yards) over at the mouth,
but within eight or ten cables' length every way, having
ten or twelve fadome water, more or lesse, full of good
fish, the soile also very fruitfull." Drake had been there
"within a year and few days before," and had left the
shore clear of tangle, with alleys and paths by which men
might walk in the woods, after goodly fowls or otherwise;
but a year of that steaming climate had spoiled his
handiwork. The tangle of many-blossomed creepers and
succulent green grasses had spread across the paths "as
that we doubted at first whether this were the same place
or no." We do not know where this romantic harbour
lies, for the Gulf of Darien is still unsurveyed. We know

only that it is somewhere nearly equidistant from Santiago de Tolu (to the east) and Nombre de Dios (to the west). Roughly speaking, it was 120 miles from either place, so that "there dwelt no Spaniards within thirty-five leagues." Before the anchors were down, and the sails furled Drake ordered out the boat, intending to go ashore. As they neared the landing-place they spied a smoke in the woods—a smoke too big to come from an Indian's fire. Drake ordered another boat to be manned with musketeers and bowmen, suspecting that the Spaniards had found the place, and that the landing would be disputed. On beaching the boats they discovered "evident markes" that a Plymouth ship, under the command of one John Garret, had been there but a day or two before. He had left a plate of lead, of the sort supplied to ships to nail across shot-holes, "nailed fast to a mighty great tree," some thirty feet in girth. On the lead a letter had been cut:

CAPTAIN DRAKE,

if you fortune to come to this Port, make hast away; for the Spanyards which you had with you here the last year, have bewrayed this place, and taken away all that you left here. I departed from hence this present 7 of July, 1572.

Your very loving friend,

JOHN GARRET.

The smoke was from a fire which Garret and his men had kindled in a great hollow tree, that was probably rotted into touchwood. It had smouldered for five days or more, sending up a thick smoke, to warn any coming to the harbour to proceed with caution.

The announcement that the place was known to the Spaniards did not weigh very heavily upon Drake; nor

is it likely that he suffered much from the loss of his
hidden stores, for nothing of any value could have been
left in such a climate. He determined not to leave
"before he had built his Pinnaces," and therefore, as
soon as the ships were moored, he ordered the pieces to
be brought ashore "for the Carpenters to set up." The
rest of the company was set to the building of a fort
upon the beach by the cutting down of trees, "and haling
them together with great Pullies and halsers." The fort
was built in the form of a pentagon, with a sort of sea-gate
opening on the bay, for the easy launching of the pinnaces. This gate could be closed at night by the drawing
of a log across the opening. They dug no trench, but
cleared the ground instead, so that for twenty yards all
round the stockhouse there was nothing to hinder a
marksman or afford cover to an enemy. Beyond that
twenty yards the forest closed in, with its wall of living
greenery, with trees "of a marvellous height" tangled
over with the brilliant blossoms of many creepers. The
writer of the account seems to have been one of the
building party that sweated the logs into position. "The
wood of those trees," he writes, "is as heavie, or heavier,
than Brasil or Lignum Vitæ, and is in colour white."

The very next day an English barque came sailing into
the anchorage, with two prizes in her wake—"a Spanish
Carvell of Sivell," which had despatches aboard her for
the Governor of Nombre de Dios, and a shallop with oars,
picked up off Cape Blanco to the eastward. She was the
property of Sir Edward Horsey, at that time Governor
of the Isle of Wight, a gallant gentleman, who received
"sweetmeats and Canarie wine" from French pirates
plying in the Channel. Her captain was one James
Rawse, or Rause; and she carried thirty men, some of
whom had been with Drake the year before. Captain
Rause, on hearing Drake's intentions, was eager "to

joyne in consort with him." We may well imagine that Drake cared little for his company; but conditions were agreed upon, an agreement signed, and the two crews set to work together. Within seven days the pinnaces had been set up, and launched, and stored with all things necessary. Then early one morning (the 20th of July) the ships got their anchors, and hoisted sail for Nombre de Dios, arriving three days later at the Isles of Pines, a group of little islands covered with fir-trees, not far to the west of the mouth of the Gulf of Darien. At the Pine Islands they found two frigates of Nombre de Dios, "lading plank and timber from thence," the soft fir wood being greatly in demand on the mainland, where the trees were harder, and difficult to work. The wood was being handled by negroes, who gave Drake some intelligence of the state of affairs at the little town he intended to attack. They said that the town was in a state of siege, expecting to be attacked at any moment by the armies of the Cimmeroons, who had "neere surprised it" only six weeks before. The Cimmeroons were "a black people, which about eighty yeares past, fledd from the Spaniards their Masters, by reason of their cruelty, and are since growne to a nation, under two Kings of their owne: the one inhabiteth to the west, th'other to the East of the way from Nombre de Dios to Panama." They were much dreaded by the Spaniards, with whom they were at constant war. The late alarm had caused the Governor to send to Panama for troops, and "certaine souldiers" were expected daily to aid in the defence of the town.

Having gathered this intelligence Drake landed the negroes on the mainland, so that they might rejoin their countrymen if they wished to do so. In any case, by landing them so far from home he prevented them from giving information of his being in those waters. "For hee was loath to put the towne to too much charge (which hee knew they would willingly bestowe) in providing before hand, for his entertainment." But being anxious to avoid all possibility of discovery " he hastened his going thither, with as much speed and secrecy as possibly he could." It had taken him three days to get to the Isles of Pines from his secret harbour—a distance certainly not more than 120 miles. He now resolved to leave the three ships and the carvel—all four grown more or less foul-bottomed and slow—in the care of Captain Rause, with just sufficient men to work them. With the three dainty pinnaces and the oared shallop that Rause had taken, he hoped to make rather swifter progress than he had been making. He took with him in the four boats fifty-three of his own company and twenty of Captain Rause's men, arranging them in order according to the military text-book: "six Targets, six Firepikes, twelve Pikes, twenty-four Muskets and Callivers, sixteene Bowes, and six Partizans, two Drums, and two Trumpets"—making seventy-four men in all, the seventy-fourth being the commander, Drake. Having furnished the boats for the sea with his usual care Drake parted company, and sailed slowly to the westward, making about fifteen miles a day under oars and sails. Perhaps he sailed only at night, in order to avoid discovery and to rest his men. Early on the morning of the 28th July they landed "at the Island of Cativaas," or Catives, off the mouth of the St Francis River. Here Drake delivered them "their severall armes, which hitherto he had kept very faire and safe in good caske," so that neither the heavy dew nor the sea-water should rust them or wet the powder. He drilled them on the shore before the heat of the sun became too great, and after the drill he spoke to them "after his manner," declaring "the greatnes of the hope of good things that was there, the weaknesse of the towne being unwalled, and the hope he had of prevailing to recompence his wrongs

. . . especially . . . as hee should be utterly undiscovered."
In the afternoon, when the sun's strength was past, they
set sail again, standing in close to the shore "that wee
might not be descried of the watch-house." By sunset
they were within two leagues of the point of the bay to
the north-north-east of the town ; and here they lowered
their sails, and dropped anchor, "riding so untill it was
darke night." When the night had fallen they stood in
shore again, "with as much silence as wee could," till they
were past the point of the harbour "under the high land,"
and "there wee stayed all silent, purposing to attempt the
towne in the dawning of the day, after that wee had re-
posed ourselves for a while."

NOMBRE DE DIOS

Nombre de Dios was founded by Diego di Niqueza
early in the sixteenth century, about the year 1510.
It received its name from a remark the founder made
on his first setting foot ashore: "Here we will found a
settlement in the name of God." It was never a large
place, for the bay lay exposed to the prevalent winds,
being open to the north and north-east. There was fair
holding ground ; but the bay was shallow and full of rocks,
and a northerly gale always raised such a sea that a
ship was hardly safe with six anchors out. The district
was very unhealthy, and the water found there was bad
and in little quantity. There was, however, a spring of
good water on an island at the mouth of the harbour.
To the shoreward there were wooded hills, with marshy
ground on their lower slopes, feeding a little river empty-
ing to the north of the town. The houses came right down
to the sea, and the trees right down to the houses, so that
"tigers [i.e. jaguars] often came into the town," to carry

away dogs, fowls, and children. Few ships lay there without burying a third of their hands ; for the fever raged there, as it rages in some of the Brazilian ports at the present time. The place was also supposed to favour the spread of leprosy. The road to Panama entered the town at the south-east ; and there was a gate at this point, though the town was never walled about. The city seems to have been built about a great central square, with straight streets crossing at right angles. Like Cartagena and Porto Bello, it was as dull as a city of the dead until the galleons came thither from Cartagena to take on board " the chests of gold and silver" received from the Governor of Panama and the golden lands to the south. When the galleons anchored, the merchants went ashore with their goods, and pitched sailcloth booths for them in the central square, and held a gallant fair till they were sold—most of the bartering being done by torchlight, in the cool of the night. Panama was distant some fifty-five miles ; and the road thither was extremely bad, owing to the frequent heavy rains and the consequent flooding of the trackway. At the time of Drake's raid, there were in all some sixty wooden houses in the place, inhabited in the *tiempo muerto*, or dead time, by about thirty people. "The rest," we read, "doe goe to Panama after the fleet is gone." Those who stayed must have had a weary life of it, for there could have been nothing for them to do save to go a-fishing. The fever never left the place, and there was always the dread of the Cimmeroons. Out in the bay there was the steaming water, with a few rotten hulks waiting to be cast ashore, and two or three rocky islets sticking up for the sea to break against. There was nothing for an inhabitant to do except to fish, and nothing for him to see except the water, with the dripping green trees beside it, and, perhaps, an advice boat slipping past for Cartagena. Once a year an express came to the bay

from Panama to say that the Peru fleet had arrived at
that port. A letter was then sent to Cartagena or to San
Juan d'Ulloa to order the great galleons there anchored
to come to collect the treasure, and convey it into Spain.
Before they dropped anchor in the Nombre de Dios bay
that city was filled to overflowing by soldiers and merchants from Panama and the adjacent cities. Waggons
of maize and cassava were dragged into the streets, with
numbers of fowls and hogs. Lodgings rose in value, until
a "middle chamber" could not be had for less than
1000 crowns. Desperate efforts were made to collect
ballast for the supply ships. Then the treasure trains
from Panama began to arrive. Soldiers marched in,
escorting strings of mules carrying chests of gold and
silver, goatskins filled with bezoar stones, and bales of
vicuna wool. The town became musical with the bells
of the mules' harness. Llamas spat and hissed at the
street corners. The Plaza became a scene of gaiety and
bustle. Folk arrived hourly by the muddy track from
Panama. Ships dropped anchor hourly, ringing their
bells and firing salutes of cannon. The grand fair then
began, and the city would be populous and stirring till
the galleons had cleared the harbour on the voyage to
Spain. As soon as the fleet was gone the city emptied
as rapidly as it had filled. The merchants and merry-
makers vanished back to Panama, and the thirty odd
wretched souls who stayed, began their dreary vigil until
the next year, when the galleons returned. In 1584, on
the report of Antonio Baptista, surveyor to the King of
Spain, the trade was removed to Porto Bello, a beautiful
bay, discovered and named by Columbus, lying some
twenty miles farther to the west. It is a good harbour
for all winds, and offers every convenience for the careen-
ing of vessels. The surveyor thought it in every way a
superior harbour. "Neither," he writes, "will so many

die there as there daily doe in Nombre de Dios." By
the middle of the seventeenth century the ruins of the
old town were barely discernible; but all traces of them
have long since disappeared. Dampier (writing of the
year 1682) says that: " I have lain ashore in the place
where that City stood; but it is all overgrown with
Wood; so as toe leave noe sign that any Town hath been
there." A thick green cane brake has overgrown the
Plaza. The battery has crumbled away. The church bell
which made such a clatter has long since ceased to sound.
The latest Admiralty Chart ignores the place.

The Cimmeroons frequently attacked the city while
it was in occupation. Once they captured and destroyed
it.

Drake visited the town a second time in 1595. It was
then a "bigge" town, having large streets and "houses
very hie, all built of timber," "one church very faire," and
"a show in their shops of great store of merchandises that
had been there."[1] There was a mill above the town,
and a little watch-house "upon the top of another hill
in the woods." To the east there was a fresh river "with
houses, and all about it gardens." The native quarter was
some miles away in the woods. Drake burned the town,
a deed which caused the inhabitants to migrate to Porto
Bello. It was at Nombre de Dios that Drake contracted
the flux of which he died. The town witnessed his first
triumph and final discomfiture.

[1] This was eleven years after the royal mandate ordering the transference of
the main trade of the place to Porto Bello. Perhaps the town retained much
of the trade, in spite of the mandate, as the transference involved the making
of a new mule track across the bogs and crags between Venta Cruz and Porto
Bello. Such a track would have taken several years to lay.

[NOTE.

Note.—The authorities for this and the following chapters are:
1. "Sir Francis Drake Reviv'd" (first published in 1626), by Philip Nichols, Preacher, helped, no doubt, by Drake himself and some of his company. 2. The scanty notice of the raid given in Hakluyt. 3. The story of Lopez Vaz, a Portuguese, also in Hakluyt.

For the description of Nombre de Dios I have trusted to the account of Drake's last voyage printed in Hakluyt, vol. iii. p. 587. In the same collection there is a translation from a very interesting report by a Spanish commissioner to the King of Spain. This paper gives reasons for the transference of the town to Porto Bello. One or two Ruttiers, or Mariner's Guides, make mention of the port, and of these the best is given in Hakluyt. It is also mentioned (but very curtly) in Herrera's History, in Dampier's Voyages, and in the account left by Champlain after his short visit to Panama. I know of no plan or picture of the place. The drawing reproduced here, from Schenk's "Hecatompolis," is purely imaginary, however pretty. For my remarks on "Cruces," or Venta Cruz, I am indebted to friends who have lived many years in Panama, and to an interesting article in *The Geographical Journal* (December-July 1903, p. 325), by Colonel G. E. Church, M. Am. Soc. C.E.

CHAPTER II

THE ATTACK ON NOMBRE DE DIOS

The treasure of the Indies—The Bastimentos—A Spanish herald

IT may now have been ten o'clock at night, and we may reckon that the boats were still four or five miles from the town, the lights of which, if any burned, must have been plainly visible to the south and south-south-west. To many of those who rocked there in the bay the coming tussle was to be the first engagement. The night wind may have seemed a little chilly, and the night and the strange town full of terrors. The men fell to talking in whispers, and the constraint and strangeness of it all, the noise of the clucking water, the cold of the night, and the thought of what the negro lumbermen had said, began to get upon their nerves. They talked of the strength of the town (and indeed, although it was an open bay, without good water, it had at that time much of the importance of Porto Bello, in the following century). They talked "especially" of the reported troop of soldiers from Panama, for Spanish infantry were the finest in the world, and the presence of a company in addition to the garrison would be enough to beat off the little band in the boats. Drake heard these conversations, and saw his young men getting out of hand, and "thought it best to put these conceits out of their heads." As the moon rose he persuaded them "that it was the day dawning"—a fiction made the more easy by the intervention of the high land between the watchers and the horizon. By the

15

growing light the boats stole farther in, arriving "at the
towne, a large hower sooner than first was purposed. For
wee arrived there by three of the clock after midnight."
It happened that a "ship of *Spaine*, of sixtie Tunnes, laden
with Canary wines and other commodities" had but newly
arrived in the bay, "and had not yet furld her sprit-saile."
It was the custom for ships to discharge half of their
cargoes at one of the islands in the bay, so as to draw less
water when they ventured farther in. Perhaps this ship of
Spain was about to discharge her butts and tierces. At
any rate her men were on deck, and the light of the moon
enabled them to see the four pinnaces, "an extraordinary
number" in so small a port, rowing hard, "with many
Oares," towards the landing. The Spaniards sent away
their "Gundeloe," or small boat (gondola, as we should
say), to warn the townsmen; but Drake edged a little to
the west, cutting in between the boat and the shore,
so as to force her "to goe to th'other side of the Bay."
Drake's boats then got ashore upon the sands, not
more than twenty yards from the houses, directly under
a battery.. There was no quay, and no sea-sentry save a
single gunner, asleep among the guns, who fled as they
clambered up the redoubt. Inside the little fort there
were six great pieces of brass ordnance, some demi- some
whole culverin, throwing shot of 10-18 lbs. weight for a
distance of a mile. It did not take long to dismount
these guns, and spike them, by beating soft metal
nails into the touch-holes, and snapping them off flush
with the orifice. But though the men worked quickly
the gunner was quicker yet. He ran through the narrow
streets, shouting the alarm, and the town woke up like
one man, expecting that the Cimmeroons were on them
from the woods. Someone ran to the church, and set the
great bell swinging. The windows went up, and the
doors slammed, as the townsfolk hurried to their weapons,

and out into the streets. The place rang with cries and with the rapid beating of the drums, for the drummers ran about the streets beating vigorously to rouse out the soldiers. Drake made the battery harmless and set a guard of twelve men over the boats on the sand. He then marched hurriedly to the little hill commanding the bay, to the east of the houses; for he had heard some talk of a battery being placed there, "which might scour round about the town," and he wished to put it out of action before venturing upon the city. He left half his company, about thirty men, to keep the foot of the hill, and climbed to the summit, where he found a "very fit place prepared," but no guns in position. He returned to the company at the foot of the mount, and bade his brother, with John Oxnam, or Oxenham, a gallant captain, and sixteen men, "to go about, behind the King's Treasure House, and enter near the easter end of the Market Place." He himself with the rest would pass up the broad street into the market-place with sound of drum and trumpet. The firepikes, "divided half to the one, and half to the other company, served no less for fright to the enemy than light of our men, who by this means might discern every place very well as if it were near day." The drums beat up gallantly, the trumpets blew points of war, and the poor citizens, scared from their beds, and not yet sure of their enemy, stood shivering in the dawn, "marvelling what the matter might be." In a few moments the two companies were entering the Plaza, making a dreadful racket as they marched, to add to the confusion of the townsfolk, who thought them far stronger than they really were. The soldiers of the garrison, with some of the citizens, fell into some sort of order "at the south east end of the Market Place, near the Governor's House, and not far from the gate of the town." They chose this position because it secured them a retreat, in the event of a repulse, along the road to Panama. The western end of the Plaza had been hung with lines, from which lighted matches dangled, so that the enemy might think that troops were there, "whereas indeed there were not past two or three that taught these lines to dance," and even these ran away as soon as the firepikes displayed the fraud. The church bell was still ringing at the end of the Plaza, and the townsfolk were still crying out as they ran for Panama, when Drake's party stormed into the square from the road leading to the sea. As they hove in sight the Spanish troops gave them "a jolly hot volley of shot," aimed very low, so as to ricochet from the sand. Drake's men at once replied with a volley from their calivers and a flight of arrows, "fine roving shafts," which did great execution. Without waiting to reload they at once charged in upon the Spaniards, coming at once "to push of pike" and point and edge. The hurry of the surprise was such that the Spaniards had no side-arms, and when once the English had closed, their troops were powerless. As the parties met, the company under Oxenham came into the Plaza at the double, by the eastern road, with their trumpets blowing and the firepikes alight. The Spaniards made no further fight of it. They flung their weapons down, and fled along the forest road. For a little distance the cheering sailors followed them, catching their feet in muskets and linstocks, which the troops had flung away in their hurry.

Having dispersed the enemy, the men reformed in the Plaza, "where a tree groweth hard by the Cross." Some hands were detailed to stop the ringing of the alarm bell, which still clanged crazily in the belfry ; but the church was securely fastened, and it was found impossible to stop the ringing without setting the place on fire, which Drake forbade. While the men were trying to get into the church, Drake forced two or three prisoners to show him the Governor's house, where the mule trains from Panama were unloaded. Only the silver was stored in that place; for the gold, pearls, and jewels, " being there once entered by the King's officer," were locked in a treasure-house, "very strongly built of lime and stone," at a little distance from the Cross, not far from the water-side. At the Governor's house they found the door wide open, and "a fair gennet ready saddled" waiting for the Governor to descend. A torch or candle was burning on the balcony, and by its light the adventurers saw "a huge heap of silver" in the open space beneath the dwelling-rooms. It was a pile of bars of silver, heaped against the wall in a mass that was roughly estimated to be seventy feet in length, ten feet across, and twelve feet high—each bar weighing about forty pounds. The men were for breaking their ranks in order to plunder the pile; but Drake bade them stand to their arms. The King's treasure-house, he said, contained more gold and pearls than they could take away; and presently, he said, they would break the place open, and see what lay within. He then marched his men back into the Plaza.

All this time the town was filled with confusion. Guns were being fired and folk were crying out in the streets. It was not yet light, and certain of the garrison, who had been quartered outside the city, ran to and fro with burning matches, shouting out "Que gente? Que gente?" The town at that time was very full of people, and this noise and confusion, and the sight of so many running figures, began to alarm the boat guard on the beach. One Diego, a negro, who had joined them on the sands, had told them that the garrison had been reinforced only eight days before by 150 Spanish soldiers.

This report, coupled with the anxiety of their position, seems to have put the boat party into a panic. They sent off messengers to Drake, saying that the pinnaces were "in danger to be taken," and that the force would be overwhelmed as soon as it grew light enough for the Spaniards to see the littleness of the band which had attacked them. Diego's words confirmed the statements of the lumbermen at the Isles of Pines. The men of Drake's party were young. They had never fought before. They had been on the rack, as it were, for several days. They were now quite out of hand, and something of their panic began to spread among the party on the Plaza. Before Drake could do more than despatch his brother, with John Oxenham, to reassure the guard, and see how matters stood, the situation became yet more complicated. "A mighty shower of rain, with a terrible storm of thunder and lightning," burst furiously upon them, making such a roaring that none could hear his own voice. As in all such storms, the rain came down in a torrent, hiding the town from view in a blinding downpour. The men ran for the shelter of "a certain shade or penthouse, at the western end of the King's Treasure House," but before they could gain the cover some of their bowstrings were wetted "and some of our match and powder hurt." As soon as the shelter had been reached, the bowstrings were shifted, the guns reprimed, and the match changed upon the linstocks. While the industrious were thus employed, a number of the hands began talking of the reports which had reached them from the boats. They were "muttering of the forces of the town," evidently anxious to be gone from thence, or at least stirring. Drake heard the muttered talk going up and down the shed, and promptly told the men that he had brought them to the mouth of the Treasure of the World, and that if they came away without it they might blame nobody but themselves.

At the end of a "long half-hour" the storm began to abate, and Drake felt that he must put an end to the

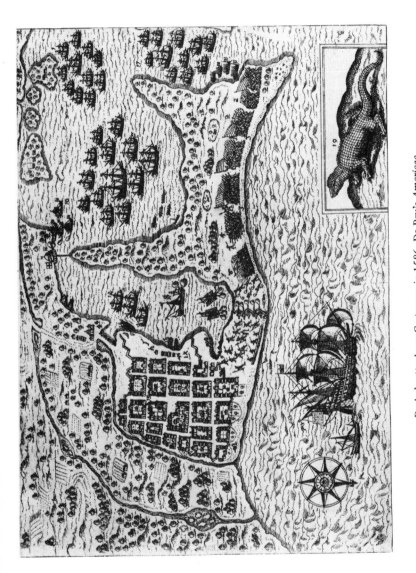

Drake's attack on Cartagena in 1586. De Bry's *Americae.*

panic. It was evidently dangerous to allow the men any
" longer leisure to demur of those doubts," nor was it safe
to give the enemy a chance of rallying. He stepped forward, bidding his brother, with John Oxenham and his
party, to break open the King's treasure-house, while he,
with the remainder of the hands, maintained the Plaza.
" But as he stepped forward his strength and sight and
speech failed him, and he began to faint for want of
blood." He had been hit in the leg with a bullet at
the first encounter, yet in the greatness of his heart he
had not complained, although suffering considerable pain.
He had seen that many of his men had "already gotten
many good things" from the booths and houses in the Plaza,
and he knew very well that these men would take the
first opportunity to slink away down to the boats. He
had, therefore, said nothing about his wound, nor was it
light enough for his men to see that he was bleeding.
On his fainting they noticed that the sand was bloody,
"the blood having filled the very first prints which our
footsteps made"—a sight which amazed and dismayed
them, for they "thought it not credible" that a man
should "spare so much blood and live." They gave him
a cordial to drink, "wherewith he recovered himself," and
bound his scarf about his leg "for the stopping of the
blood." They then entreated him "to be content to go
with them aboard," there to have his wound probed and
dressed before adventuring farther. This did not satisfy
Drake, for he knew very well that if the Spaniards rallied,
the town would be lost, for it was "utterly impossible,
at least very unlikely, that ever they should, for that
time, return again, to recover the state in which they
now were." He begged them to leave him where he
was, and to get the treasure, for "it were more honourable
for himself to jeopard his life for so great a benefit, than
to leave off so high an enterprise unperformed." But to

this the men would not listen. With Drake, their captain, alive "they might recover wealth sufficient" at any time, but with Drake dead "they should hardly be able to recover home." Those who had picked up a little booty in the raid were only too glad of an excuse to get to the boats, while those who were most eager to break the treasure-house, would not allow Drake to put his life in hazard. Drake, poor man, was spent with loss of blood, and could not reason with them, so that, "with force mingled with fair entreaty, they bare him aboard his pinnace, and so abandoned a most rich spoil for the present, only to preserve their Captain's life." It was just daybreak when they got to the boats, so that they were able to take stock of each other in the early morning light before shoving off from the beach. They had lost but one man, "a trumpeter," who was shot dead in the Plaza in the first assault, "his Trumpet still in his hand." Many were wounded, but the Captain's wound seems to have been the most serious. As they rowed out from the town the surgeons among them provided remedies and salves for the wounded. As they neared the open sea the men took the opportunity to attack "the aforesaid ship of wines," for "the more comfort of the company." They made her a prize with no great trouble, but before they got her clear of the haven they received a shot or two from the dismantled battery. One of the culverins which they had tumbled to the ground was remounted by some of the garrison, "so as they made a shot at us." The shot did not hit the mark, and the four boats, with their prize, got clear away to the Isle of Bastimentos, or Isle of Victuals, about a league to the westward of the harbour. They stayed there for the next two days, to cure the wounded men and to refresh themselves, "in the goodly gardens which we there found." The island was stocked with dainty roots and fruits, "besides great plenty of poultry," for it served the citizens as a farm and market-garden, "from which their fresh provisions were derived." Soon after they had come to anchor, and established themselves among the fruit-trees, a flag of truce came off from the Governor of the city. It was carried by a Spanish captain, who had come to Nombre de Dios with the company of troops from Panama. He was a handsome gentleman, of a delicate carriage and of an elaborate politeness. He was come, of course, as a spy, but he began with the assurance that he came "of mere good will," to see the heroes who had attempted the town with so small a party. At the first, he said, the townsfolk had thought them Frenchmen, from whom they looked for little mercy, but that afterwards, when the arrows had shown them that they were English, they had less fear, for they knew the humanity of that race. Although, he said, his curiosity to see such brave folk were sufficient warrant for his adventuring among them, he had also a commission from the Governor. That gentleman wished to know whether their captain was the same Captain Drake, of whom some of the townsfolk talked as being so kind to his prisoners. He then asked whether the arrows used in the battle in the Plaza had been poisoned, for many Spaniards had been wounded by them, and would fain know how to treat the wounds. Lastly he wished to know whether they were in need of victuals or other necessaries, pledging the Governor's word that he would do all he could to supply anything they wanted. The questions seem to us a little transparent, and so they seemed to Drake, but Drake was always a courteous and ceremonious gentleman. He replied that he was the Captain Drake they meant; that "it was never his manner to use poisoned arrows"; that the wounds could be cured by the usual methods; and that as for wants, the Isle of Bastimentos would supply

him. He wanted nothing, he said, " but some of that
special commodity which that country yielded." And,
therefore, he advised the Governor " to hold open his eyes,
for before he departed, if God lent him life and leave, he
meant to reap some of their harvest, which they got out
of the earth, and send into Spain to trouble all the earth."
The answer seems to have nettled the Spanish spy, for he
asked (" if he might, without offence, move such a question ")
why the English had left the town when 360 tons of
silver, with gold to a far greater value, had been lying
at their mercy. Drake showed him the " true cause " of
his unwilling retreat to the pinnaces. The answer moved
the Spaniard to remark that " the English had no less
reason in departing, than courage in attempting,"—a remark
made with a mental note that the townsfolk would be well
advised to leave this Drake alone on his island, without
sending boats out to attack him. Drake then entertained
the spy to dinner, " with great favour and courteous entertainment, and such gifts as most contented him." As
he made his way to his boat after dinner he vowed and
protested that " he was never so much honoured of any
in his life." He must have had a curious story for the
Governor when he got ashore to the town.

As soon as the trumpets had sounded the departure
of the flag of truce, Drake sent for Diego, the negro, who
had joined the boat party in the morning. From Diego
he learned many " intelligences of importance," none of
them, perhaps, more grateful to Drake than the news that
his name was highly honoured among the Maroons or
Cimmeroons. Diego begged that Drake would give him
an opportunity of treating with the chiefs of these savages,
as by their help, he said, they " might have gold and
silver enough." The matter was debated among the
company, while Drake gave effect to another of his plans.
Not more than thirty miles away along the coast was a

certain river, "the River of Chagres," which trended in a south-easterly direction towards Panama across the isthmus. It was navigable to within six leagues of Panama, and at the point to which it was navigable there stood "a little town called Venta Cruz." When the road from Panama to Nombre de Dios was impracticable, owing to the rains, or the raids of the Maroons, the treasure was carried to Venta Cruz, and there shipped aboard swift vessels, built for oars and sails, which carried the precious stuff to Nombre de Dios. Drake had a mind to look into Venta Cruz to surprise some of the treasure on its way. He, therefore, sent away his brother, with two pinnaces and a steady man named Ellis Hixom, to examine the Chagres River, and to bring back a report of its fitness for boats such as theirs. Having seen them stand to the west, Drake ordered his men aboard early in the morning of the 31st July. The sweeps were shipped and the sails hoisted, and the pinnaces made off with their captured wine ship to rejoin Captain Rause at the Isles of Pines, or Port Plenty. They arrived at their haven on the evening of the 1st of August, after a sail of thirty-six hours. Captain Rause was angry that the raid had not been more successful, and felt that it was useless to stay longer in those seas, now that the Spaniards knew that they were on the coast. He waited till the pinnaces returned from Chagres River, as some of his hands were in them ; but as soon as they arrived he parted company, after dissolving partnership with Drake. Drake seems to have been glad to see him go.

CHAPTER III

THE CRUISE OFF THE MAIN

The cruise of the pinnaces—Cartagena—The secret haven—Death
of John Drake

WHILE they were waiting for the pinnaces Drake
had the ships set in order, the arms scoured, and
everything made ready for the next adventure. He had
taken Nombre de Dios so easily that he felt confident
of treating Cartagena, the chiefest town in those waters,
in the same way. On the 7th of August he set sail
for Cartagena with his two ships and three pinnaces,
making no attempt upon the mainland as he sailed, as
he did not wish to be discovered. He met with calms
and light airs on the passage, and did not arrive off
Cartagena until the evening of the 13th August. He
came to anchor in seven-fathom water between the islands
of Charesha (which we cannot now identify) and St
Barnards, now known as San Barnardo. As soon as the
sails were furled, Drake manned his three pinnaces, and
rowed about the island into the harbour of Cartagena,
"where, at the very entry, he found a frigate at anchor."
He hooked on to her chains, and boarded her, finding
her an easy spoil, for she had been left in the care of
"only one old man." They asked this old sailor where
the rest of the company had gone. He answered that
they were gone ashore in their gundeloe that evening,
to fight about a mistress, adding that about two hours
before, a pinnace had gone past under sail, with her oars
out, and the men rowing furiously. Her men had hailed

26

his vessel as they passed, asking whether any French or English men had been there. Upon answer that there had been none they bade him look to himself, and rowed on up the coast. Within an hour of their going past the harbour the city batteries had fired many cannon, as though some danger were toward. One of the old man's mates had then gone aloft "to descry what might be the cause." He had looked over the narrow neck of land which shuts the harbour from the sea, and had espied "divers frigates and small shipping bringing themselves within the Castle." This report showed Drake that he had been discovered, but the information did not greatly move him. He gathered from the old mariner that a great ship of Seville lay moored just round the next point, with her yards across, "being bound the next morning for St Domingo," or Hispaniola. Drake "took this old man into his pinnace to verify that which he had informed, and rowed towards this ship." As he drew near, the Spanish mariners hailed them, asking "whence the shallops came." Drake answered: "From Nombre de Dios." His answer set the Spaniards cursing and damning him for a heretic English buccaneer. "We gave no heed to their words," says the narrative, but hooked on to the chains and ports, on the starboard bow, starboard quarter, and port beam, and laid her aboard without further talk. It was something of a task to get on board, for the ship stood high in the water, being of 240 tons, (and as far as we can judge) in ballast. Having gained the ship's waist they tossed the gratings and hatch covers down into the lower decks. The Spaniards gave up the ship without fighting, and retired, with their weapons, to the hold. Two or three of their younger seamen went forward, and hid in the manger, where they were found as soon as the dark decks were lit by a lantern from the pinnaces. The raiders then cut the ship's cables, and towed her "without the island into the sound right afore the town," just beyond the shot of the citizens' great guns. As they towed her out, the town took the alarm, the bells were rung, thirty great cannon were fired, and the garrison, both horse and foot, well armed with calivers, marched down "to the very point of the wood," to impeach them "if they might" in their going out to sea. The next morning (Drake being still within the outer harbour) he captured two Spanish frigates "in which there were two, who called themselves King's Scrivanos [notaries] the one of Cartagena, the other of Veragua." The boats, which were sparsely manned, had been at Nombre de Dios at the time of the raid. They were now bound for Cartagena with double letters of advice, "to certify that Captain Drake had been at Nombre de Dios, and taken it; and had it not been that he was hurt with some blessed shot, by all likelihood he had sacked it. He was yet still upon the coast," ran the letter, "and they should therefore carefully prepare for him."

Sailing out of the haven (by the Boca Chica, or Little Mouth) Drake set his pinnaces ashore, and stood away to the San Barnardo Islands, to the south of the town, where he found "great store of fish" as a change of diet for his men. He then cruised up and down among the islands, considering what he should attempt. He had been discovered at the two chief cities on the Main, but he had not yet made his voyage (*i.e.* it had not yet paid expenses), and until he had met with the Maroons, and earned "a little comfortable dew of Heaven," he meant to stay upon the coast. He, therefore, planned to diminish his squadron, for with the two ships to keep it was difficult to man the pinnaces, and the pinnaces had proved peculiarly fitted for the work in hand. With one ship destroyed, and the other converted into a storeship, his movements would, he thought, be much less hampered; "but knowing the affection of his company, how loath they were to leave either of their ships, being both so good sailers and so well furnished; he purposed in himself some policy to make them most willing to effect what he intended." He, therefore, sent for Thomas Moone, who was carpenter aboard the *Swan*, and held a conference with him in the cabin. Having pledged him to secrecy, he gave him an order to scuttle that swift little ship in the middle of the second watch, or two in the morning. He was "to go down secretly into the well of the ship, and with a spike-gimlet to bore three holes, as near the keel as he could, and lay something against it [oakum or the like] that the force of the water entering, might make no great noise, nor be discovered by a boiling up." Thomas Moone "at the hearing hereof" was utterly dismayed, for to him the project seemed flat burglary as ever was committed. Why, he asked, should the Captain want to sink so good a ship, a ship both "new and strong," in which they had sailed together in two "rich and gainfull" voyages? If the Captain's brother (John Drake, who was master of the *Swan*) and the rest of the company (twenty-six hands in all) should catch him at such practices he thought verily they would heave him overboard. However, Drake promised that the matter should be kept secret "till all of them should be glad of it." On these terms Moone consented to scuttle the *Swan* that night.

The next morning, a little after daybreak, Drake called away his pinnace, "proposing to go a-fishing." Rowing down to the *Swan* he hailed her, asking his brother to go with him. John Drake was in his bunk at the time, and replied that "he would follow presently," or if it would please him to stay a very little he would attend him. Drake saw that the deed was done; for the *Swan* was slowly settling. He would not stay for his brother, but asked casually, "as making no great account of it," why their barque was so deep in the sea. John Drake thought little of the question, but sent a man down to the steward, who had charge of the hold, to inquire "whether there were any water in the ship, or what other cause might be?" The steward, "hastily stepping down at his usual scuttle," was wet to the waist before he reached the foot of the ladder. Very greatly scared he hurried out of the hold, "as if the water had followed him," crying out that the ship was full of water. John Drake at once called all hands to mend ship, sending some below to find the leak and the remainder to the pumps. The men turned to "very willingly," so that "there was no need to hasten them," and John Drake left them at their work while he reported the "strange chance" to his brother. He could not understand how it had happened. They had not pumped twice in six weeks before, and now they had six feet of water in the hold. He hoped his brother would give him "leave from attending him in fishing," as he wished to find the leak without delay. Drake offered to send the *Pascha's* men abroad to take a spell at the pumps, but this John Drake did not wish. He had men enough, he said; and he would like his brother to continue his fishing, so that they might have fresh fish for dinner. On getting back to the *Swan* he found that the pumps had gained very little on the leak, "yet such was their love to the bark, . . . that they ceased not, but to the utmost of their strength laboured all that they might, till three in the afternoon." By that time the *Pascha's* men, helped by Drake himself, had taken turn about at the pump brakes, and the pumping had been carried on for eight or nine hours without ceasing. The pumping had freed her only about a foot and a half, and the leak was still undiscovered.

The men were tired out, for the sun was now at his hottest, and Drake adds slyly that they "had now a less liking of her than before, and greater content to hear of some means for remedy." We gather from what follows, that when he asked them what they wished to do, they left it all to him. He, therefore, suggested that John Drake should go aboard the *Pascha* as her captain. He himself, he said, would shift into a pinnace; while the *Swan* should be set on fire, and abandoned as soon as her gear was taken out of her. The pinnaces came aboard the sinking ship, and the men pillaged her of all her stores. Powder, tar, and the like were scattered about her decks; and she was then set on fire, and watched until she sank. Thus "our Captain had his desire, and men enough for his pinnaces."

The next morning, the 16th August, the squadron bore away for the Gulf of Darien, to find some secret harbour where they might leave the ship at anchor, "not discoverable by the enemy," who thereby might imagine them quite departed from the coast. Drake intended to take two of the pinnaces along the Main as soon as they had hidden away the *Pascha*, for he was minded to go a cruise up the Rio Grande, or Magdalena River. In his absence John Drake was to take the third pinnace, with Diego, the negro, as a guide, to open up communications with the Cimmeroons. By the 21st of August they arrived in the Gulf; and Drake sought out a secret anchorage, far from any trade route, where the squadron might lie quietly till the fame of their being on the coast might cease. They found a place suited to their needs, and dropped their anchors in its secret channels, in "a fit and convenient road," where a sailor might take his ease over a rum bowl. Drake took his men ashore, and cleared a large plot of ground "both of trees and brakes" as a site for a little village, trimly thatched with palm leaves, which was built by Diego, the negro, after the Indian fashion, for the "more comfort of the company." The archers made themselves butts to shoot at, because they had "many that delighted in that exercise and wanted not a fletcher to keep the bows and arrows in order." The rest of the company, "every one as he liked best," disported merrily at bowls and quoits, fleeting the time carelessly as they did in the Golden Age. "For our Captain allowed one half of the company to pass their time thus, every other day interchangeable," the other half of the crew being put to the provision of fresh food and the necessary work aboard the vessels. Drake took especial interest in trying the powers of the pinnaces, trimming them in every conceivable way, so as to learn their capacity under any circumstance. The smiths set up their forge, "being furnished out of England with anvil, iron, and coals" (surely Drake never forgot anything), which stood the expedition "in great stead," for, no doubt, there was much iron-work that needed repair. The country swarmed with conies, hogs, deer, and fowl, so that the men lived upon fresh meat, or upon the fish in the creeks, "whereof there was great plenty." The woods were full of wholesome fruits, though, perhaps, the water of the neighbouring rivers was not quite all that could be wished. They stayed in this pleasant haven for fifteen days, at the end of which Drake took his two pinnaces, leaving John Drake behind in charge of the *Pascha* and the remaining pinnace, and sailed away along the coast to explore the Rio Grande. He kept the pinnaces far out at sea to avoid discovery, and landed on the 8th of September about six miles to the westward of the river's mouth, in order to obtain some fresh beef from the Indian cowherds. The district was then rich pasture-land, as rich as the modern pastures in Argentina. It was grazed over by vast herds of cattle, savage and swift, which the

Spaniards placed in charge of Indian cowboys. When the beeves were slaughtered, their meat was dried into charqui, or "boucanned," over a slow fire, into which the hide was thrown. It was then sent down to Cartagena, for the provisioning of the galleons going home. The province (Nueva Reyna) was less pestilential than its westward neighbours. Sugar was grown there in the semi-marshy tracts near the river. Gold was to be found there in considerable quantities, and there were several pearl fisheries upon the coasts. The district was more populous than any part of Spanish America, for it was not only healthier, but more open, affording little cover for Maroons.

On landing, Drake met some Indians in charge of a herd of steers. They asked him in broken Spanish "What they would have." Drake gave them to understand that he wished to buy some fresh meat, upon which they picked out several cattle "with ease and so readily, as if they had a special commandment over them, whereas they would not abide us to come near them." The Indians have just that skill in handling cattle which the negroes have in handling mules. They did Drake this service willingly, "because our Captain, according to his custom, contented them for their pains with such things as they account greatly of." He left them in high good humour, promising him that if he came again he should have what he desired of them. Drake left the shore as soon as his pinnaces were laden with fresh meat, and sailed on up the coast till he reached the lesser, or western, mouth of the Rio Grande, "where we entered about three of the clock." The river runs with a great fierceness, so that the hands were able to draw fresh water "for their beverage" a mile and a half from the mouth. It was a current almost too fierce to row against in the hot sun, so that five hours' hard rowing only brought them six miles on their way upstream.   They then moored the pinnaces to a great tree that grew on the bank. They ate their suppers in that place, hoping to pass a quiet evening, but with the darkness there came such a terrible thunderstorm "as made us not a little to marvel at," though Drake assured the younger men that in that country such storms soon passed. It wetted them to the bone, no doubt, but within three-quarters of an hour it had blown over and become calm. Immediately the rain had ceased, the air began to hum with many wings, and forth came "a kind of flies of that country, called mosquitoes, like our gnats," which bit them spitefully as they lay in the bottoms of the boats. It was much too hot to lie beneath a blanket, and the men did not know how to kindle a "smudge" of smouldering aromatic leaves. They had no pork fat nor paraffin to rub upon their hands and faces, according to the modern practice, and "the juice of lemons," which gave them a little relief, must have been a poor substitute. "We could not rest all that night," says the narrative. At daybreak the next morning they rowed away from that place, "rowing in the eddy" along the banks, where the current helped them. Where the eddy failed, as in swift and shallow places, they hauled the boats up with great labour by making a hawser fast to a tree ahead, and hauling up to it, as on a guess-warp. The work of rowing, or warping, was done by spells, watch and watch, "each company their half-hour. glass," till about three in the afternoon, by which time they had come some fifteen miles. They passed two Indians who sat in a canoe a-fishing ; but the Indians took them to be Spaniards, and Drake let them think so, for he did not wish to be discovered. About an hour later they espied "certain houses on the other side of the river," a mile or so from them, the river being very broad—so great, says the narrative, "that a man can scantly be discerned from side to side." A Spaniard, who had charge of those houses, espied them from the vantage of the bank, and promptly kindled a smoke "for a signal to turn that way," being lonely up there in the wilds, and anxious for news of the world. As they rowed across the current to him he waved to them "with his hat and his long hanging sleeves" to come ashore, but as soon as he perceived them to be foreigners he took to his heels, and fled from the river-side. The adventurers found that he was a sort of store or warehouse keeper, in charge of five houses "all full of white rusk, dried bacon, that country cheese (like Holland cheese in fashion—*i.e.* round—but far more delicate in taste, of which they send into Spain as special presents), many sorts of sweetmeats, and conserves; with great store of sugar: being provided to serve the fleet returning to Spain." As they loaded their pinnaces with these provisions they talked with a poor Indian woman, who told them that about thirty trading vessels were expected from Cartagena. The news caused them to use despatch in their lading, so that by nightfall they were embarked again, and rowing down-stream against the wind. The Spaniards of Villa del Rey, a city some two miles inland from the storehouses, endeavoured to hinder their passage by marching their Indians to the bushes on the river-bank, and causing them to shoot their arrows as the boats rowed past. They did not do any damage to the adventurers, who rowed downstream a few miles, and then moored their boats for the night. Early the next morning they reached the mouth of the river, and here they hauled ashore to put the pinnaces in trim. The provisions were unloaded, and the boats thoroughly cleansed, after which the packages were stowed securely, so as to withstand the tossings of the seas. The squadron then proceeded to the westward, going out of their course for several miles in order to overhaul a Spanish barque. They "imagined she had some gold or treasure going for Spain," but on search in her hold they could find only sugar and hides. They, therefore, let her go, and stood off again for the secret harbour. The next day they took some five or six small frigates, bound from Santiago de Tolu to Cartagena, with ladings of "live hogs, hens, and maize, which we call Guinea wheat." They examined the crews of these ships for news "of their preparations for us," and then dismissed them, reserving only two of the half-dozen prizes "because they were so well stored with good victuals." Three days later they arrived at the hidden anchorage, which Drake called Port Plenty, because of abundance of "good victuals" that they took while lying there. Provision ships were passing continually, either to Nombre de Dios or Cartagena, with food for the citizens or for the victualling of the plate fleets. "So that if we had been two thousand, yea, three thousand, persons, we might with our pinnaces easily have provided them sufficient victuals of wine, meal, rusk, cassavi (a kind of bread made of a root called Yucca, whose juice is poison, but the substance good and wholesome), dried beef, dried fish, live sheep, live hogs, abundance of hens, besides the infinite store of dainty fresh fish, very easily to be taken every day." So much food was taken, that the company, under the direction of Diego, the negro, were forced to build "four several magazines or storehouses, some ten, some twenty leagues asunder," on the Main, or on the islands near it, for its storage. They intended to stay upon the coast until their voyage was "made," and, therefore, needed magazines of the kind for the future plenishing of their lazarettoes. We read that Diego, the negro, was of special service to them in the building of these houses, for, like all the Maroons, he was extremely skilful at the craft. They were probably huts of mud and wattle, thatched with palm leaves, "with a Sort of Door made of Macaw-Wood,

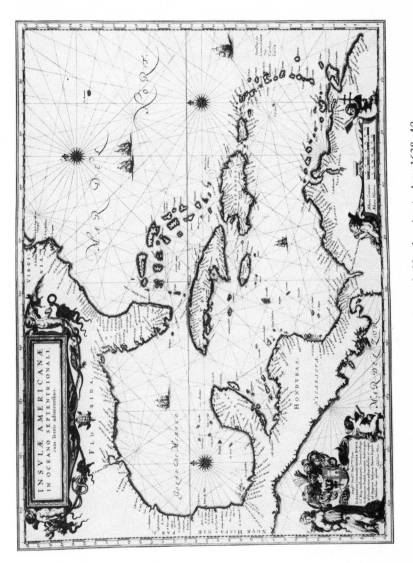

West Indies. Blaeu's : *Le Theatre du Monde*... Amsterdam; 1638—40

and Bamboes." From these magazines Drake relieved two French ships "in extreme want"; while his men and their allies the Cimmeroons lived at free quarters all the time they stayed there.

While the Captain had been cruising up the Magdalena, his brother, John Drake, had been westward along the coast with Diego, "the Negro aforesaid," in his pinnace. Diego had landed on the coast to talk with "certain of the Cimmeroons," who exchanged hostages with Drake's party, and agreed upon a meeting-place at a little river midway between the Cabezas, or "Headlands," and the anchorage. Drake talked with these hostages as soon as he arrived from the seas. He found them two "very sensible men," most ready to help him against the common enemy. They told him that "their Nation conceited great joy of his arrivall"; for they had heard of Nombre de Dios and of his former raids upon the coast, and gladly welcomed the suggested alliance. Their chief and tribe, they said, were encamped near the afore-mentioned little river, the Rio Diego, to await Drake's decision. Having compared the talk of these men with the reports he had gathered from the Indian cowherds and Spanish prisoners, he consulted his brother (who had seen the Maroons at the Rio Diego camp), and asked "those of best service with him" what were fittest to be done. John Drake advised that the ships should proceed to the westward, to the Rio Diego, for near the mouth of that stream he had discovered a choice hiding-place. It could be reached by many channels, but only by the most careful pilotage, for the channels were full of rocks and shoals. The channels twisted sluggishly among a multitude of islands, which were gorgeous with rhododendron shrubs, and alive with butterflies, blue and scarlet, that sunned themselves, in blots of colour, upon the heavy green leaves. Among the blossomed branches there were parrots screaming, and the little humming-birds, like flying jewels, darting from flower to flower. Up above them the great trees towered, shutting out the sight of the sea, so that a dozen ships might have lain in that place without being observed from the open water. The description of this hiding-place moved Drake to proceed thither at once with his two pinnaces, the two Maroons, and his brother John, giving orders for the ship to follow the next morning. The pinnaces arrived there the next day, and found the Cimmeroons encamped there, some of them at the river's mouth, the others "in a wood by the river's side." A solemn feast was prepared, at which the Maroons gave "good testimonies of their joy and good will" towards the adventurers. After the feast, the tribe marched away to the Rio Guana, intending to meet with another tribe, at that time camped among the hills. The pinnaces returned from Rio Diego, wondering why the ship had not arrived, and anxious for her safety. They found her, on the 16th September, in the place where they had left her, "but in far other state," for a tempest had set her on her side, and sorely spoiled her trim, so that it took two days to repair the damage done. A pinnace was then despatched to the Rio Diego an-chorage, to go "amongst the shoals and sandy places, to sound out the channel." On the 19th of September the *Pascha* was warily piloted to moorings, "with much ado to recover the road among so many flats and shoals." Her berth was about five leagues from the Cativaas, or Catives, "betwixt an island and the Main"—the island being about half-a-mile from the shore, some three acres in extent, "flat, and very full of trees and bushes."

The anchors were hardly in the ground, when the friendly tribe of Cimmeroons appeared upon the shore, with several others whom they had met in the mountains. They were all fetched aboard, " to their great comfort and our content," and a council was held forthwith. Drake then asked the chiefs how they could help him to obtain some gold and silver. They replied that nothing could be done for another five months, because the autumn, the rainy season, was upon them, during which time no treasure would be moved from Panama. Had they known that he wanted gold, they said, they would have satisfied him, for they had taken a great store from the Spaniards in a foray, and had flung it into the rivers, which were now too high for them to hope to recover it by diving. He must, therefore, wait, they said, till the rains had ceased in the coming March, when they could attack a treasure train together. The answer was a little unexpected, but not unpleasant, for Drake was willing to remain on the coast for another year if need were. He at once resolved to build himself a fort upon the island, "for the planting of all our ordnance therein, and for our safeguard, if the enemy in all this time, should chance to come." The Cimmeroons cut down a number of Palmito boughs and branches, and soon had two large sheds built, both trim and watertight, for the housing of the company. The boats were then sent ashore to the Main to bring over timber for the building of the fortress. This stronghold was built in the shape of a triangle, with a deep ditch all round it.

The building was a full thirteen feet in height, built of tree boles from the Main, with earth from the trench to take the place of mortar. The ship's guns were hoisted out of the ship and rafted over to the fortress, and there mounted at the embrasures. For platforms for the guns they used the planks of one of the frigates captured near Cartagena. When the heavy work of lumber handling had been finished, but before the fort was ready for use, Drake took John Oxenham, with two of the pinnaces, upon a cruise to the east. He feared that a life of ease ashore would soon make his mariners discontented and eager to be home. It was, therefore, necessary to invent distractions for them. Instead of going at once towards his quarry he sailed along leisurely, close to the coast, stopping a night at one little island for a feast on a kind of bird like spur-kites, the flesh of which was very delicate. He stopped another night at another island, because "of a great kind of shellfish of a foot long," which the company called whelks. As soon as these delectable islands had been left astern, the pinnaces "hauled off into the sea," across the bright, sunny water, blue and flashing, gleaming with the silver arrows of the flying-fish, in order to make the Isles of San Barnardo. They chased two frigates ashore before they came to moorings, after which they scrubbed and trimmed their boats, spent a day fishing from the rocks, and set sail again for Santiago de Tolu. Here they landed in a garden, close to the city, to the delight of some Indians who were working there. After bargaining together for the garden stuff the Indians left their bows and arrows with the sailors while they ran to pluck "many sorts of dainty fruits and roots," such as the garden yielded. Drake paid for the green stuff, and had it taken aboard, after inquiring strictly as to the state of the country and the plate fleets.· The company then rowed away for Cartagena, eating their "mellions and winter cherries" with a good appetite. They rowed through the Boca Chica, or Little Mouth, into the splendid harbour, where they set sail, "having the wind large," towards the inner haven and the city. They anchored "right over against the goodly Garden Island," where the fruit was a sore temptation to the seamen, who longed to rob the trees. Drake would not allow them to land, for he feared an ambush, and, indeed, a few hours later, as they passed by the point of the island, they were fired at from the orchards with "a volley of a hundred shot," one of which wounded a sailor.   There was little to be done in the harbour, so they put to sea again.   They took a barque the next morning about six miles from the port.   She was a ship of fifty tons, laden with soap and sweetmeats, bound from St Domingo towards Cartagena. She was armed with "swords, targets and some small shot, besides four iron bases."   Her captain and passengers had slipped ashore in the boat as soon as they had spied the pinnaces, but the captain's silken flag, woven in colours, with his coat-of-arms, had been left behind as a spoil.   Having sent her company ashore, "saving a young Negro two or three years old, which we brought away," they sailed her into Cartagena harbour, with the pinnaces towing astern.   They anchored at the mouth of the inner haven to await events.   During the afternoon the Scrivano, or King's notary, aforementioned, rode down "to the point by the wood side" with a little troop of horsemen. The Scrivano displayed a flag of truce, and came aboard, to worry Drake with his oily lawyer's manner and elaborate, transparent lies.   He promised to obtain fresh meat for him as a slight return for "his manifold favours, etc." but Drake saw that it was but a plot of the Governor's to keep him in the port till they could trap him.   He thanked the supple liar, kept a good lookout throughout the night, and stood to sea as soon as the sun rose.   He took two frigates the next day, just outside the harbour.   They were small boats in ballast, one of twelve, one of fifty tons, bound for St Domingo.   He brought them to anchor in a bravery, "within saker shot of the east Bulwark," and then dismissed their mariners ashore.   On the 21st October, the morning after this adventure, the Spaniards sent a flag of truce to the headland at the mouth of the Boca Chica. Drake manned one of his pinnaces, and rowed ashore to see what they wanted.   When about 200 yards from the point the Spaniards fled into the wood, as though

afraid of the boat's guns—hoping, no doubt, that Drake
would follow, and allow them to ambush him. Drake
dropped his grapnel over the stern of the pinnace, and
veered the boat ashore, little by little, till the bows grated
on the sand. As she touched he leaped boldly ashore, in
sight of the Spanish troops, "to declare that he durst set
his foot a land." The Spaniards seem to have made a rush
towards him, whereupon he got on board again, bade his
men warp the boat out by the cable, and "rid awhile,"
some 100 yards from the shore, in the smooth green
water, watching the fish finning past the weeds. Seeing
that Drake was less foolish than they had hoped, the
Spaniards came out upon the sands, at the edge of the
wood, and bade one of their number take his clothes off,
to swim to the boat with a message. The lad stripped,
and swam off to the boat, "as with a Message from the
Governor," asking them why they had come to the coast,
and why they stayed there. Drake replied that he had
come to trade, "for he had tin, pewter, cloth, and other
merchandise that they needed," with which reply the
youth swam back to the soldiers. After some talk upon
the sands, the men-at-arms sent him back with an answer.
"The King," they said, "had forbidden them to traffic
with any foreign nation, for any commodities, except
powder and shot; of which, if he had any store, they
would be his merchants." Drake answered that he had
come all the way from England to exchange his commodities for gold and silver, and had little will to return
"without his errand." He told them that, in his opinion,
they were "like to have little rest" if they would not
traffic with him fairly in the way of business. He then
gave the messenger "a fair shirt for a reward," and
despatched him back to his masters. The lad rolled the
shirt about his head in the Indian fashion, and swam back
"very speedily," using, perhaps, the swift Indian stroke.

He did not return that day, though Drake waited for him until sunset, when the pinnace pulled slowly back to the two frigates, "within saker shot [or three-quarters of a mile] of the east Bulwark." The adventurers lay there all that night, expecting to be attacked. The guns were loaded, and cartridges made ready, and a strict lookout was kept. At dawn they saw two sails running down towards them from the Boca Chica on a fresh easterly breeze. Drake manned his two pinnaces, leaving the frigates empty, expecting to have a fight for their possession. Before he came within gunshot of the Spaniards he had to use his oars, for the wind fell, thereby lessening the advantage the Spanish had. As the boats neared each other Drake's mariners "saw many heads peeping over board" along the gunwales of the enemy. They perceived then that the two ships had been manned to occupy Drake's attention, while another squadron made a dash from the town, "from the eastern Bulwark," to retake his two prizes. But Drake "prevented both their drifts." He bade John Oxenham remain there with the one pinnace, "to entertain these two Men of war," while he, with the other, rowed furiously back to the two prizes. Quick as he had been the Spaniards had been quicker. They had rowed out in a large canoe, which had made two trips, so that one frigate was now full of Spaniards, who had cut her cables, while the canoe towed her towards the batteries. As Drake ranged up alongside, the towline was cast adrift by the men in the canoe; while the gallants on the deck leaped overboard, to swim ashore, leaving their rapiers, guns, and powder flasks behind them. Drake watched them swim out of danger, and then set the larger ship on fire. The smaller of the two he scuttled where she lay, "giving them to understand by this, that we perceived their secret practices." As soon as the frigates were disposed of, the pinnace returned to John Oxenham, who was lying to by the two men-of-war, waiting for them to open fire. As the Captain's pinnace drew near, the wind shifted to the north, and blew freshly, so that both the English boats, being to shoreward of the enemy, were forced to run before it, into the harbour, " to the great joy of the Spaniards," who thought they were running away. Directly they were past the point, "and felt smooth water," they obtained the weather-gage, exchanged a few shots, and dropped their anchors, keeping well to windward of the enemy. The Spaniards also anchored ; but as the wind freshened into "a norther" they thought it best to put ashore, and, therefore, retired to the town.

For the next four days it blew very hard from the west, with cold rain squalls, to the great discomfort of all hands, who could keep neither warm nor dry. On the fifth day (27th October) a frigate came in from the sea, and they at once attacked her, hoping to find shelter aboard her after the four days of wet and cold. The Spaniards ran her ashore on the point by the Boca Chica, "unhanging her rudder and taking away her sails, that she might not easily be carried away." However, the boats dashed alongside, intending to board her. As they came alongside, a company of horse and foot advanced on to the sands from the woods, opening fire on them as soon as they had formed. The pinnaces replied with their muskets and heavy guns, sending a shot "so near a brave cavalier" that the whole party retreated to the coverts. From the thick brush they were able to save the frigate from capture without danger to themselves ; so Drake abandoned her, and set to sea again, in the teeth of the gale, intending to win to Las Serenas, some rocks six miles to sea, off which he thought he could anchor, with his masts down, until the weather moderated. But when he arrived off the rocks, a mighty sea was beating over them, so that he had to run back to Cartagena, where he remained six days, "notwithstanding the Spaniards grieved greatly at our abode there so long."

On the 2nd of November the Governor of Cartagena made a determined attempt to destroy him or drive him out to sea. He manned three vessels—"a great shallop, a fine gundeloe and a great canoe"—with Spanish musketeers and Indians with poisoned arrows. These attacked with no great spirit, for as soon as the pinnaces advanced they retreated, and presently "went ashore into the woods," from which an ambush "of some sixty shot" opened a smart fire. As the ambush began to blaze away from the bushes, Drake saw that two pinnaces and a frigate, manned with musketeers and archers, were warping towards him from the town, in the teeth of the wind. As this second line of battle neared the scene of action, the Spaniards left the ambush in the wood, and ran down the sands to the gundeloe and canoe, which they manned, and again thrust from the shore. Drake then stood away into the haven, out of shot of the shore guns, and cast anchor in the great open space, with the two pinnaces lying close together, one immediately ahead of the other. He rigged the sides of the pinnaces with bonnets, the narrow lengths of canvas which were laced to the feet of sails to give them greater spread. With these for his close-fights, or war-girdles, he waved to the Spaniards to attack. They rowed up cheering, all five boats of them, "assuring their fellows of the day." Had they pushed the attack home, the issue might have been different, but the sight of the close-fights frightened them. They lay on their oars "at caliver-shot distance," and opened a smart musketry fire, "spending powder apace," without pausing, for two or three hours. One man was wounded on Drake's side. The Spanish loss could not be told, but Drake's men could plainly see that the Spanish pinnaces had been shot through and through. One lucky shot went into a Spanish powder tub, which thereupon exploded. Drake at once weighed anchor, intending to run them down while they were in confusion. He had the wind of them, and would have been able to do this without difficulty, but they did not wait his coming. They got to their oars in a hurry, and rowed to their defence in the woods—the fight being at an end before the frigate could warp to windward into action.

Being weary of these continual fruitless tussles, "and because our victuals grew scant," Drake sailed from the port the following morning, in slightly better weather, hoping to get fresh provisions at the Rio Grande, where he had met with such abundance a few days before. The wind was still fresh from the west, so that he could not rejoin his ship nor reach one of his magazines. He took two days in sailing to the Magdalena, but when he arrived there he found the country stripped. "We found bare nothing, not so much as any people left," for the Spaniards had ordered everyone to retire to the hills, driving their cattle with them, "that we might not be relieved by them." The outlook was now serious, for there was very little food left, and that of most indifferent quality, much of it being spoiled by the rains and the salt water. On the day of their landfall they rowed hard for several hours to capture a frigate, but she was as bare of food as they. "She had neither meat nor money," and so "our great hope" was "converted into grief." Sailors get used to living upon short allowance. The men tightened their belts to stay their hunger, and splashed salt water on their chests to allay their thirst. They ran for Santa Martha, a little city to the east, where they hoped "to find some shipping in the road, or limpets on the rocks, or succour against the storm in that good harbour." They found no shipping there, however, and little succour against the storm. They anchored "under the western point, where is high land," but they could not venture in, for the town was

strongly fortified (later raiders were less squeamish). The
Spaniards had seen them come to moorings, and managed
to send some thirty or forty musketeers among the rocks,
within gunshot of them. These kept up a continual
musket fire, which did bodily hurt to none, but proved
a sad annoyance to sailors who were wearied and out
of victuals. They found it impossible to reply to the
musketry, for the rocks hid the musketeers from view.
There was nothing for it but to "up kedge and cut," in
the hope of finding some less troublous berth. As they
worked across the Santa Martha bay the culverins in the
city batteries opened fire. One shot "made a near
escape," for it fell between the pinnaces as they lay
together in "conference of what was best to be done."

The company were inclined to bring the cruise to an
end, and begged that they might " put themselves a land,
some place to the Eastward, to get victuals." They
thought it would be better to trust to the courtesy of
the country people than to keep the seas as they were,
in the cold and heavy weather, with a couple of leaky,
open boats. Drake disliked this advice, and recommended
that they should run on for Rio de la Hacha, or even as
far as Curaçoa, where they would be likely to meet with
victual ships indifferently defended. The men aboard
John Oxenham's pinnace answered that they would
willingly follow him throughout the world, but they
did not see, they said, how the pinnaces could stand
such weather as they had had. Nor did they see how
they were going to live with such little food aboard,
for they had "only one gammon of bacon and thirty
pounds of biscuit for eighteen men "—a bare two days'
half allowance. Drake replied that they were better off
than he was, "who had but one gammon of bacon and
forty pounds of biscuit for his twenty-four men ; and
therefore [he went on] he doubted not but they would

take such part as he did, and willingly depend upon
God's Almighty providence, which never faileth them
that trust in Him." He did not wait for any further
talk, but hoisted his fore-sail and put his helm up for
Curaçoa, knowing that the other pinnace would not refuse
to follow him. With "sorrowful hearts in respect of the
weak pinnace, yet desirous to follow their captain," the
weary crew stood after him on the same course. They
had not gone more than three leagues when, lo!—balm
in Gilead—"a sail plying to the westward" under her fore-
sail and main-sail. There was "great joy" in that hunger-
bitten company, who promptly "vowed together, that we
would have her, or else it should cost us dear." Coming
up with her they found her to be a Spanish ship of more
than ninety tons. Drake "waved amain" to her, the usual
summons to surrender; but she "despised our summons,"
and at once opened fire on them, but without success, for
the sea was running very high. The sea was too high
for them to board her so they set small storm-sails, and
stood in chase, intending to "keep her company to her
small content till fairer weather might lay the sea." They
followed her for two hours, when "it pleased God" to
send a great shower, which, of course, beat down the sea
into "a reasonable calm," so that they could pepper her
with their guns "and approach her at pleasure." She
made but a slight resistance after that, and "in short
time we had taken her; finding her laden with victuals
well powdered [salted] and dried: which at that present
we received as sent us of God's great mercy."

After a stormy night at sea, Drake sent Ellis Hixom,
"who had then charge of his pinnace, to search out some
harbour along the coast." Hixom soon discovered a
little bay, where there was good holding ground, with
sufficient depth of water to float the prize. They entered
the new port, and dropped their anchors there, promising

the Spaniards their clothes, as well as their liberty, if they would but bring them to a clear spring of water and a supply of fresh meat. The Spaniards, who knew the coast very well, soon brought them to an Indian village, where the natives "were clothed and governed by a Spaniard." They stayed there all the day, cutting wood for their fire, filling water casks, and storing the purchased meat. The Indians helped them with all their might, for Drake, following his custom, gave them "content and satisfaction" for the work they did for him. Towards night Drake called his men aboard, leaving the Spanish prisoners ashore, according to his promise, "to their great content." The wood, water casks, and sides of meat were duly stored, the anchors were brought to the bows, and the adventurers put to sea again towards the secret harbour. That day one of their men died from "a sickness which had begun to kindle among us, two or three days before." What the cause of this malady was "we knew not of certainty," but "we imputed it to the cold which our men had taken, lying without succour in the pinnaces." It may have been pleurisy, or pneumonia, or some low fever. The dead man was Charles Glub, "one of our Quarter Masters, a very tall man, and a right good mariner, taken away to the great grief of Captain and company"—a sufficiently beautiful epitaph for any man. "But howsoever it was," runs the touching account, "thus it pleased God to visit us, and yet in favour to restore unto health all the rest of our company that were touched with this disease, which were not a few."

The 15th of November broke bright and fine, though the wind still blew from the west. Drake ordered the *Minion*, the smaller of his two pinnaces, to part company, "to hasten away before him towards his ships at Port Diego . . . to carry news of his coming, and to put all things in a readiness for our land journey if they heard anything of the Fleet's arrival." If they wanted wine, he said, they had better put in at San Barnardo, and empty some of the caches in the sand there, where they had buried many bottles. Seven days later Drake put in at San Barnardo for the same commodity, "finding but twelve *botijos* of wine of all the store we left, which had escaped the curious search of the enemy who had been there, for they were deep in the ground." Perhaps the crew of the *Minion* were the guilty ones. About the 27th of November the Captain's party arrived at Port Diego, where they found all things in good order, "but received very heavy news of the death of John Drake, our Captain's brother, and another young man called Richard Allen, which were both slain at one time [on the 9th October, the day Drake left the isle of shell-fish] as they attempted the boarding of a frigate." Drake had been deeply attached to this brother, whom he looked upon as a "young man of great hope." His death was a sore blow to him, all the more because it happened in his absence, when he could neither warn him of the risks he ran nor comfort him as he lay a-dying.

He had been in the pinnace, it seems, with a cargo of planks from the Spanish wreck, carrying the timber for the platform of the battery. It was a bright, sunny morning, and the men were rowing lazily towards the fort, "when they saw this frigate at sea." The men were in merry heart, and eager for a game at handystrokes. They were "very importunate on him, to give chase and set upon this frigate, which they deemed had been a fit booty for them." He told them that they "wanted weapons to assail"; that, for all they knew, the frigate might be full of men and guns; and that their boat was cumbered up with planks, required for his brother's service. These answers were not enough for them, and "still they urged him with words and supposals." "If you will needs," said he ;—

" Adventure. It shall never be said that I will be hind-most, neither shall you report to my brother that you lost your voyage by any cowardice you found in me." The men armed themselves as they could with stretchers from the boat, or anything that came to hand. They hove the planks overboard to make a clear fighting space, and "took them such poor weapons as they had : viz., a broken pointed rapier, one old visgee, and a rusty caliver. John Drake took the rapier and made a gauntlet of his pillow, Richard Allen the visgee, both standing at the head of the pinnace called Eion. Robert took the caliver, and so boarded." It was a gallant, mad attempt, but utterly hopeless from the first. The frigate was " armed round about with a close fight of hides," and "full of pikes and calivers, which were discharged in their faces, and deadly wounded those that were in the fore ship, John Drake in the belly, and Richard Allen in the head." Though they were both sorely hurt, they shoved the pinnace clear with their oars, and so left the frigate, and hurried home to their ship, where "within an hour after" this young man of great hope ended his days, "greatly lamented of all the company." He was buried in that place, with Richard Allen his shipmate, among the brilliant shrubs, over which the parrots chatter.

For the next four or five weeks the company remained at Fort Diego with the Maroons, their allies. They fared sumptuously every day on the food stored within the magazine ; while "daily out of the woods" they took wild hogs, the "very good sort of a beast called warre," that Dampier ate, besides great store of turkeys, pheasants, and numberless guanas, "which make very good Broath." The men were in good health, and well contented ; but a day or two after the New Year (January 1573) "half a score of our company fell down sick together, and the most of them died within two or three days." They did not know

what the sickness was, nor do they leave us much information to enable us to diagnose it. They called it a
calenture, or fever, and attributed it to "the sudden
change from cold to heat, or by reason of brackish water
which had been taken in by our pinnace, through the
sloth of their men in the mouth of the river, not rowing
further in where the water was good." We cannot wonder
that they died from drinking the water of that sluggish
tropical river, for in the rainy season such water is often
poisonous to the fish in the sea some half-a-mile from
the shore. It comes down from the hills thick with
pestilential matter. It sweeps away the rotting leaves
and branches, the dead and drowned animals, from the
flooded woods and savannahs. "And I believe," says
Dampier, "it receives a strong Tincture from the Roots
of several Kind of Trees, Herbs, etc., and especially where
there is any stagnancy of the Water, it soon corrupts ; and
possibly the Serpents and other poisonous Vermin and
Insects may not a little contribute to its bad qualities."
Whatever it was, the disease raged among the men with
great violence—as many as thirty being down with it at
the one time. Among those who died was Joseph Drake,
another brother of the Captain, "who died in our Captain's
arms." The many deaths caused something like a panic
among the men, and Drake, in his distress, determined
to hold a post-mortem upon his brother's corpse " that the
cause [of the disease] might be the better discerned, and
consequently remedied." The operation was performed
by the surgeon, "who found his liver swollen, his heart
as it were sodden, and his guts all fair." The corpse of
one dead from yellow-fever displays very similar symptoms ;
and the muddy foreshore on which they were camped
would, doubtless, swarm with the yellow-fever mosquito.
The sick seem to have recovered swiftly—a trait observable
in yellow-fever patients. This, says the narrative, " was the

An engagement between buccaneers and Spanish galleons. *Exquemeling.*

first and last experiment that our Captain made of anatomy in this voyage." The surgeon who made this examination "over-lived him not past four days"—a fact which very possibly saved the lives of half the company. He had had the sickness at its first beginning among them, but had recovered. He died, we are told, " of an over-bold practice which he would needs make upon himself, by receiving an over-strong purgation of his own device, after which taken he never spake ; nor his Boy recovered the health which he lost by tasting it, till he saw England." He seems to have taken the draught directly after the operation, as a remedy against infection from the corpse. The boy, who, perhaps, acted as assistant at the operation, may have thought it necessary to drink his master's heel-taps by way of safeguard.

While the company lay thus fever-stricken at the fort, the Maroons had been wandering abroad among the forest, ranging the country up and down "between Nombre de Dios and us, to learn what they might for us." During the last few days of January 1573 they came in with the news that the plate fleet "had certainly arrived in Nombre de Dios." On the 30th of January, therefore, Drake ordered the *Lion*, one of the three pinnaces, to proceed "to the seamost islands of the Cativaas," a few miles from the fort, to "descry the truth of the report" by observing whether many frigates were going towards Nombre de Dios from the east, as with provisions for the fleet. The *Lion* remained at sea for a few days, when she captured a frigate laden with "maize, hens, and pompions from Tolu." She had the Scrivano of Tolu aboard her, with eleven men and one woman. From these they learned that the fleet was certainly at Nombre de Dios, as the Indians had informed them. The prisoners were "used very courteously," and "diligently guarded from the deadly hatred of the Cimmeroons," who used every means in their power to obtain them from the English, so that "they might cut their throats to revenge their wrongs and injuries." Drake warned his allies not to touch them "or give them ill countenance"; but, feeling a little doubtful of their safety, he placed them aboard the Spanish prize, in charge of Ellis Hixom, and had the ship hauled ashore to the island, "which we termed Slaughter Island (because so many of our men died there)." He was about to start upon "his journey for Panama by land," and he could not follow his usual custom of letting his prisoners go free.

CHAPTER IV

THE ROAD TO PANAMA

The Maroons—The native city—The great tree—Panama—The
silver train—The failure—Venta Cruz

WHEN the Spanish prize had been warped to her
berth at Slaughter Island, Drake called his men
together, with the chiefs of the Maroons, to a solemn
council of war about the fire. He then discussed with
them, with his usual care, the equipment necessary for an
undertaking of the kind in hand. He was going to cross
the isthmus with them, those "20 leagues of death and
misery," in order to surprise one of the recuas, or treasure
trains, as it wandered north upon the road from Panama
to Nombre de Dios. It was, as he says, "a great and long
journey," through jungles, across swamps, and up precipitous crags. Any error in equipment would be paid
for in blood. It was essential, therefore, that they should
strictly debate "what kind of weapons, what store of
victuals, and what manner of apparel" would be fittest for
them. The Maroons "especially advised" him "to carry as
great store of shoes as possibly he might, by reason of
so many rivers with stone and gravel as they were to
pass." This advice was followed by all hands, who provided themselves with a good store of boots and spare
leather, thereby saving themselves from much annoyance
from jiguas, or jiggers, and the venomous leeches of the
swamps. The sickness had destroyed twenty-eight of the
company. Three had died of wounds or in battle, and
one had died from cold and exposure in the pinnace. Of

the remaining forty-two Drake selected eighteen of the best. A number were still ill abed, and these he left behind in the care of Ellis Hixom and his little band of shipkeepers. The dried meat and biscuit were then packed carefully into bundles. The eighteen took their weapons, with such necessaries as they thought they might require. Drake called Hixom aside, and gave him "straight charge, in any case not to trust any messenger that should come in his name with any tokens, unless he brought his hand-writing: which he knew could not be counterfeited by the Cimaroons or Spaniards." A last farewell was taken; thirty brawny Cimmeroons swung the packs upon their shoulders, shaking their javelins in salute. The ship-keepers sounded "A loath to depart," and dipped their colours. The forty-eight adventurers then formed into order, and marched away into the forest on their perilous journey.

Having such stalwart carriers, the English were able to march light, "not troubled with anything but our furniture." The Maroons carried "every one of them two sorts of arrows" in addition to the packs of victuals, for they had promised to provide fresh food upon the march for all the company. "Every day we were marching by sun-rising," says the narrative, taking the cool of the morning before the sun was hot. At "ten in the forenoon" a halt was called for dinner, which they ate in quiet "ever near some river." This halt lasted until after twelve. Then they marched again till four, at which time they sought out a river-bank for their camping ground. Often they slept in old huts built by the Indians "when they travelled through these woods," but more frequently the Maroons built them new ones, having a strange skill in that craft. Then they would light little fires of wood inside the huts, giving a clear red glow, with just sufficient smoke to keep away mosquitoes. They would sup pleasantly together there, snugly sheltered from the rain if any fell; warm if it were cold, as on the hills; and cool if it were hot, as in the jungle. When the Indians had lit their little "light Wood" candles these huts must have been delightful places, full of jolly talk and merry music. Outside, by the river-brink, the frogs would croak; and, perhaps, the adventurers heard "the shriekings of Snakes and other Insects," such as scared Lionel Wafer there about a century later. Those who ventured out into the night were perplexed by the innumerable multitude of fireflies that spangled the darkness with their golden sparks. In the mornings the brilliant blue and green macaws aroused them with their guttural cries "like Men who speak much in the Throat." The chicaly bird began his musical quick cuckoo cry, the corrosou tolled out his bell notes, the "waggish kinds of Monkeys" screamed and chattered in the branches, playing "a thousand antick Tricks." Then the sun came up in his splendour above the living wall of greenery, and the men buckled on their gear, and fell in for the road.

As they marched, they sometimes met with droves of peccary or warree. Then six Maroons would lay their burdens down, and make a slaughter of them, bringing away as much of the dainty wild pork as they could carry. Always they had an abundance of fresh fruit, such as "Mammeas" ("very wholesome and delicious"), "Guavas, Palmitos, Pinos, Oranges, Lemons and divers others." Then there were others which were eaten "first dry roasted," as "Plantains, Potatoes, and such like," besides bananas and the delicious sapadilloes. On one occasion "the Cimaroons found an otter, and prepared it to be drest: our Captain marvelling at it. Pedro, our chief Cimaroon, asked him, "Are you a man of war, and in want; and yet doubt whether this be meat, that hath blood? Herewithal [we read] our Captain rebuked himself secretly, that he had so slightly considered of it before."

After three days' wandering in the woods the Maroons brought them to a trim little Maroon town, which was built on the side of a hill by a pretty river. It was surrounded by "a dyke of eight feet broad, and a thick mud wall of ten feet high, sufficient to stop a sudden surpriser. It had one long and broad street, lying east and west, and two other cross streets of less breadth and length," containing in all some "five or six and fifty households." It was "kept so clean and sweet, that not only the houses, but the very streets were pleasant to behold"—a thing, doubtless, marvellous to one accustomed to an Elizabethan English town. "In this town we saw they lived very civilly and cleanly," for, as soon as the company marched in, the thirty carriers "washed themselves in the river and changed their apparel," which was "very fine and fitly made," after the Spanish cut. The clothes, by all accounts, were only worn on state occasions. They were long cotton gowns, either white or rusty black, "shap'd like our Carter's Frocks."

The town was thirty-five leagues from Nombre de Dios and forty-five from Panama. It had been surprised the year before Drake came there (1572) by 150 Spanish troops under "a gallant gentleman," who had been guided thither by a recreant Maroon. He attacked a little before the dawn, and cut down many women and children, but failed to prevent the escape of nearly all the men. In a little while they rallied, and attacked the Spaniards with great fury, killing their guide and four-fifths of their company. The wretched remnant straggled back as best they could "to return answer to them which sent them." The natives living there at the time of Drake's visit kept a continual watch some three miles from the town, to prevent a second surprise. Any Spaniards whom they met they "killed like beasts."

The adventurers passed a night in the town, and stayed until noon of the day following. The Maroons told them stories of their battles with the Spaniards, while Drake inquired into "their affection in religion." He learned that they had no kind of priests; "only they held the Cross in great reputation"—having, perhaps, learned so much of Christianity from the Spaniards. Drake seems to have done a little earnest missionary work, for he persuaded them "to leave their crosses, and to learn the Lord's Prayer, and to be instructed in some measure concerning God's true worship." After dinner on the 7th of February the company took to the roads again, refusing to take any of the countless recruits who offered their services. Four Maroons went on ahead to mark a trail by breaking branches or flinging a bunch of leaves upon the ground. After these four, marched twelve more Maroons as a sort of vanguard. Then came Drake with his men and the two Maroon chiefs. Another troop of twelve Maroons brought up the rear. The Maroons marched in strict silence, "which they also required us to keep," for it is the custom among nearly all savage folk to remain silent on the trail.

The way now led them through parts less swampy, and, therefore, less densely tangled over than those nearer the "North Sea." "All the way was through woods very cool and pleasant," says the narrative, "by reason of those goodly and high trees, that grow there so thick." They were mounting by slow degrees to the "ridge between the two seas," and the woodland was getting clear of undergrowth. As later buccaneers have noted, the upper land of the isthmus is wooded with vast trees, whose branches shut out the sun. Beneath these trees a man may walk with pleasure, or indeed ride, for there is hardly any undergrowth. The branches are so thick together that the lower ground receives no sunlight, and, therefore,

little grows there. The heat of the sun is shut out, and
" it is cooler travelling there . . . in that hot region, than
it is in . . . England in the summer time." As the men
began to ascend, the Maroons told them that not far away
there grew a great tree about midway between the oceans,
" from which we might at once discern the North Sea
from whence we came, and the South Sea whither we
were going." On the 11th of February, after four days of
slow but steady climbing, they " came to the height of the
desired hill, a very high hill, lying East and West, like a
ridge between the two seas." It was ten o'clock in the
forenoon, the hour at which the dinner halt was made.
Pedro, the Maroon chief, now took Drake's hand, and
" prayed him to follow him if he was desirous to see at
once the two seas which he had so longed for." Drake
followed Pedro to the hilltop, to the " goodly and great
high Tree," of which the Maroons had spoken. He found
that they had hacked out steps upon the bole, " to ascend
up near unto the top," where they had built a pleasant
little hut of branches thatched from the sun, " wherein ten
or twelve men might easily sit." " South and north of
this Tree " the Maroons had felled certain trees " that the
prospect might be the clearer." At its base there was a
number of strong houses " that had been built long before," perhaps by an older people than the Cimmeroons.
The tree seems to have been a place of much resort among
that people, as it lay in their paths across the isthmus, and
towards the west.

Drake climbed the tree with Pedro to the little sunny
bower at the top. A fresh breeze which was blowing, had
blown away the mists and the heat haze, so that the
whole isthmus lay exposed before him, in the golden
sunlight. There to the north, like a bright blue jewel,
was " the Atlantic Ocean whence now we came." There
to the south, some thirty miles away, was " that sea of

which he had heard such golden reports." He looked at the wonderful South Sea, and "besought Almighty God of His goodness, to give him life and leave to sail once in an English ship, in that sea." The prayer was granted to him, for in five years' time he was off that very coast with such a spoil as no ship ever took before. Having glutted his eyes with the sight, Drake called up all his English followers, and "acquainted John Oxenham especially with this his petition and purpose, if it would please God to grant him that happiness." Oxenham answered fervently that "unless our Captain did beat him from his company, he would follow him, by God's grace." He fulfilled his vow a few months later, with disaster to himself and his associates.

"Thoroughly satisfied with the sight of the seas," the men descended to their dinner with excellent appetite. They then pushed on lightly as before, through continual forest, for another two days. On the 13th of February, when they had gained the west side of the Cheapo River, the forest broke away into little knots of trees green and goodly, which showed like islands in a rolling ocean of green grass. They were come to the famous savannahs, over which roamed herds of black cattle, swift and savage. Everywhere about them was the wiry stipa grass, and "a kind of grass with a stalk as big as a great wheaten reed, which hath a blade issuing from the top of it, on which though the cattle feed, yet it groweth every day higher, until the top be too high for an ox to reach." The inhabitants of the country were wont to burn the grass every year, but "after it is thus burnt" it "springeth up fresh like green corn" within three days. "Such," says the narrative, "is the great fruitfulness of the soil: by reason of the evenness of the day and the night, and the rich dews which fall every morning." As the raiders advanced along this glorious grass-land they sometimes caught sight of Panama. Whenever they topped a rise they could see the city, though very far away ; and at last, "on the last day," they saw the ships riding in the road, with the blue Pacific trembling away into the sky beyond them. Now was the woodcock near the gin, and now the raiders had to watch their steps. There was no cover on those rolling sweeps of grass. They were within a day's journey of the city. The grass-land (as Drake gathered from his guides) was a favourite hunting-ground of the city poulterers, for there, as Drake puts it, "the Dames of Panama are wont to send forth hunters and fowlers, for taking of sundry dainty fowl, which the land yieldeth." Such a body of men as theirs might readily be detected by one of these sportsmen, and one such detection would surely ruin the attempt. They therefore, crept like snakes "out of all ordinary way," worming themselves through the grass-clumps till they came to a little river-bed, in which a trickle of water ran slowly across the sun-bleached pebbles. They were minded to reach a grove or wood about a league from Panama. The sun beat upon them fiercely, and it was necessary for them to travel in the heat of the day. In that open country the midday heat was intense, but they contrived to gain the shelter of the wood by three that afternoon. "This last day," says the narrative, "our Captain did behold and view the most of all that fair city, discerning the large street which lieth directly from the sea into the land, South and North."

Having gained the shelter of the wood, Drake chose out a Maroon "that had served a master in Panama" to venture into the city as a spy. He dressed the man "in such apparel as the Negroes of Panama do use to wear," and sent him off to the town an hour before night, "so that by the closing in of the evening he might be in the city." He gave the man strict charge to find out "the certain night, and the time of the night, when the carriers laded the Treasure from the King's Treasure House to

Nombre de Dios." The first stage of the journey (from Panama to Venta Cruz) was always undertaken in the cool of the night, "because the country is all champion, and consequently by day very hot." From Venta Cruz to Nombre de Dios "they travel always by day and not by night, because all that way is full of woods and therefore very cool." Drake's plan was to waylay one of the treasure trains on the night journey towards Venta Cruz. The Maroon soon returned to the little wood where the men were lying. He had entered the town without trouble, and had met with some old companions, who had told him all he wished to know. A treasure train was to start that very night, for a great Spanish gentleman, the treasurer of Lima, "was intending to pass into Spain" in a swift advice ship which stayed for him at Nombre de Dios. "His daughter and family" were coming with him, "having fourteen mules in company, of which eight were laden with gold, and one with jewels." After this troop, two other recuas, "of fifty mules in each," would take the road, carrying victuals and wine for the fleet, "with some little quantity of silver."

As soon as the news had been conveyed to Drake, he marched his men away from Panama towards Venta Cruz, some four leagues' journey. He halted them about two leagues to the south of Venta Cruz, in a clump of tall grass, and then examined a Spanish prisoner whom his scouts had caught. Two of the Maroons, stealing forward along the line of march, had scented the acrid smoke of a burning match carried by some arquebusier. They had crept up "by scent of the said match," and had heard a sound of snoring coming from the grass by the roadside. A Spanish sentry had fallen asleep upon his post, "and being but one they fell upon him, stopped his mouth from crying, put out his match," and bound him so effectually "that they well near strangled him." He was in the pay of the King's treasurer, who had hired him, with others, to guard the treasure train upon its march from Venta Cruz. He had fallen asleep while waiting for the mules to arrive, as he knew that he would get no sleep until the company he marched with was safe in Nombre de Dios. He was in terror of his life, for he believed that he had fallen into the hands of the Maroons, from whom he might expect no mercy. When he learned that he was a prisoner to Francis Drake he plucked up courage, "and was bold to make two requests unto him." First, he asked that Drake would order the Maroons to spare his life, for he knew that they "hated the Spaniards, especially the soldiers, extremely," but a word from such a Captain would be enough to save him. The second request was also personal. He assured them, upon the faith of a soldier, that "they should have that night more gold, besides jewels, and pearls of great price, than all they could carry"; if not, he swore, let them deal with him as they would. But, he added, if the raiders are successful, "then it might please our Captain to give unto him, as much as might suffice for him and his mistress to live upon, as he had heard our Captain had done to divers others"—promising, in such a case, to make his name as famous as any of them which had received the like favour.

Being now "at the place appointed" Drake divided his men into two companies. With eight Englishmen and fifteen Cimmeroons he marched to some long grass about fifty paces from the road. He sent John Oxenham, with Pedro and the other company of men, to the other side of the road, at the same distance from it, but a little farther to the south, in order that, "as occasion served, the former company might take the foremost mules by the heads," while Oxenham's party did that service for those which followed. The arrangement also provided "that if we should have need to use our weapons that night, we might be sure not to endamage our fellows." Having reached their stations, the men lay down to wait, keeping as quiet as they could. In about an hour's time they heard the clanging of many mule bells, making a loud music, in the direction of Venta Cruz. Mules were returning from that town to Panama; for with the fleet at Nombre de Dios there was much business between the two seaports, and the mule trains were going and coming several times a day. As they listened, they heard more mule bells ringing far away on the road from Panama. The treasurer with his company was coming.

Now, Drake had given strict orders that no man should show himself, or as much as budge from his station, "but let all that came from Venta Cruz [which was nothing but merchandise] to pass quietly." Yet one of the men, probably one of Oxenham's men, of the name of Robert Pike, now disobeyed those orders. "Having drunken too much aqua-vitæ without water," he forgot himself. He rose from his place in the grass, "enticing a Cimaroon with him," and crept up close to the road, "with intent to have shown his forwardness on the foremost mules." Almost immediately a cavalier came trotting past from Venta Cruz upon a fine horse, with a little page running at the stirrup. As he trotted by, Robert Pike "rose up to see what he was." The Cimmeroon promptly pulled him down, and sat upon him; but his promptness came too late to save the situation. All the English had put their shirts over their other apparel, "that we might be sure to know our own men in the pell mell in the night." The Spanish cavalier had glanced in Robert Pike's direction, and had seen a figure rising from the grass "half all in white" and very conspicuous. He had heard of Drake's being on the coast, and at once came to the conclusion that that arch-pirate had found his way through the woods to reward himself for his disappointment at Nombre de Dios. He was evidently a man of great presence of mind. He put spurs to his horse, and galloped off down the road, partly to escape the danger, but partly also to warn the treasure train, the bells of which were now clanging loudly at a little distance from the ambuscade.

Drake heard the trotting horse's hoofs clatter out into a furious gallop. He suspected that he had been discovered, "but could not imagine by whose fault, neither did the time give him the leasure to search." It was a still night, and he had heard no noise, yet something had startled the cavalier. Earnestly hoping that the rider had been alarmed by the silence of the night and the well-known danger of the road, he lay down among the grass again to wait for the mules to come. The bells clanged nearer and nearer, till at last the mules were trotting past the ambush. The captains blew their whistles to the attack. The raiders rose from the grass-clumps with a cheer. There was a rush across the narrow trackway at the drivers, the mules were seized, and in a moment, two full recuas were in the raiders' hands.

So far all had gone merrily. The sailors turned to loot the mule packs, congratulating themselves upon their glorious good fortune. It must have been a strange scene to witness—the mules scared and savage, the jolly seamen laughing as they pulled the packs away, the Maroons grinning and chattering, and the harness and the bells jingling out a music to the night. As the packs were ripped open a mutter of disappointment began to sound among the ranks of the spoilers. Pack after pack was found to consist of merchandise—vicuna wool, or dried provender for the galleons. The amount of silver found amounted to a bare two horse loads. Gold there was none. The jewels of the King's treasurer were not to be discovered. The angry sailors turned upon the muleteers for an explanation. The chief muleteer, "a very sensible fellow," was taken to Drake, who soon learned from him the reason why the catch was so poor. The cavalier who had noticed Robert Pike was the saviour of the treasure As soon as the figure half all in white had risen ghost-like by the road, he had galloped to the treasure mules to report what he had seen to the treasurer. The thing he had seen was vague, but it was yet too unusual to pass unnoticed. Drake, he said, was a person of devilish resource, and it was highly probable, he thought, that the pirates had come "in covert through the woods" to recoup themselves for their former disappointments. A white shirt was the usual uniform for men engaged in night attacks. No Maroon would wear such a thing in that locality, and, therefore, it would be well to let the food train pass ahead of the treasure. The loss of the food train would be a little matter, while it would surely show them whether an ambush lay in wait or not. The treasurer had accordingly drawn his company aside to allow the food mules to get ahead of him. As soon as the noise upon the road advised him that the enemy had made their spring, he withdrew quietly towards Panama. "Thus," says the narrative, "we were disappointed of a most rich booty : which is to be though God would not should be taken, for that, by all likelihood, it was well gotten by that Treasurer."

We are not told what happened to Robert Pike, but it is probable that he had a bad five minutes when the muleteer's story reached the sailors. It was bad enough to have marched all day under a broiling sun, and to lose a royal fortune at the end ; but that was not all, nor nearly all : they were now discovered to the enemy, who lay in considerable force in their front and rear. They were wearied out with marching, yet they knew very well that unless they " shifted for themselves betimes " all the Spaniards

of Panama would be upon them. They had a bare two
or three hours' grace in which to secure themselves.
They had marched four leagues that night, and by marching back those same four leagues they might win to
cover by the morning. If they marched forward they
might gain the forest in two leagues ; but Venta Cruz lay
in the road, and Venta Cruz was guarded day and night
by a company of Spanish troops. To reach the forest
by the latter road they would have to make a way with
their swords, but with men so tired and out of heart
it seemed the likelier route of the two. It was better,
Drake thought, "to encounter his enemies while he had
strength remaining, than to be encountered or chased
when they should be worn out with weariness." He
bade all hands to eat and drink from the provisions found
upon the mules, and while they took their supper he
told them what he had resolved to do. He called upon
Pedro, the Maroon, by name, asking "whether he would
give his hand not to forsake him." Pedro swore that
he would rather die at his feet than desert him in such
a pass—a vow which assured Drake of the loyalty of
his allies. As soon as supper was over, he bade the men
mount upon the mules, so that they might not weary
themselves with marching. An hour's trot brought them
to the woods within a mile of Venta Cruz, where they
dismounted, and went afoot, after bidding the muleteers
not to follow if they cared for whole skins. The road
was here some ten or twelve feet broad, "so as two Recuas
may pass one by another." It was paved with cobbles,
which had been beaten into the mud by Indian slaves.
On either side of it was the dense tropical forest, "as thick
as our thickest hedges in England that are oftenest cut."
Among the tangle, about half-a-mile from the town, the
Spaniards had taken up a strong position. The town
guard of musketeers had been reinforced by a number

The sacking of Puerto Principe, Cuba, by Morgan's buccaneers in 1668. *Exquemeling.*

of friars from a religious house. They lay there, hidden in the jungle, blowing their matches to keep them burning clearly. Two Maroons, whom Drake had sent forward as scouts, crept back to him with the news that the enemy were there in force, for they had smelt the reek of the smouldering matches and heard the hushed noise of many men moving in the scrub. Drake gave orders that no man should fire till the Spaniards had given them a volley, for he thought they would first parley with him, "as indeed fell out." Soon afterwards, as the men neared the Spanish ambush, a Spanish captain rose from the road, and "cried out, Hoo!" Drake answered with, "Hallo!" —the sailor's reply to a hail. The Spaniard then put the query "Que gente?" to which Drake answered "Englishmen." The Spaniard, "in the name of the King of Spain his master," then charged him to surrender, passing his word as a gentleman soldier that the whole company should be treated courteously. Drake made a few quick steps towards the Spaniard, crying out that "for the honour of the Queen of England, his mistress, he must have passage that way." As he advanced, he fired his pistol towards him, in order to draw the Spanish fire. Immediately the thicket burst out into flame; for the ambush took the shot for a signal, and fired off their whole volley. Drake received several hail-shot in his body. Many of the men were wounded, and one man fell sorely hurt. As the volley crackled out its last few shots, Drake blew his whistle, as a signal to his men to fire. A volley of shot and arrows was fired into the thicket, and the company at once advanced, "with intent to come to handy strokes." As they stormed forward to the thicket, the Spaniards fled towards a position of greater strength. Drake called upon his men to double forward to prevent them. The Maroons at once rushed to the front, "with their arrows ready in their bows, and their manner of country dance or leap, singing Yó péhó! Yó péhó, and so got before us where they continued their leap and song after the manner of their own country wars." The Spaniards heard the war-cry ringing out behind them, and fell back rapidly upon the town. Near the town's end a party of them rallied, forming a sort of rearguard to cover the retreat. As they took up a position in the woods, the Maroons charged them upon both flanks, while the English rushed their centre. There was a mad moment of fighting in the scrub. A Maroon went down with a pike through the body, but he contrived to kill the pikeman before he died. Several Englishmen were hurt. The Spaniards' loss is not mentioned, but it was probably severe. They broke and fled before the fury of the attack, and the whole body of fighting men, "friars and all," were thrust back into the town by the raiders. As they ran, the raiders pressed them home, shouting and slaying. The gates were open. The Spanish never had another chance to rally, and the town was taken with a rush a very few minutes after the captain's challenge in the wood.

VENTA CRUZ

Venta Cruz, the modern Cruces, stood, and still stands, on the west or left bank of the Chagres River. It marks the highest point to which boats may penetrate from the North Sea. Right opposite the town the river broadens out to a considerable width, affording berths for a number of vessels of slight draught. At the time of Drake's raid it was a place of much importance. The land route from Panama to Nombre de Dios was, as we have said, boggy, dangerous, and pestilential. The freight charges for mule transport across the isthmus were excessive, ranging from twenty-five to thirty dollars of assayed silver for a mule load of 200 pounds weight—a charge which works out at nearly £70 a ton. Even in the dry season the roads were bad, and the mule trains were never safe from the Maroons. Many merchants, therefore, sent their goods to Venta Cruz in flat-bottomed boats of about fifteen tons. These would sail from Nombre de Dios to the mouth of the Chagres River, where they struck sail, and took to their sweeps. The current was not very violent except in the upper reaches, and the boats were generally able to gain Venta Cruz in a few days—in about three days in dry weather and about twelve in the rains. A towing-path was advocated at one time; but it does not seem to have been laid, though the river-banks are in many places flat and sandy, and free from the dense undergrowth of the tropics. As soon as the boats arrived at Venta Cruz they were dragged alongside the jetty on the river-bank, and their cargoes were transferred to some strong stone warehouses. In due course the goods were packed on mules, and driven away down the road to Panama, a distance of some fifteen or eighteen miles, which the mules would cover in about eight hours. The town at the time of Drake's raid contained about forty or fifty houses, some of them handsome stone structures decorated with carven work. The river-bank was covered with a great many warehouses, and there were several official buildings, handsome enough, for the Governor and the King's officers. There was a monastery full of friars, "where we found above a thousand bulls and pardons, newly sent from Rome." Perhaps there was also some sort of a barrack for the troops. The only church was the great church of the monastery. The town was not fortified, but the houses made a sort of hedge around it; and there were but two entrances—the one from the forest, by which Drake's party entered; the other leading over a pontoon bridge towards the hilly woods beyond the Chagres. Attached to the monastery, and tended by the monks and their servants, was a sort of sanatorium and lying-in hospital. Nombre de Dios was so unhealthy, so full of malaria and yellow fever, "that no Spaniard or white woman" could ever be delivered there without the loss of the child on the second or third day. It was the custom of the matrons of Nombre de Dios to proceed to Venta Cruz or to Panama to give birth to their children. The babes were left in the place where they were born, in the care of the friars, until they were five or six years old. They were then brought to Nombre de Dios, where "if they escaped sickness the first or second month, they commonly lived in it as healthily as in any other place." Life in Venta Cruz must have been far from pleasant. The Maroons were a continual menace, but the town was too well guarded, and too close to Panama, for them to put the place in serious danger. The inhabitants had to keep within the township; for the forest lay just beyond the houses, and lonely wanderers were certain to be stabbed by lurking Maroons or carried off by jaguars. In the season the mule trains were continually coming and going, either along the swampy track to Nombre de Dios or from Nombre de Dios to Panama. Boats came sleepily up the Chagres to drop their anchors by the jetty, with news from the Old World and the commodities which the New World did not yield. It must, then, have been one of the most eventful places in the uncomfortable isthmus; but no place can be very pleasant which has an annual rainfall of 120 inches and a mean annual temperature of about 80°. The country adjacent is indescribably beautiful; the river is clear and brilliant; the woods are gorgeous with many-coloured blossoms, and with birds and butterflies that gleam in green and blue among the leaves. During the rains the river sometimes rises forty feet in a night, and sweeps into the town with masses of rotting verdure from the hills. There is always fever in the place, but in the rainy season it is more virulent than in the dry. At present the town has few white inhabitants. The fair stone houses which Drake saw are long since gone, having been destroyed in one of the buccaneering raids a century later. The modern town is a mere collection of dirty huts, inhabited by negroes, half-breeds, and Indians.

CHAPTER V

BACK TO THE MAIN BODY

The treasure train—The spoil—Captain Tetû hurt

A S soon as the town was in his hands, Drake set guards on the bridge across the Chagres and at the gate by which he had entered the town. He gave orders to the Maroons that they were not to molest women or unarmed men. He gave them free permission to take what they would from the stores and houses, and then went in person to comfort some gentlewomen "which had lately been delivered of children there." They were in terror of their lives, for they had heard the shouts and firing, and had thought that the Maroons were coming. They refused to listen to the various comforters whom Drake had sent to them, and "never ceased most earnestly entreating" that Drake himself would come to them. Drake succeeded in reassuring them that nothing "to the worth of a garter" would be taken from them. They then dried their tears, and were comforted.

The raiders stayed in the town about an hour and à half, during which time they succeeded in getting together a little comfortable dew of heaven—not gold, indeed, nor silver, but yet "good pillage." Drake allowed them this latitude so that they might not be cast down by the disappointment of the night. He gave orders, however, that no heavy loot should be carried from the town, because they had yet many miles to go, and were still in danger of attack. While the men were getting their spoils together, ready for marching, and eating a hasty breakfast

74

in the early morning light, a sudden fusillade began at
the Panama gate. Some ten or twelve cavaliers had
galloped in from Panama, supposing that the pirates
had left the town. They had come on confidently, right
up to the muzzles of the sentries' muskets. They had
then been met with a shattering volley, which killed and
wounded half their number and sent the others scattering
to the woods. Fearing that they were but a scouting
party, and that a troop of horse might be following to
support them, Drake gave the word to fall in for the
road. The spoil, such as it was, was shouldered; Drake
blew a blast upon his whistle; the men formed up into
their accustomed marching order, and tramped away from
Venta Cruz, across the Chagres bridge, just as the dawn
set the parrots screeching and woke the monkeys to their
morning song. They seem to have expected no pursuit;
but Drake was not a man to run unnecessary risks. His
men, including the Maroons, were "grown very valiant,"
yet they were granted no further chance to show their
valour. Drake told them that they had now been "well
near a fortnight" from the ship, with her company of sick
and sorry sailors. He was anxious to rejoin her without
delay, so the word was given to force the marching. He
refused to visit the Indian villages, though the Maroons
begged him earnestly to do so. His one wish was to
rejoin Ellis Hixom. He "hustled" his little company
without mercy, encouraging them "with such example
and speech that the way seemed much shorter." He
himself, we are told, "marched most cheerfully," telling
his comrades of the golden spoils they would win before
they sailed again for England. There was little ease
on that march to the coast, for Drake would allow no
one to leave the ranks. When provisions ran out they
had to march on empty stomachs. There was no hunting
of the peccary or the deer, as on the jolly progress west-

ward. "We marched many days with hungry stomachs,"
says the narrative, and such was the hurry of the march
that many of the men "fainted with sickness of weariness."
Their clothes were hanging on their backs in shreds and
tatters. Their boots had long since cracked and rotted.
Many of them were marching with their feet wrapped up
in rags. Many of them were so footsore they could
scarcely put their feet upon the ground. Swaying, limping, utterly road-weary, they came tottering into a little
village which the Maroons had built as a rest-house for
them, about three leagues from the ship. They were
quite exhausted. Their feet were bloody and swollen.
The last stages had been marched with great bodily
suffering, "all our men complaining of the tenderness
of their feet." Drake complained also, "sometimes without cause, but sometimes with cause indeed ; which made
the rest to bear the burden the more easily." Some of
the men were carried in by the Maroons. Indeed, the
Maroons had saved the whole party from collapse, for
they not only built them shelter huts at night, carried
the weary, and found, or made, them a road to travel
by, but they also bore the whole burden of the company's
arms and necessaries. Their fellows who had stayed with
Ellis Hixom had built the little town in the woods, for
the refreshment of all hands, in case they should arrive
worn out with marching. At sunset on the evening of
Saturday, the 22nd of February, the weary crew arrived
at the little town, to the great joy of the Maroons who
kept watch and ward there. The tired men lay down
to rest, while Drake "despatched a Cimaroon with a
token and certain order to the Master."
    The day had dawned before this messenger arrived upon
the sands near which the ship was moored. He hailed
her, crying out that he came with news, and immediately
a boat pushed off, manned by men "which longed to hear

of our Captain's speeding." As soon as he appeared before Ellis Hixom, he handed over Drake's golden toothpick, "which he said our Captain had sent for a token to Ellis Hixom, with charge to meet him at such a river." The sight of the golden toothpick was too much for Ellis Hixom. He knew it to be his Captain's property, but coming as it did, without a sign in writing, it convinced him that "something had befallen our Captain otherwise than well." The Maroon saw him staring "as amazed," and told him that it was dark when Drake had packed him off, so that no letter could be sent, "but yet with the point of his knife, he wrote something upon the toothpick, ' which,' he said, ' should be sufficient to gain credit to the messenger.'" Looking closely at the sliver of gold, Hixom saw a sentence scratched upon it: "By me, Francis Drake," which convinced him that the message was genuine. He at once called away one of the pinnaces, storing her with "what provision he could," and promptly set sail for the mouth of the Tortugos River, a few miles along the coast, to the west of where he lay, for there Drake intended to await him.

At about three o'clock that afternoon, Drake marched his men, or all who were fit to march, out of the forest to the sandy beach at the river's mouth. Half-an-hour later the tattered ragamuffins saw the pinnace running in to take them off, "which was unto us all a double rejoicing : first that we saw them, and next, so soon." The whole company stood up together on the beach to sing some of the psalms of thanksgiving—praising God "most heartily, for that we saw our pinnace and fellows again." To Ellis Hixom and his gang of shipkeepers the raiders appeared "as men strangely changed," though Drake was less changed than the others, in spite of the wound he got at Venta Cruz. The three weeks' march in that abominable country, and the last few days of "fasting and sore travail," would have been enough to "fore pine and waste" the very strongest, while "the grief we drew inwardly, for that we returned without that gold and treasure we hoped for, did no doubt show her print and footsteps in our faces." The next day the pinnace rowed "to another river in the bottom of the bay" to pick up the stragglers who had stayed to rest with the Maroons. The company was then reunited in the secret haven. Wonderful tales were told of the journey across the isthmus, of the South Sea, with its lovely city, and of the rush through the grass in the darkness, when the mule bells came clanging past, that night near Venta Cruz. The sick men recovering from their calentures "were thoroughly revived" by these tales. They importuned Drake to take them with him on the next foray; for Drake gave out that he meant not to leave off thus, but would once again attempt the same journey. In the general rejoicing and merry-making it is possible that Robert Pike remained aloof in the darkness of the 'tween decks, deprived of his allowance of aqua-vitæ.

Drake noted the eager spirit among his men, and determined to give it vent. He called them together to a consultation, at which they discussed what was best to be done until the mule trains again set forth from Panama. There was Veragua, "a rich town lying to the Westward, between Nombre de Dios and Nicaragua, where is the richest mine of fine gold that is on this North side." At Veragua also there were little rivers, in which "oftentimes they find pieces of gold as big as peas." Then, if Veragua were thought ill of, as too difficult, there were treasure ships to intercept as they wallowed home for Spain from Nombre de Dios. Or the men might keep themselves employed in capturing victual frigates for the stocking of the ship before they attacked another recua. This last scheme was flouted by many as unnecessary. They had food enough, they said, and what they lacked the country would supply, but the treasure, the comfortable dew of heaven, for which they had come so far, was the main thing, and to get that they were ready to venture on the galleons, soldiers or no soldiers. At this point the Maroons were called in to give their opinion. Most of them had served the Spaniards as slaves in one town or another of the Main. Several of them had worked under the whip of a wealthy Spaniard in Veragua, a creature of the name of Pezoro, who was "bad and cruel, not only to his slaves, but unto all men." This gentleman lived in a strong stone house at a little distance from the town. He had amassed a vast quantity of treasure, for he owned a gold mine, which he worked with 100 slaves. He lived with a guard of soldiers, but the Maroons felt confident that by attacking from the shore side of the house they could easily break in upon him. His gold was stored in his house "in certain great chests." If they succeeded in surprising the house, it would be an easy matter to make a spoil of the whole. Drake did not care for the scheme, as it involved a long march through the woods. He hesitated to put his men to so much labour, for he had now seen something of this woodland marching, and knew how desperate a toil it was. He thought that they would be better employed in gathering victuals and looking out for treasure transports. They might practise both crafts at the same time by separating into two companies. John Oxenham, in the *Bear* frigate, could sail "Eastwards towards Tolu, to see what store of victuals would come athwart his halse." In the meanwhile he would take the *Minion* pinnace to the west, to "lie off and on the Cabezas" in order to intercept any treasure transports coming from Veragua or Nicaragua to Nombre de Dios. Those of the Maroons who cared to stay aboard the *Pascha* were free to do so. The rest were dismissed "most courteously" with "gifts and favours" of the sorts most pleasing to them, such as knives, iron, coloured ribbons and cloth.

The companies were picked; the pinnaces received their stores; sails were bent and set, and the two boats sailed away to their stations. Off the Cabezas the *Minion* fell in with a frigate from Nicaragua "in which was some gold and a Genoese pilot." Drake treated this pilot in his usual liberal manner till he won him over to his interests. He had been in Veragua harbour, he said, but eight days before. He knew the channel perfectly, so that he could carry Drake in, at night if need were, at any state of the tide. The townsfolk, he said, were in a panic on account of Drake's presence in those seas; they were in such a state of terror that they could not decide upon a scheme to defend the town in case he attacked it. Signor Pezoro was thinking of removing himself to the South Seas. The harbour lay open to any enemy, for the only guns in the place were up at the town, about fifteen miles from the haven's mouth. If Drake made a sudden dash, he said, he would be able to cut out a frigate in the harbour. She was fitting for the sea there, and was very nearly ready to sail. She had aboard her "above a million of gold," which, with a little promptness and courage, might become the property of the raiders. On hearing of this golden booty, Drake thought of all that the Maroons had told him. He was minded to return to the anchorage, to fetch off some of those who had lived with Senor Pezoro, in order that he might have a check upon the pilot's statements, and a guide, if need were, to the city. The Genoese dissuaded him from this scheme, pointing out that a return to the ship would waste several days, during which the frigate might get away to sea. Drake, therefore, took the packets of gold from the Nicaraguan prize, and dismissed her "somewhat lighter to hasten her journey." He then got his oars out, and made all haste to the west, under a press of sail, "to get this harbour, and to enter it by night." He hoped to cut out the treasure ship and to have a look at the house of Senor Pezoro—two investments which would "make" the voyage if all went well. But as the boat drew near to the mouth of the harbour "we heard the report of two Chambers, and farther off, about a league within the bay, two others as it were answering them." The Spaniards had espied the boat, and had fired signal guns to warn thè shipping and the town. The report of the guns called the Spaniards to arms—an exercise they were more ready to since the Governor of Panama had warned them to expect Drake. "The rich Gnuffe Pezoro," it was thought, had paid the cost of the sentries. "It was not God's will that we should enter at that time," says the narrative. The wind shifted opportunely to the westward ; and Drake put his helm up, and ran away to the east, where he picked up the *Bear*, "according to appointment." Oxenham had had a very prosperous and pleasant cruise, for off Tolu he had come across a victual frigate "in which there were ten men [whom they set ashore], great store of maize, twenty - eight fat hogs, and two hundred hens." The lading was discharged into the *Pascha* on the 19th and 20th of March as a seasonable refreshment to the company. The frigate pleased Drake, for though she was small (not twenty tons, in fact) she was strong, new, and of a beautiful model. As soon as her cargo was out of her, he laid her on her side, and scraped and tallowed her "to make her a Man of war." He then fitted her with guns from the *Pascha*, and stored her with provisions for a cruise. The Spaniards taken in her had spoken of "two little galleys built in Nombre de Dios, to waft [tow] the Chagres Fleet to and fro." They were "not yet both launched," and the Chagres fleet lay waiting for them within the mouth of the Chagres River. Drake "purposed now to adventure for that Fleet." The day on

which he made his plan was Easter Sunday, the 22nd
March. " And to hearten his company " for that bold
attempt " he feasted them that Easter Day with great
cheer and cheerfulness " on the dainties taken from the
Spaniards.

The next day, he manned " the new tallowed frigate of
Tolu," and sailed away west (with Oxenham in the *Bear*
in company) " towards the Cativaas," where they landed
to refresh themselves. As they played about upon the sand,
flinging pebbles at the land-crabs, they saw a sail to the
westward coming down towards them. They at once
repaired aboard, and made sail, and " plied towards " the
stranger, thinking her to be a Spaniard. The stranger
held on her course as though to run the raiders aboard,
" till he perceived by our confidence that we were no
Spaniards, and conjectured we were those Englishmen
of whom he had heard long before." He bore up suddenly
under the lee of the English ships, " and in token of
amity shot off his lee ordnance "—a salute which Drake
at once acknowledged by a similar discharge. As the
ships neared each other, the stranger hailed Drake, saying
that he was Captain Tetû, or Le Testu, a Frenchman of
Newhaven (or Havre), in desperate want of water. He
had been looking for Drake, he said, for the past five
weeks, " and prayed our Captain to help him to some
water, for that he had nothing but wine and cider aboard
him, which had brought his men into great sickness "—
gastritis or dysentery. Drake at once sent a boat aboard
with a cask or two of drink, and some fresh meat, " willing
him to follow us to the next port, where he should have
both water and victuals."

As soon as they had brought their ships to anchor, the
French captain sent Drake " a case of pistols, and a fair
gilt scimitar (which had been the late King's of France)
whom Monsieur Montgomery hurt in the eye." The

Frenchman had received it from "Monsieur Strozze," or Strozzi, a famous general of banditti. Drake accepted the gift in the magnificent manner peculiar to him, sending the bearer back to Tetû with a chain of gold supporting a tablet of enamel. Having exchanged gifts, according to the custom of the sea, Captain Tetû came off to visit Drake. He was a Huguenot privateer, who had been in France at the time of the Massacre of St Bartholomew, the murder of Coligny, "and divers others murders." He had "thought those Frenchmen the happiest which were farthest from France," and had, therefore, put to sea to escape from persecution. He was now cruising off the Spanish Main, "a Man of war as we were." He had heard much of Drake's spoils upon the coast, and "desired to know" how he too might win a little Spanish gold. His ship was a fine craft of more than eighty tons, manned by seventy men and boys. He asked Drake to take him into partnership, so that they might share the next adventure.

The offer was not very welcome to Drake, for the French company was more than double the strength of the English. Drake had but thirty-one men left alive, and he regarded Tetû with a good deal of jealousy and a good deal of distrust. Yet with only thirty-one men he could hardly hope to succeed in any great adventure. If he joined with the French, he thought there would be danger of their appropriating most of the booty after using him and his men as their tools. The English sailors were of the same opinion; but it was at last decided that Tetû, with twenty picked hands, should be admitted to partnership, "to serve with our Captain for halves." It was something of a risk, but by admitting only twenty of the seventy men the risk was minimised. They were not enough to overpower Drake in case they wished to make away with all the booty, yet they made him sufficiently strong to attempt the schemes he had in hand. An agreement was, therefore, signed; a boat was sent to the secret anchorage to bring the Cimmeroons; and the three ships then sailed away to the east, to the magazines of food which Drake had stored some weeks before.

Here they lay at anchor for five or six days to enable the sick Frenchmen to get their health and strength after their weeks of misery. The Huguenot ship was revictualled from the magazines and then taken with the *Bear* into the secret haven. The third pinnace, the *Lion*, had been sunk a few days before, but the other two, the *Eion* and the *Minion*, with the new Tolu frigate, were set in order for the next adventure. Drake chose fifteen of his remaining thirty hands, and sent them down into the pinnaces with a few Maroons. The twenty Frenchmen joined him, under their captain, and the expedition then set sail for Rio Francisco, fifteen miles from Nombre de Dios. As they sailed, the Maroons gave out that the frigate was too deep a ship to cross the Rio Francisco bar, which had little water on it at that season of the year. They, therefore, sailed her back, and left her at the Cabezas, " manned with English and French, in the charge of Richard Doble," with strict orders not to venture out until the return of the pinnaces.

Putting her complement into the pinnaces, they again set sail for the mouth of the Francisco River. They crossed the bar without difficulty, and rowed their boats upstream. They landed some miles from the sea, leaving the pinnaces in charge of some Maroons. These had orders to leave the river, and hide themselves in the Cabezas, and to await the raiders at the landing-place, without fail, in four days' time.

As soon as Drake had landed, he ordered the company in the formation he had used on his march to Panama. He enjoined strict silence upon all, and gave the word

Cap.ᵗ GEORGE LOWTHER and his Company at Port
Mayo *in the Gulph of Matique.*

Captain George Lowther, a buccaneer of the early eighteenth century. In 1723
Lowther's ship was forced to surrender to the South Sea Company's ship *Eagle*.
Lowther escaped but shot himself a few days later. *Johnson.*

to march. They set forward silently, through the cane-brakes and lush undergrowth, upon the long, seven leagues march to the town of Nombre de Dios. They marched all day uncomplainingly, so that at dusk they had crept to within a mile of the trackway, a little to the south of the town. They were now on some gently rising ground, with the swamps and Nombre de Dios at their feet. It made a good camping-ground; and there they passed the night of the 31st of March, resting and feasting "in great stillness, in a most convenient place." They were so close to the town that they could hear the church bells ringing and the clatter of the hammers in the bay, where the carpenters were at work upon the treasure ships. They were working there busily, beating in the rivets all night, in the coolness, to fit the ships for sea. Nearer to them, a little to the west, was the trackway, so that they could hear the mule trains going past to Panama with a great noise of ringing bells.

Early on the morning of the 1st of April they heard a great clang of bells among the woods. The mule trains were coming in from Venta Cruz—three mule trains according to the Cimmeroons, laden with "more gold and silver than all of us could bear away." The adventurers took their weapons, and crept through the scrub to the trackway "to hear the bells." In a few minutes, when each side of the track had been manned by the adventurers, the treasure trains trotted up with a great clang and clatter. There were three complete recuas, "one of 50 mules, the other two of 70 each, every of which carried 300 lbs. of silver; which in all amounted to near thirty tons." The trains were guarded by a half company of Spanish foot, "fifteen to each company." The soldiers marched by the side of the trains, blowing on their matches to keep the smouldering ends alight. As the leading mules came up with the head of the ambush

Drake blew a blast upon his whistle. The raiders rose from their hiding-place, and fired a volley of shot and arrows at the troops. At the same moment tarry hands were laid upon the heads of the leading mules, so that "all the rest stayed and lay down as their manner is." The Spanish soldiers, taken by surprise, were yet a credit to their colours. They fell into confusion at the first assault, but immediately rallied. A brisk skirmish began, over the bodies of the mules, with sharp firing of muskets and arrows. Captain Tetû was hit in the belly with a charge of hail-shot; a Maroon was shot dead; and then the sailors cleared the road with a rush, driving the Spanish pell-mell towards the town. Then with feverish hands they cast adrift the mule packs "to ease some of the mules, which were heaviest loaden, of their carriage." They were among such wealth as few men have looked upon at the one time. How much they took will never now be known, but each man there had as much pure gold, in bars and quoits, as he could carry. They buried about fifteen tons of silver "partly in the burrows which the great land-crabs had made in the earth, and partly under old trees which were fallen thereabout, and partly in the sand and gravel of a river, "not very deep of water." Some of it, no doubt, remains there to this day.

In about two hours' time, they were ready to return to their pinnaces. They formed into order, and hurried away towards the woods, making as much haste as the weight of plunder would allow. As they gained the shelter of the forest they heard a troop of horse, with some arquebusiers, coming hurriedly to the rescue of the mules. They attempted no pursuit, for no Spaniard cared to enter the forest to attack a force in which Maroons were serving. The raiders were, therefore, able to get clear away into the jungle. All that day and the next day they hurried eastward through the scrub.

They made a brief pause, as they tramped, to lay down Captain Tetû, whose wound prevented him from marching. He could go no farther, and begged that he might be left behind in the forest, " in hope that some rest would recover him better strength." Two French sailors stayed with him to protect him.

CHAPTER VI

THE ADVENTURE OF THE RAFT

Drake's voyage to the Catives—Homeward bound—The interrupted
sermon

WHEN the retreating force had gone about two
leagues, they discovered that a Frenchman was
missing from the ranks. He had not been hurt in the
fight; but there was no time to search for him (as a matter
of fact, he had drunk too much wine, and had lost
himself in the woods), so again they pressed on to the
pinnaces and safety. On the 3rd of April, utterly worn
out with the hurry of the retreat, they came to the
Francisco River. They were staggering under the weight
of all their plunder, and, to complete their misery, they
were wet to the skin with a rain-storm which had raged
all night. To their horror they found no pinnaces awaiting
them, but out at sea, not far from the coast, were seven
Spanish pinnaces which had been beating up the inlets for
them. These were now rowing as though directly from
the rendezvous at the Cabezas, so that the draggled band
upon the shore made no doubt that their pinnaces had
been sunk, their friends killed or taken, and the retreat
cut off.

Drake's chief fear, on seeing these Spanish boats, was
that "they had compelled our men by torture to confess
where his frigate and ships were." To the disheartened
folk about him it seemed that all hope of returning home
was now gone, for they made no doubt that the ships were
by this time destroyed. Some of them flung down their

gold in despair while all felt something of the general panic. The Maroons recommended that the march should be made by land, "though it were sixteen days' journey," promising them that, if the ships were taken, they might sojourn among them in the forest as long as they wished. The sailors were in too great "distress and perplexity to listen to counsel ; but Drake had a genius for handling situations of the kind, and he now came forward to quell the uproar. The men were babbling and swearing in open mutiny, and the case demanded violent remedy. He called for silence, telling the mutineers that he was no whit better off than they were ; that it was no time to give way to fear, but a time to keep a stiff upper lip, and play the man. He reminded them that, even if the Spaniards had taken the pinnaces, "which God forbid," " yet they must have time to search them, time to examine the mariners, time to execute their resolution after it is determined." " Before all these times be taken," he exclaimed angrily, " we may get to our ships if ye will." They might not hope to go by land, he said, for it would take too long, and the ways would be too foul. But why should they not go by water ? There was the river at their feet, roaring down in full spate, tumbling the trunks of trees destroyed in last night's storm. Why in the world should they not make a raft of the trees, "and put ourselves to sea "? " I will be one," he concluded, " who will be the other ? " The appeal went home to the sailors. An Englishman named John Smith at once came forward, with a couple of Frenchmen " who could swim very well." The Maroons formed into a line beside the river, and the tree trunks were caught and hauled ashore to form the body of the raft. The branches were trimmed with the hatchets they had brought to clear a path through the forest. The boles were fastened together with thongs stolen from the recua, and with the pliant bejuca growing all about them.

The men worked merrily, convinced that Drake would find a way to bring the ship to them. As soon as the raft was built, a mast was stepped in her, on which a biscuit sack was hoisted for a sail. A young tree, working in a crutch, served them as a steering oar. The four men went aboard, a line was laid out to the bar, and the curious raft was hauled off into the sea. The last of the storm of the night before was still roaring up aloft. A high sea was running, and the wind blew strong from the west. Drake put his helm up, and stood off before it, crying out to the company that "if it pleased God, he should put his foot in safety aboard his frigate, he would, God willing, by one means or other get them all aboard, in despite of all the Spaniards in the Indies."

Those who have sailed on a raft in calm water will appreciate the courage of Drake's deed. The four men aboard her had to squat in several inches of salt water, holding on for their lives, while the green seas came racing over them "to the arm pits" at "every surge of the wave." The day was intensely hot in spite of the wind, and "what with the parching of the sun and what with the beating of the salt water, they had all of them their skins much fretted away." With blistered and cracking faces, parched with the heat and the salt, and shivering from the continual immersion, they sailed for six hours, making about a knot and a half an hour. When they had made their third league "God gave them the sight of two pinnaces" beating towards them under oars and sail, and making heavy weather of it. The sight of the boats was a great joy to the four sufferers on the raft. They edged towards them as best they could, crying out that all was safe, "so that there was no cause of fear." It was now twilight, and the wind, already fierce, was blowing up into a gale. In the failing light, with the spray sweeping into their eyes, the men aboard the pinnaces could not see the raft, nor could they make headway towards her with the wind as it was. As Drake watched, he saw them bear up for a cove to the lee of a point of land, where they could shelter for the night. He waited a few moments to see if they would put forth again, but soon saw that they had anchored. He then ran his raft ashore to windward of them, on the other side of the headland. He was very angry with the pinnaces' hands for their disobedience of orders. Had they done as he had commanded them, they would have been in the Francisco River the night before, and all the pains and danger of the raft would have been unnecessary. Drake, therefore, resolved to play a trick upon them. As soon as he landed, he set off running to the haven where the boats lay, followed by John Smith and the two Frenchmen—all running " in great haste," " as if they had been chased by the enemy." The hands in the pinnaces saw the four men hurrying towards them, and at once concluded that the Spaniards had destroyed the expedition, and that these four hunted wretches were the sole survivors. In an agony of suspense they got the four men into the boats, eagerly asking where the others were, and in what state. To these inquiries "he answered coldly, ' Well '"—an answer which convinced them that their mates were either dead or in the hands of the Spaniards. Drake watched their misery for a little while, and then being " willing to rid all doubts, and fill them with joy," he took from the bosom of his shirt " a quoit of gold," giving thanks to God that the voyage was at last "made." Some Frenchmen were in the boat, and to these he broke the news of Captain Tetû's wound and how he had been left behind in the forest, " and two of his company with him." He then bade the men to get the grapnels up, as he was determined to row to the Rio Francisco that night. After the anchors were raised, and the oars shipped, a few hours of desperate rowing brought them to the river's mouth, where the company had camped about a fire. By the dawn of the next day the whole expedition was embarked, and the pinnaces (their planking cracking with the weight of treasure) were running eastward with a fresh wind dead astern. They picked up the frigate that morning, and then stood on for the ships, under sail, with great joy. Soon they were lying safe at anchor in the shelter of the secret haven at Fort Diego. All the gold and silver were laid together in a heap, and there in the full view of all hands, French and English, Drake weighed it on the steward's meat scales, dividing it into two equal portions, to the satisfaction of everyone. The French took their portion aboard their ship as soon as it had been allotted to them. They then begged Drake for some more sea-stores, to fit them for the sea, and he gave them a quantity of provisions from his secret magazines. They then filled their water casks, and stood away to the west, to cruise for a few days off the Cabezas in the hope of obtaining news of Captain Tetû.

As soon as they had gone, Drake ordered his old ship, the *Pascha*, to be stripped of all things necessary for the fitting of the frigate, the Spanish prize. The long months at Port Diego had left her very foul, and it was easier to dismantle her than to fit her for the sea. While she was being stripped to equip the frigate, Drake organised another expedition to recover Captain Tetû and the buried silver. His men would not allow him to take a part in this final adventure, so Oxenham, and one Thomas Sherwell, were placed in command. Drake accompanied them as far as the Francisco River, taking an oar in one of the pinnaces which conveyed them. As they rowed lightly up the stream, the reeds were thrust aside, and one of Captain Tetû's two comrades came staggering out, and fell upon his knees. In a broken voice he thanked

God that ever Drake was born to deliver him thus, after he had given up all hope.

He told them that he had been surprised by the Spaniards half-an-hour after he had taken up his post beside his wounded captain. As the Spaniards came upon them, he took to his heels, followed by his mate. He had been carrying a lot of pillage, but as he ran he threw it all away, including a box of jewels, which caught his mate's eye as it fell in the grass. "His fellow took it up, and burdened himself so sore that he could make no speed," so that the Spaniards soon overtook him, and carried him away with Captain Tetû. Having taken two of the three Frenchmen, the Spaniards were content to leave the chase, and the poor survivor had contrived to reach the Rio Francisco after several days of wandering in the woods. As for the silver which they had buried so carefully in the sands, "he thought that it was all gone . . . for that . . . there had been near two thousand Spaniards and Negroes there to dig and search for it." Notwithstanding this report, John Oxenham with a company of twenty-seven men, marched west to view the place. He found that the earth "every way a mile distant had been digged and turned up," for the Spaniards had put their captives to the torture to learn what had been done with the treasure. Most of it had been recovered by this means, "yet nevertheless, for all that narrow search," a little of the dew of heaven was still glimmering in the crab-holes. The company was able to rout out some quantity of refined gold, with thirteen bars of silver, weighing some forty pounds apiece. With this spoil upon their backs, they returned to the Rio Francisco, where the pinnaces took them off to the frigate.

Now that the voyage was made, it was "high time to think of homeward," before the Spaniards should fit out men-of-war against them. Drake was anxious to give the *Pascha* to the Spanish prisoners, as some compensation for their weeks of captivity. He could not part with her, however, till he had secured another vessel to act as tender, or victualler, to his little frigate. He determined to make a cast to the east, as far as the Rio Grande, to look for some suitable ship. The Huguenot privateer, which had been lying off the Cabezas, sailed eastward in his company, having abandoned Captain Tetû and his two shipmates to the mercies of the Spaniards. They stood along the coast together as far as the Isles of San Barnardo, where the French ship parted company. The Spanish plate fleet, with its guard of galleons, was riding at the entry to Cartagena, and the Frenchmen feared that by coming too near they might be taken. They, therefore, saluted Drake with guns and colours, and shaped their course for Hispaniola and home.

But Drake held on in his way in a bravery, determined to see the Rio Grande before returning home. He sailed past Cartagena almost within gunshot, "in the sight of all the Fleet, with a flag of St George in the main top of our frigate, with silk streamers and ancients down to the water, sailing forward with a large wind." Late that night they arrived off the mouth of the Rio Grande, where they shortened sail, "and lay off and on." At midnight the wind veered round to the eastward, so that the victuallers at anchor in the river were able to set sail for Cartagena. About two o'clock in the morning a frigate slipped over the bar under small sail, and ran past Drake towards the west. The English at once opened fire upon her with their shot and arrows, to which the Spaniards replied with their quick-firing guns. While the English gunners plied her with missiles a pinnace laid her aboard, at which the Spaniards leaped overboard

and swam for the shore.   The newly taken frigate proved
to be some seven or eight tons larger than the one
in which the English had come to the east.   She was
laden with maize, hens, and hogs, and a large quantity
of honey from the wild bees of Nueva Reyna.   As
soon as the day dawned, the two frigates sailed
away again to the Cabezas to prepare for the voyage
home.

The prize's cargo was discharged upon the beach.   Both
frigates were then hove down, and the Spanish prisoners
(taken some weeks before) were allowed to depart aboard
the *Pascha*.   The barnacles were scrubbed and burned
off the frigates; their bends were resheathed and re-
tallowed; the provisions were stowed in good trim;
water casks were filled; and all things set in order for
the voyage.   The dainty pinnaces, which had done them
such good service, and carried them so many weary miles,
were then torn to pieces, and burned, " that the Cimaroons
might have the iron-work."   Lastly, Drake asked Pedro
and three Maroon chiefs to go through both the frigates
"to see what they liked."   He wished them to choose
themselves some farewell gifts, and promised them that
they should have what they asked, unless it were essential
to the safety of the vessels.   We are not told the choice
of the three Maroon chiefs, but we read that Pedro chose
the "fair gilt scimitar," the gift of Captain Tetû. which
had once belonged to Henri II. of France.   Drake had not
meant to part with it, but Pedro begged for it so prettily,
through the mouth of one Francis Tucker, that Drake
gave it him "with many good words," together with a
quantity of silk and linen for the wives of those who
had marched with him.   They then bade adieu to the
delighted Pedro and his fellows, for it was time to set
sail for England.   With a salute of guns and colours,
with the trumpets sounding, and the ships' companies

to give a cheer, the two little frigates slipped out of their harbour, and stood away under all sail for Cape St Antonio. They took a small barque laden with hides upon the way, but dismissed her as being useless to them after they had robbed her of her pump. At Cape St Antonio they salted and dried a number of turtles, as provisions for the voyage. Then they took their departure cheerfully towards the north, intending to call at Newfoundland to fill with water. The wind blew steadily from the south and west to blow them home, so that this scheme was abandoned. Abundant rain supplied their water casks, the wind held steady, the sun shone, and the blue miles slipped away. "Within twenty-three days" they passed "from the Cape of Florida to the Isles of Scilly," the two Spanish frigates being admirable sailers. With the silk streamers flying in a bravery the two ships sailed into Plymouth "on Sunday, about sermon time, August the 9th, 1573." There they dropped anchor to the thunder of the guns, to the great joy of all the townsfolk. "The news of our Captain's return . . . did so speedily pass over all the church, and surpass their minds with desire and delight to see him, that very few or none remained with the Preacher, all hastening to see the evidence of God's love and blessing towards our Gracious Queen and country, by the fruit of our Captain's labour and success. *Soli Deo Gloria.*"

We may take leave of him at this point, with the Plymouth bells ringing him a welcome and the worshippers flocking down to see him land.

Note.—"There were at the time," says the narrative, "belonging to Cartagena, Nombre de Dios, Rio Grande, Santa Marta, Rio de la Hacha, Venta Cruz, Veragua, Nicaragua, the Honduras, Jamaica, etc. ; above 200 frigates ; some of 120 tons, others but of 10 or 12 tons, but the most of 30 or 40 tons, which all had intercourse between Cartagena and Nombre de Dios. The most of which, during our abode in those parts, we took ; and some of them twice or thrice each."

Most of these frigates were provision ships, but in all of them, no doubt, there was a certain amount of gold and silver, besides uncut jewels or pearls from the King's Islands. We do not know the amount of Drake's plunder, but with the spoil of all these frigates, added to the loot of the recua, it must have been very considerable. He may have made as much as £40,000, or more, or less. It is as well to put the estimate low.

CHAPTER VII

JOHN OXENHAM

The voyage—His pinnace—Into the South Sea—Disaster—His unhappy end

THE John Oxenham, or Oxnam, who followed Drake to Nombre de Dios, and stood with him that sunny day watching the blue Pacific from the tree-top, was a Devonshire gentleman from South Tawton. He was of good family and well to do. He may, perhaps, have given money towards the fitting out of Drake's squadron. It is at least certain that he held in that voyage a position of authority considerably greater than that of "soldier, mariner, and cook"—the rates assigned to him by Sir Richard Hawkins. On his return from the Nombre de Dios raid, he disappears, and it is uncertain whether he followed Drake to Ireland, or settled down at home in Devonshire. He did not forget the oath he had sworn to his old Captain, to follow him to the South Sea in God's good time. But after waiting a year or two, and finding that Drake was not ready to attempt that adventure, he determined to go at his own charge, with such men as he could find. He was well known in the little Devon seaports as a bold sailor and fiery sea-captain. He was "a fine figure of a man," and the glory of Drake's raid was partly his. He was looked upon as one of the chief men in that foray. He had, therefore, little difficulty in getting recruits for a new voyage to the Main.

In the year 1574 he set sail from Plymouth in a fine ship of 140 tons, with a crew of seventy men and boys.

He made a fair passage to the Main, and anchored in Drake's old anchorage—either that of the secret haven, in the Gulf of Darien, or that farther west, among the Catives. Here he went ashore, and made friends with the Maroons, some of whom, no doubt, were old acquaintances, still gay with beads or iron-work which he had given them two years before. They told him that the treasure trains "from Panama to Nombre de Dios" were now strongly guarded by Spanish soldiers, so that he might not hope to win such a golden booty as Drake had won, by holding up a recua on the march. Oxenham, therefore, determined "to do that which never any man before enterprised"—by leaving his ship, marching over the watershed, building a pinnace in the woods, and going for a cruise on the South Sea. He dragged his ship far into the haven, struck her topmasts, and left her among the trees, beached on the mud, and covered with green boughs so as to be hidden from view. Her great guns were swung ashore, and buried, and the graves of them strewn with leaves and brushwood. He then armed his men with their calivers and their sacks of victual, "and so went with the Negroes," dragging with them two small guns, probably quick-firing guns, mounted on staves of wood or iron. Hawkins says that he left four or five men behind him as shipkeepers. After a march of "about twelve leagues into the maine-land" the Maroons brought him to a river "that goeth to the South Sea." Here the party halted, and built themselves little huts of boughs to live in while they made themselves a ship.

They cut down some trees here, and built themselves a pinnace "which was five and fortie foot by the keele." They seem to have brought their sails and tackling with them, but had they not done so they could have made shift with the rough Indian cloth and the fibrous, easily twisted bark of the maho-tree. Having built this little ship, they went aboard of her, and dropped downstream to the Pacific—the first English crew, but not the first Englishman, to sail those waters. Six negroes came with them to act as guides. As soon as they had sailed out of the river's mouth, they made for the Pearl Islands, or Islands of the King, "which is five and twentie leagues from Panama." Here they lay very close, in some snug inlet hidden from the sea. Some of them went inland to a rocky cliff, to watch the seas for ships coming northward from Peru with treasure from the gold and silver mines. The islands are in the fairway between Panama and Lima, but ten days passed before the watchers saw a sail, and cried out to those in the boat. "There came a small Barke by, which came from Peru, from a place called Quito"; and the pinnace dashed alongside of her, and carried her by the sword, before her sailors learned what was the matter. She was laden with "sixtie thousand pezos of golde, and much victuals.". John Oxenham took her lading, and kept the barque by him, while he stayed on at the islands. At the end of six days, another "barke" came by, from Lima, "in whiche he tooke an hundred thousand pezos of silver in barres." This was plunder enough to "make" any voyage, and with this John Oxenham was content. Before he sailed away, however, he marched upon one or two of the Pearl fisheries, where he found a few pearls, He then sailed northward to the river's mouth taking his prizes with him, with all the prisoners.

At the river's mouth he very foolishly "sent away the two prizes that hee tooke"—a piece of clemency which knotted the rope under his ear. He then sailed up the river, helping his pinnace by poles, oars, and warps, but making slow progress.

Before he reached this river, the negroes of the Pearl Islands sent word to the Governor of Panama that English

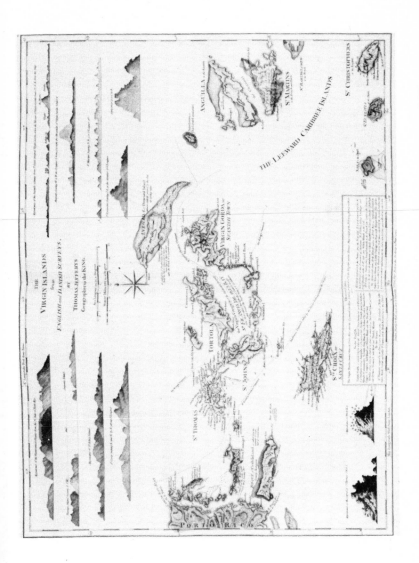

Chart of the Virgin Islands. Thomas Jefferys': *The West India Atlas...*, London; 1775.

pirates had been in those seas plundering their fisheries. "Within two days" the Governor despatched four galleys, "with negroes to rowe," and twenty-five musketeers in each galley, under the Captain John de Ortega, to search the Pearl Islands very thoroughly for those robbers. They reached the islands, learned in which direction the pirate ships had gone, and rowed away north to overtake them. As they came near the land, they fell in with the two prizes, the men of which were able to tell them how the pirates had gone up the river but a few days before.

John de Ortega came to the river's mouth with his four galleys, and "knew not which way to take, because there were three partitions in the river, to goe up in." He decided at last to go up the greatest, and was actually rowing towards it, when "he saw comming down a lesser river many feathers of hennes, which the Englishmen had pulled to eate." These drifting feathers, thrown overboard so carelessly, decided the Spanish captain. He turned up the lesser river "where he saw the feathers," and bade his negroes give way heartily. Four days later, he saw the English pinnace drawn up on the river-bank "upon the sands," guarded by six of her crew. The musketeers at once fired a volley, which killed one of the Englishmen, and sent the other five scattering to the cover of the woods. There was nothing in the pinnace but bread and meat. All the gold pezoes and the bars of silver had been landed.

The presence of the boat guard warned the Spanish captain that the main body of the pirates was near at hand. He determined to land eighty of his musketeers to search those woods before returning home. "Hee had not gone half a league" before he found one of the native huts, thatched with palm leaves, in which were "all the Englishmen's goods and the gold and silver also." The Englishmen were lying about the hut, many of them unarmed, with no sentry keeping a lookout for them. Taken by surprise as they were, they ran away into the woods, leaving all things in the hands of the Spaniards. The Spaniards carried the treasure back to the galleys, and rowed slowly down the river "without following the Englishmen any further."

It appeared later, that Oxenham had ordered his men to carry the gold and silver from the place where they had hauled the pinnace ashore, to the place where the ship was hidden. To this the mariners joyfully assented, "for hee promised to give them part of it besides their wages." Unfortunately, they wished this "part of it" paid to them at once, before they shifted an ingot—a want which seemed to reflect upon John Oxenham's honour. He was naturally very angry "because they would not take his word" to pay them something handsome when he reached home. He was a choleric sea-captain, and began, very naturally, to damn them for their insolence. "He fell out with them, and they with him," says Hakluyt. One of them, stung by his Captain's curses, "would have killed the Captaine" there and then, with his caliver,[1] or sailor's knife. This last act was too much. Oxenham gave them a few final curses, and told them that, if such were their temper, they should not so much as touch a quoit of the treasure, but that he would get Maroons to carry it. He then left them, and went alone into the forest to find Maroons for the porterage. As he came back towards the camp, with a gang of negroes, he met the five survivors of the boat guard "and the rest also which ran from the house," all very penitent and sorry now that the mischief had been done. They told him of the loss of the treasure, and looked to him for guidance and advice, promising a better behaviour in the future. Oxenham told them that if they helped

---

[1] *Caliver*, a light, hand musket. A musket without a crutch, or rest.

him to recover the treasure, they should have half of it, "if they got it from the Spaniards." "The Negroes promised to help him with their bows and arrows," and with this addition to their force they set off down the river-bank in pursuit.

After three days' travelling, they came upon the Spaniards, in camp, on the bank of the river, apparently in some strong position, sheltered with trees. Oxenham at once fell on "with great fury," exposing himself and his men to the bullets of the musketeers. The Spaniards were used to woodland fighting. Each musketeer retired behind a tree, and fired from behind it, without showing more than his head and shoulders, and then but for a moment. The Englishmen charged up the slope to the muzzles of the guns, but were repulsed with loss, losing eleven men killed and five men taken alive. The number of wounded is not stated. The negroes, who were less active in the charge, lost only five men. The Spaniards loss was two killed "and five sore hurt." The English were beaten off the ground, and routed. They made no attempt to rally, and did not fall on a second time.

The Spanish captain asked his prisoners why they had not crossed the isthmus to their ship in the days before the pursuit began. To this the prisoners answered with the tale of their mutinies, adding that their Captain would not stay longer in those parts now that his company had been routed. The Spaniards then buried their dead, retired on board their galleys, and rowed home to Panama, taking with them their prisoners and the English pinnace. When they arrived in that city, the prisoners were tortured till they confessed where their ship was hidden. Advice was then sent to Nombre de Dios, where four pinnaces were at once equipped to seek out the secret haven. They soon found the ship, "and brought her

to Nombre de Dios," where her guns and buried stores
were divided among the King's ships employed in the
work of the coast. While this search for the ship
was being made, the Viceroy of Peru sent out 150
musketeers to destroy the "fiftie English men" remaining alive. These troops, conducted by Maroons, soon
found the English in a camp by the river, "making of
certaine Canoas to goe into the North Sea, and there
to take some Bark or other." Many of them were sick
and ill, "and were taken." The rest escaped into the
forest, where they tried to make some arrangement with
the negroes. The negroes, it seems, were angry with
Oxenham for his failure to keep his word to them. They
had agreed to help him on condition that they might
have all the Spanish prisoners to torture "to feed their
insatiable revenges." Oxenham had released his prisoners,
as we have seen, and the Maroons had been disappointed
of their dish of roasted Spaniards' hearts. They were
naturally very angry, and told John Oxenham, when
he came to them for help, that his misfortunes were
entirely due to his own folly. Had he kept his word,
they said, he would have reached his ship without suffering these reverses. After a few days, being weary of
keeping so many foreigners, they betrayed the English
sailors to the Spaniards. "They were brought to
Panama," to the justice of that city, who asked John
Oxenham "whether hee had the Queene's licence, or the
licence of any other Prince or Lord, for his attempt."
To this John Oxenham answered that he had no licence
saving his sword. He was then condemned to death
with the rest of his company, with the exception of two
(or five) ships' boys. After a night or two in Panama
prison, within sound of the surf of the Pacific, the mariners
were led out, and shot. Oxenham and the master and
the pilot were sent to Lima, where they were hanged

as pirates in the square of the city. A force of musketeers was then sent into the interior, to reduce the Maroons "which had assisted those English men." The punitive force " executed great justice," till " the Negroes grew wise and wary," after which there was no more justice to be done. The ships' boys, who were spared, were probably sold as slaves in Lima, or Panama. They probably lived in those towns for the rest of their lives, and may have become good Catholics, and wealthy, after due probation under the whip.

Sir Richard Hawkins, who was in Panama in 1593, and who may have heard a Spanish version of the history, tells us that aboard the treasure ship taken by Oxenham were " two peeces of speciall estimation : the one a table of massie gold, with emralds . . . a present to the King ; the other a lady of singular beautie." According to Sir Richard, John Oxenham fell in love with this lady, and it was through her prayers that he released the other prisoners. He is said to have "kept the lady" when he turned the other prisoners away. The lady's "sonne, or a nephew," who was among those thus discharged, made every effort to redeem his mother (or aunt). He prayed so vehemently and "with such diligence," to the Governor at Panama, that the four galleys were granted to him "within few howers." The story is not corroborated ; but Oxenham was very human, and Spanish beauty, like other beauty, is worth sinning for.

A year or two later, Captain Andrew Barker of Bristol, while cruising off the Main, captured a Spanish frigate "between Chagre and Veragua." On board of her, pointing through the port-holes, were four cast-iron guns which had been aboard John Oxenham's ship. They were brought to England, and left in the Scilly Islands, A.D. 1576.

Note.—The story of John Oxenham is taken from " Purchas his Pilgrimes," vol. iv. (the original large 4to edition) ; and from Hakluyt, vol. iii. p. 526. Another version of the tale is given in Sir R. Hawkins' " Observations." He is also mentioned in Hakluyt's account of Andrew Barker.

CHAPTER VIII

THE SPANISH RULE IN HISPANIOLA

Rise of the buccaneers—The hunters of the wild bulls—Tortuga—
Buccaneer politics—Buccaneer customs

IN 1492, when Columbus landed on Hayti, he found
there about 1,000,000 Indians, of a gentle refine-
ment of manners, living peaceably under their kings or
caciques. They were "faint-hearted creatures," "a barbarous sort of people, totally given to sensuality and a
brutish custom of life, hating all manner of labour,
and only inclined to run from place to place." The
Spaniards killed many thousands of them, hunted a
number with their bloodhounds, sent a number to work
the gold-mines, and caused about a third of the population
to commit suicide or die of famine. They discouraged
sensuality and a distaste for work so zealously that
within twenty years they had reduced the population to
less than a twentieth part of its original 1,000,000 of souls.
They then called the island Hispaniola, and built a city,
on the south coast, as the capital. This city they called
Nueva Ysabel, in honour of the Queen of Spain, but the
name was soon changed to that of St Domingo.[1]

Those Indians who were not enslaved, retired to the
inmost parts of the island, to the shelter of the thickest
woods, where they maintained themselves by hunting.
The swine and cattle, which had belonged to their fellows
in their prosperous days, ran wild, and swarmed all over
the island in incredible numbers. The dogs of the

[1] See particularly Burney, Exquemeling, Edwards, and Hazard.

caciques also took to the woods, where they ranged in packs of two or three score, hunting the wild swine and the calves. The Spaniards seem to have left the interior of the island to the few survivors, as they had too few slaves to cultivate it. They settled themselves at St Domingo, and at various places upon the coast, such as Santiago and St John of Goave. They planted tobacco, sugar, chocolate, and ginger, and carried on a considerable trade with the cities on the Main and in the mother country.

Hayti, or Hispaniola, is in the fairway of ships coming from Europe towards the Main. It was at one time looked upon as the landfall to be made before proceeding west to Vera Cruz or south to Cartagena. The French, English, and Hollanders, who visited those seas " maugre the King of Spain's beard," discovered it at a very early date. They were not slow to recognise its many advantages. The Spanish, who fiercely resented the presence of any foreigners in a part of the world apportioned to Spain by the Pope, did all they could to destroy them whenever they had the opportunity. But the Spanish population in the Indies was small, and spread over a vast area, and restricted, by Government rules, to certain lines of action. They could not patrol the Indies with a number of guarda costas sufficient to exclude all foreign ships, nor could they set guards, in forts, at every estancia or anchorage in the vast coast-line of the islands. Nor could they enforce the Spanish law, which forbade the settlers to trade with the merchants of other countries. It often happened that a ship from France, Holland, or England arrived upon the coasts of Hispaniola, or some other Spanish colony, off some settlement without a garrison. The settlers in these out-of-the-way places were very glad to trade with such ships, for the freight they brought was cheaper and of better quality than that which paid duty to their King. The goods were landed,

and paid for. The ships sent their crews ashore to fill
fresh water or to reprovision, and then sailed home for
Europe, to return the next year with new goods. On
the St Domingo or Hispaniola coasts there are countless creeks and inlets, making good harbours, where these
smuggling ships might anchor or careen. The land was
well watered and densely wooded, so that casks could be
filled, and firewood obtained, without difficulty on any
part of the coast. Moreover, the herds of wild cattle and
droves of wild boars enabled the ships to reprovision
without cost. Before the end of the sixteenth century, it
had become the custom for privateers to recruit upon the
coast of Hispaniola, much as Drake recruited at Port
Plenty. The ships used to sail or warp into some snug
cove, where they could be laid upon the careen to allow
their barnacles to be burned away. The crews then landed,
and pitched themselves tents of sails upon the beach, while
some of their number took their muskets, and went to kill
the cattle in the woods. In that climate, meat does not
keep for more than a few hours, and it often happened
that the mariners had little salt to spare for the salting
of their kill. They, therefore, cured the meat in a manner
they had learned from the Carib Indians. The process
will be described later on.

The Spanish guarda costas, which were swift small
vessels like the frigates Drake captured on the Main,
did all they could to suppress the illegal trafficking.
Their captains had orders to take no prisoners, and every
"interloper" who fell into their hands was either hanged,
like Oxenham, or shot, like Oxenham's mariners. The
huntsmen in the woods were sometimes fired at by parties
of Spaniards from the towns. There was continual war
between the Spaniards, the surviving natives, and the
interlopers. But when the Massacre of St Bartholomew
drove many Huguenots across the water to follow the

fortunes of captains like Le Testu, and when the news of Drake's success at Nombre de Dios came to England, the interlopers began to swarm the seas in dangerous multitudes. Before 1580, the western coast of Hispaniola had become a sort of colony, to which the desperate and the adventurous came in companies. The ships used to lie at anchor in the creeks, while a number of the men from each ship went ashore to hunt cattle and wild boars. Many of the sailors found the life of the hunter passing pleasant. There were no watches to keep, no master to obey, no bad food to grumble at, and, better still, no work to do, save the pleasant work of shooting cattle for one's dinner. Many of them found the life so delightful that they did not care to leave it when the time came for their ships to sail for Europe. Men who had failed to win any booty on the "Terra Firma," and had no jolly drinking-bout to look for on the quays at home, were often glad to stay behind at the hunting till some more fortunate captain should put in in want of men. Ship-wrecked men, men who were of little use at sea, men "who had disagreed with their commander," began to settle on the coast in little fellowships.[1] They set on foot a regular traffic with the ships which anchored there. They killed great quantities of meat, which they exchanged (to the ships' captains) for strong waters, muskets, powder and ball, woven stuffs, and iron-ware. After a time, they began to preserve the hides, "by pegging them out very tite on the Ground,"—a commodity of value, by which they made much money. The bones they did not seem to have utilised after they had split them for their marrow. The tallow and suet were sold to the ships—the one to grease the ships' bottoms when careened, the other as an article for export to the European countries. It was a wild life, full of merriment and danger. The Spaniards killed a

[1] See Exquemeling, Burney, and the Abbé Raynal.

number of them, both French and English, but the casualties on the Spanish side were probably a good deal the heavier. The huntsmen became more numerous. For all that the Spaniards could do, their settlements and factories grew larger. The life attracted people, in spite of all its perils, just as tunny fishing attracted the young gallant in Cervantes. A day of hunting in the woods, a night of jollity, with songs, over a cup of drink, among adventurous companions—*qué cosa tan bonita!* We cannot wonder that it had a fascination. If a few poor fellows in their leather coats lay out on the savannahs with Spanish bullets in their skulls, the rum went none the less merrily about the camp fires of those who got away.

In 1586, on New Year's Day to be exact, Sir Francis Drake arrived off Hispaniola with his fleet. He had a Greek pilot with him, who helped him up the roads to within gunshot of St Domingo. The old Spanish city was not prepared for battle, and the Governor made of it " a New Year's gift " to the valorous raiders. The town was sacked, and the squadron sailed away to pillage Cartagena and St Augustine. Drake's raid was so successful that privateers came swarming in his steps to plunder the weakened Spanish towns. They settled on the west and north-west coasts of Hispaniola, compelling any Spanish settlers whom they found to retire to the east and south. The French and English had now a firm foothold in the Indies. Without assistance from their respective Governments they had won the right to live there, "maugre the King of Spain's beard." In a few years' time, they had become so prosperous that the Governments of France and England resolved to plant a colony in the Caribbee Islands, or Lesser Antilles. They thought that such a colony would be of benefit to the earlier adventurers by giving them official recognition and protection. A royal colony of French and English was, therefore, established on the island of St Christopher, or St Kitts, one of the Caribbees, to the east of Hispaniola, in the year 1625. The island was divided between the two companies. They combined very amicably in a murderous attack upon the natives, and then fell to quarrelling about the possession of an island to the south.

As the Governments had foreseen, their action in establishing a colony upon St Kitts did much to stimulate the settlements in Hispaniola. The hunters went farther afield, for the cattle had gradually left the western coast for the interior. The anchorages by Cape Tiburon, or "Cape Shark," and Samana, were filled with ships, both privateers and traders, loading with hides and tallow or victualling for a raid upon the Main. The huntsmen and hidecurers, French and English, had grown wealthy. Many of them had slaves, in addition to other valuable property. Their growing wealth made them anxious to secure themselves from any sudden attack by land or sea.

At the north-west end of Hispaniola, separated from that island by a narrow strip of sea, there is a humpbacked little island, a few miles long, rather hilly in its centre, and very densely wooded. At a distance it resembles a swimming turtle, so that the adventurers on Hispaniola called it Tortuga, or Turtle Island. Later on, it was known as Petit Guaves. Between this Tortuga and the larger island there was an excellent anchorage for ships, which had been defended at one time by a Spanish garrison. The Spaniards had gone away, leaving the place unguarded. The wealthier settlers seized the island, built themselves factories and houses, and made it " their head-quarters, or place of general rendezvous." After they had settled there, they seem to have thought themselves secure.[1]   In 1638 the Spaniards attacked the place, at a time when nearly all the men were absent at the hunting.   They killed all they found upon the island, and stayed there some little time, hanging those who surrendered to them after the first encounter. Having massacred some 200 or 300 settlers, and destroyed as many buildings as they could, the Spaniards sailed away, thinking it unnecessary to leave a garrison behind them.   In this they acted foolishly, for their atrocities stirred the interlopers to revenge themselves. A band of them returned to Tortuga, to the ruins which the Spaniards had left standing.   Here they formed themselves into a corporate body, with the intention to attack the Spanish at the first opportunity.   Here, too, for the first time, they elected a commander.   It was at this crisis in their history that they began to be known as buccaneers, or people who practise the boucan, the native way of curing meat.   It is now time to explain the meaning of the word and to give some account of the modes of life of the folk who brought it to our language.

The Carib Indians, and the kindred tribes on the Brazilian coast, had a peculiar way of curing meat for preservation.   They used to build a wooden grille or grating, raised upon poles some two or three feet high, above their camp fires.   This grating was called by the Indians barbecue.   The meat to be preserved, were it ox, fish, wild boar, or human being, was then laid upon the grille.   The fire underneath the grille was kept low, and fed with green sticks, and with the offal, hide, and bones of the slaughtered animal.   This process was called boucanning, from an Indian word "boucan," which seems to have signified "dried meat" and "camp-fire."   Buccaneer, in its original sense, meant one who practised the boucan.

[1] Burney.

Meat thus cured kept good for several months. It was of delicate flavour, " red as a rose," and of a tempting smell. It could be eaten without further cookery. Sometimes the meat was cut into pieces, and salted, before it was boucanned—a practice which made it keep a little longer than it would otherwise have done. Sometimes it was merely cut in strips, roughly rubbed with brine, and hung in the sun to dry into charqui, or jerked beef. The flesh of the wild hog made the most toothsome boucanned meat. It kept good a little longer than the beef, but it needed more careful treatment, as stowage in a damp lazaretto turned it bad at once. The hunters took especial care to kill none but the choicest wild boars for sea-store. Lean boars and sows were never killed. Many hunters, it seems, confined themselves to hunting boars, leaving the beeves as unworthy quarry.

When hunting, the buccaneers went on foot, in small parties of four or five. The country in which they hunted was densely wooded, so that they could not ride. Each huntsman carried a gun of a peculiar make, with a barrel four and a half feet long and a spade-shaped stock. The long barrel made the gun carry very true. For ramrods they carried three or four straight sticks of lance wood—a wood almost as hard as iron, and much more easily replaced. The balls used, weighed from one to two ounces apiece. The powder was of the very best make known. It was exported specially from Normandy—a country which sent out many buccaneers, whose phrases still linger in the Norman patois. For powder flask they used a hollow gourd, which was first dried in the sun. When it had dried to a fitting hardness it was covered with cuirbouilli, or boiled leather, which made it watertight. A pointed stopper secured the mouth, and made a sort of handle to the whole, by which it could be secured to the strap which the hunter slung across his shoulders. Each

hunter carried a light tent, made of linen or thin canvas.
The tents rolled up into a narrow compass, like a bando-
lier, so that they could be carried without trouble.   The
woods were so thick that the leggings of the huntsmen
had to be of special strength.   They were made of bull or
boar hide, the hair worn outwards.[1]   Moccasins, or shoes
for hunting, were made of dressed bull's hide.   The clothes
worn at sea or while out hunting were " uniformly slovenly."
A big heavy hat, wide in the brim and running up into a
peak, protected the wearer from sunstroke.   A dirty linen
shirt, which custom decreed should not be washed, was the
usual wear.   It tucked into a dirty pair of linen drawers
or knickerbockers, which garments were always dyed
a dull red in the blood of the beasts killed.   A sailor's
belt went round the waist, with a long machete or sheath-
knife secured to it at the back.   Such was the attire of a
master hunter, buccaneer, or Brother of the Coast.   Many
of them had valets or servants sent out to them from
France for a term of three years.   These valets were
treated with abominable cruelty, and put to all manner of
bitter labour.   A valet who had served his time was presented with a gun and powder, two shirts and a hat—an
equipment which enabled him to enter business on his
own account.   Every hunting party was arranged on the
system of share and share alike.   The parties usually
made their plans at the Tortuga taverns.   They agreed
with the sugar and tobacco planters to supply the plantations with meat in exchange for tobacco.   They then
loaded up their valets with hunters' necessaries, and sailed
for Hispaniola.   Often they remained in the woods for a
year or two, sending their servants to the coast from time
to time with loads of meat and hides.   They hunted, as a
rule, without dogs, though some sought out the whelps of
the wild mastiffs and trained them to hunt the boars.

[1] See Burney, and Exquemeling.

They stalked their quarry carefully, and shot it from behind a tree. In the evenings they boucanned their kill, pegged out the hides as tightly as they could, smoked a pipe or two about the fire, and prepared a glorious meal of marrow, "toute chaude"—their favourite dish. After supper they pitched their little linen tents, smeared their faces with grease to keep away the insects, put some wood upon the fire, and retired to sleep, with little thought of the beauty of the fireflies. They slept to leeward of the fires, and as near to them as possible, so that the smoke might blow over them, and keep off the mosquitoes. They used to place wet tobacco leaf and the leaves of certain plants among the embers in order that the smoke might be more pungent.

When the hunt was over, the parties would return to the coast to dispose of all they carried home, and to receive all they had earned during their absence. It was a lucrative business, and two years' hunting in the woods brought to each hunter a considerable sum of money. As soon as they touched their cash, they retired to Tortuga, where they bought new guns, powder, bullets, small shot, knives, and axes "against another going out or hunting." When the new munitions had been paid for, the buccaneers knew exactly how much money they could spend in self-indulgence. Those who have seen a cowboy on a holiday, or a sailor newly home from the seas, will understand the nature of the "great liberality" these hunters practised on such occasions. One who saw a good deal of their way of life[1] has written that their chief vice, or debauchery, was that of drunkenness, "which they exercise for the most part with brandy. This they drink as liberally as the Spaniards do clear fountain water. Sometimes they buy together a pipe of wine ; this they stave at the one end, and never cease drinking till they have made an end

[1] Exquemeling.

of it.   Thus they celebrate the festivals of Bacchus so long as they have any money left." The island of Tortuga must have witnessed some strange scenes.   We may picture a squalid little "cow town," with tropical vegetation growing up to the doors.   A few rough bungalow houses, a few huts thatched with palm leaves, a few casks standing in the shade of pent roofs.   To seaward a few ships of small tonnage lying at anchor.   To landward hilly ground, broken into strips of tillage, where some wretches hoe tobacco under the lash.   In the street, in the sunlight, lie a few savage dogs.   At one of the houses, a buccaneer has just finished flogging his valet; he is now pouring lemon juice, mixed with salt and pepper, into the raw, red flesh.   At another house, a gang of dirty men in dirty scarlet drawers are drinking turn about out of a pan of brandy.   The reader may complete the sketch should he find it sufficiently attractive.

When the buccaneers elected their first captain, they had made but few determined forays against the Spaniards. The greater number of them were French cattle hunters dealing in boucanned meat, hides, and tallow.   A few hunted wild boars ; a few more planted tobacco of great excellence, with a little sugar, a little indigo, and a little manioc.   Among the company were a number of wild Englishmen, of the stamp of Oxenham, who made Tortuga their base and pleasure-house, using it as a port from which to sally out to plunder Spanish ships.   After a cruise, these pirates sometimes went ashore for a month or two of cattle hunting.   Often enough, the French cattle hunters took their places on the ships.   The sailors and huntsmen soon became amphibious, varying the life of the woods with that of a sailor, and sometimes relaxing after a cruise with a year's work in the tobacco fields.   In 1638, when the Spanish made their raid, there were considerable numbers (certainly several hundreds) of men engaged in

A buccaneer's slave with his master's gun. *Exquemeling*

these three occupations. After the raid they increased
in number rapidly ; for after the raid they began to revenge
themselves by systematic raids upon the Spaniards—a
business which attracted hundreds of young men from
France and England. After the raid, too, the French and
English Governments began to treat the planters of the
St Kitts colony unjustly, so that many poor men were
forced to leave their plots of ground there. These men
left the colonies to join the buccaneers at Tortuga, who
soon became so numerous that they might have made an
independent state had they but agreed among themselves.
This they could not do, for the French had designs upon
Tortuga. A French garrison was landed on the island,
seemingly to protect the French planters from the English,
but in reality to seize the place for the French crown.
Another garrison encamped upon the coast of the larger
island. The English were now in a position like that of
the spar in the tale.[1] They could no longer follow the
business of cattle hunting ; they could no longer find an
anchorage and a ready market at Tortuga. They were
forced, therefore, to find some other rendezvous, where
they could refit after a cruise upon the Main. They withdrew themselves more and more from the French buccaneers, though the two parties frequently combined in
enterprises of danger and importance. They seem to have
relinquished Tortuga without fighting. They were less
attached to the place than the French. Their holdings
were fewer, and they had but a minor share in the cattle
hunting. But for many years to come they regarded the
French buccaneers with suspicion, as doubtful allies.
When they sailed away from Tortuga they sought out
other haunts on islands partly settled by the English.

In 1655, when an English fleet under Penn and Venables
came to the Indies to attack the Spaniards, a body of

[1] Precarious, and not at all permanent.

English buccaneers who had settled at Barbadoes came in their ships to join the colours. In all, 5000 of them mustered, but the service they performed was of poor quality. The combined force attacked St Domingo, and suffered a severe repulse. They then sailed for Jamaica, which they took without much difficulty. The buccaneers found Jamaica a place peculiarly suited to them: it swarmed with wild cattle; it had a good harbour; it lay conveniently for raids upon the Main. They began to settle there, at Port Royal, with the troops left there by Cromwell's orders. They planted tobacco and sugar, followed the boucan, and lived as they had lived in the past at Hispaniola. Whenever England was at war with Spain the Governor of the island gave them commissions to go privateering against the Spanish. A percentage of the spoil was always paid to the Governor, while the constant raiding on the Main prevented the Spaniards from attacking the new colony in force. The buccaneers were thus of great use to the Colonial Government. They brought in money to the Treasury and kept the Spanish troops engaged. The governors of the French islands acted in precisely the same way. They gave the French buccaneers every encouragement. When France was at peace with Spain they sent to Portugal ("which country was then at war with Spain") for Portuguese commissions, with which the buccaneer captains could go cruising. The English buccaneers often visited the French islands in order to obtain similar commissions. When England was at war with Spain the French came to Port Royal for commissions from the English Governor. It was not a very moral state of affairs; but the Colonial governors argued that the buccaneers were useful, that they brought in money, and that they could be disowned at any time should Spain make peace with all the interloping countries.

The buccaneers now began "to make themselves redoubtable to the Spaniards, and to spread riches and abundance in our Colonies." They raided Nueva Segovia, took a number of Spanish ships, and sacked Maracaibo and western Gibraltar. Their captains on these raids were Frenchmen and Portuguese. The spoils they took were enormous, for they tortured every prisoner they captured until he revealed to them where he had hidden his gold. They treated the Spaniards with every conceivable barbarity, nor were the Spaniards more merciful when the chance offered.

The buccaneers, French and English, had a number of peculiar customs or laws by which their strange society was held together. They seem to have had some definite religious beliefs, for we read of a French captain who shot a buccaneer "in the church" for irreverence at Mass. No buccaneer was allowed to hunt or to cure meat upon a Sunday. No crew put to sea upon a cruise without first going to church to ask a blessing on their enterprise. No crew got drunk, on the return to port after a successful trip, until thanks had been declared for the dew of heaven they had gathered. After a cruise, the men were expected to fling all their loot into a pile, from which the chiefs made their selection and division. Each buccaneer was called upon to hold up his right hand, and to swear that he had not concealed any portion of the spoil. If, after making oath, a man were found to have secreted anything, he was bundled overboard, or marooned when the ship next made the land. Each buccaneer had a mate or comrade, with whom he shared all things, and to whom his property devolved in the event of death.[1] In many cases the partnership lasted during life. A love for his partner was usually the only tender sentiment a buccaneer allowed himself.

When a number of buccaneers grew tired of plucking

[1] Similar pacts of comradeship are made among merchant sailors to this day.

weeds[1] from the tobacco ground, and felt the allurement of the sea, and longed to go a-cruising, they used to send an Indian, or a negro slave, to their fellows up the coast, inviting them to come to drink a dram with them. A day was named for the rendezvous, and a store was cleared, or a tobacco drying-house prepared, or perhaps a tent of sails was pitched, for the place of meeting. Early on the morning fixed for the council, a barrel of brandy was rolled up for the refreshment of the guests, while the black slaves put some sweet potatoes in a net to boil for the gentlemen's breakfasts. Presently a canoa or periagua would come round the headland from the sea, under a single sail—the topgallant-sail of some sunk Spanish ship. In her would be some ten or a dozen men, of all countries, anxious for a cruise upon the Main. Some would be Englishmen from the tobacco fields on Sixteen-Mile Walk. One or two of them were broken Royalists, of gentle birth, with a memory in their hearts of English country houses. Others were Irishmen from Montserrat, the wretched Kernes deported after the storm of Tredah. Some were French hunters from the Hispaniola woods, with the tan upon their cheeks, and a habit of silence due to many lonely marches on the trail. The new-comers brought their arms with them : muskets with long single barrels, heavy pistols, machetes, or sword-like knives, and a cask or two of powder and ball. During the morning other parties drifted in. Hunters, and planters, and old, grizzled seamen came swaggering down the trackways to the place of meeting. Most of them were dressed in the dirty shirts and blood-stained drawers of the profession, but some there were who wore a scarlet cloak or a purple serape which had been stitched for a

---

[1] Exquemeling gives many curious details of the life of these strange people. See the French edition of "Histoire des Avanturiers."

Spaniard on the Main. Among the party were generally some Indians from Campeachy—tall fellows of a
blackish copper colour, with javelins in their hands for
the spearing of fish. All of this company would gather
in the council chamber, where a rich planter sat at a
table with some paper scrolls in front of him.

As soon as sufficient men had come to muster, the
planter[1] would begin proceedings by offering a certain
sum of money towards the equipment of a roving
squadron. The assembled buccaneers then asked him
to what port he purposed cruising. He would suggest
one or two, giving his reasons, perhaps bringing in an
Indian with news of a gold mine on the Main, or of a
treasure-house that might be sacked, or of a plate ship
about to sail eastward. Among these suggestions one
at least was certain to be plausible. Another buccaneer
would then offer to lend a good canoa, with, perhaps, a
cask or two of meat as sea-provision. Others would
offer powder and ball, money to purchase brandy for
the voyage, or roll tobacco for the solace of the men.
Those who could offer nothing, but were eager to contribute and to bear a hand, would pledge themselves
to pay a share of the expenses out of the profits of the
cruise. When the president had written down the list
of contributions he called upon the company to elect
a captain. This was seldom a difficult matter, for some
experienced sailor—a good fellow, brave as a lion, and
fortunate in love and war—was sure to be among them.
Having chosen the captain, the company elected sailing
masters, gunners, chirurgeons (if they had them), and
the other officers necessary to the economy of ships of
war. They then discussed the "lays" or shares to be
allotted to each man out of the general booty.

Those who lent the ships and bore the cost of the pro-

---

[1] Exquemeling gives these details.

visioning, were generally allotted one-third of all the plunder taken. The captain received three shares, sometimes six or seven shares, according to his fortune. The minor officers received two shares apiece. The men or common adventurers received each one share. No plunder was allotted until an allowance had been made for those who were wounded on the cruise. Compensation varied from time to time, but the scale most generally used was as follows[1]:—"For the loss of a right arm six hundred pieces of eight, or six slaves; for the loss of a left arm five hundred pieces of eight, or five slaves; for a right leg five hundred pieces of eight, or five slaves; for a left leg four hundred pieces of eight, or four slaves; for an eye one hundred pieces of eight, or one slave; for a finger of the hand the same reward as for the eye."

In addition to this compensation, a wounded man received a crown a day (say three shillings) for two months after the division of the spoil. If the booty were too little to allow of the declaration of a dividend, the wounded were put ashore at the port of rendezvous, and the adventurers kept the seas until they had enough to bring them home.

In the years of buccaneer prosperity, when Port Royal was full of ruffians eager to go cruising, the proceedings may often have been less regular. A voyage was sometimes arranged in the taverns, where the gangs drank punch, or rumbo, a draught of rum and water (taken half-and-half, and sweetened with crude sugar) so long as their money lasted. If a gang had a ship, or the offer of a ship, and had but little silver left them from their last cruise, they would go aboard with their muskets, shot, and powder casks, trusting to fortune to obtain stores. Nearly every ship's company had a Mosquito Indian, or more than one, to act as guide ashore, in places where

[1] Exquemeling.

a native's woodcraft was essential to a white man's safety. At sea these Indians supplied the mariners with fish, for they were singularly skilful with the fish spear. When a gang of buccaneers put to sea without provisions, they generally steered to the feeding grounds of the sea-turtles, or to some place where the sea-cows, or manatees, were found.[1] Here the Indians were sent out in small canoes, with their spears and tortoise irons. The spears were not unlike our modern harpoons. The tortoise irons were short, heavy arrow heads, which penetrated the turtle's shell when rightly thrown. The heads were attached to a stick, and to a cord which they made of a fibrous bark. When the blow had gone home, the stick came adrift, leaving the iron in the wound, with the cord still fast to it. When the turtles had been hauled aboard, their flesh was salted with the brine taken from the natural salt-pans to be found among the islands. When a manatee was killed, the hide was stripped away, and hung to dry. It was then cut into thongs, and put to various uses. The buccaneers made grummets, or rings, of it, for use in their row boats instead of tholes or rowlocks. The meat of manatee, though extremely delicate, did not take salt so readily as that of turtles. Turtle was the stand-by of the hungry buccaneer when far from the Main or the Jamaican barbecues. In addition to the turtle they had a dish of fish whenever the Indians were so fortunate as to find a shoal, or when the private fishing lines, of which each sailor carried several, were successful. Two Mosquito Indians, it was said, could keep 100 men in fish with no other weapons than their spears and irons. In coasting along the Main, a buccaneer captain could always obtain sufficient food for his immediate need, for hardly any part of the coast was destitute of land-crabs, oysters, fruit, deer, peccary, or warree. But for

[1] Dampier.

a continued cruise with a large crew this hand-to-mouth
supply was insufficient.

The buccaneers sometimes began a cruise by sailing to
an estancia in Hispaniola, or on the Main, where they
might supply their harness casks with flesh.   They used
to attack these estancias, or "hog-yards," at night.   They
began by capturing the swine or cattle-herds, and threatening them with death should they refuse to give them the
meat they needed.   Having chosen as many beeves or
swine as seemed sufficient for their purpose, they kicked
the herds for their pains, and put the meat in pickle.[1]
They then visited some other Spanish house for a supply
of rum or brandy, or a few hat-loads of sugar in the crude.
Tobacco they stole from the drying-rooms of planters
they disliked.   Lemons, limes, and other anti-scorbutics
they plucked from the trees, when fortune sent them to
the coast.   Flour they generally captured from the
Spanish.   They seldom were without a supply, for it
is often mentioned as a marching ration—"a doughboy,
or dumpling," boiled with fat, in a sort of heavy cake,
a very portable and filling kind of victual.   At sea their
staple food was flesh—either boucanned meat or salted
turtle.   Their allowance, "twice a day to every one," was
"as much as he can eat, without either weight or measure."
Water and strong liquors were allowed (while they lasted)
in the same liberal spirit.   This reckless generosity was
recklessly abused.   Meat and drink, so easily provided,
were always improvidently spent.   Probably few buccaneer ships returned from a cruise with the hands on
full allowance.   The rule was "drunk and full, or dry
and empty, to hell with bloody misers"—the proverb
of the American merchant sailor of to-day.   They knew
no mean in anything.   That which came easily might
go lightly: there was more where that came from.

[1] Exquemeling.

When the ship had been thus victualled the gang went aboard her to discuss where they should go "to seek their desperate fortunes." The preliminary agreement was put in writing, much as in the former case, allotting each man his due share of the expected spoil. We read that the carpenter who "careened, mended, and rigged the vessel" was generally allotted a fee of from twenty-five to forty pounds for his pains—a sum drawn from the common stock or "purchase" subsequently taken by the adventurers. For the surgeon "and his chest of medicaments" they provided a "competent salary" of from fifty to sixty pounds. Boys received half-a-share, " by reason that, when they take a better vessel than their own, it is the duty of the boys to set fire to the ship or boat wherein they are, and then retire to the prize which they have taken." All shares were allotted on the good old rule: "No prey, No pay," so that all had a keen incentive to bestir themselves. They were also " very civil and charitable to each other," observing "among themselves, very good orders." They sailed together like a company of brothers, or rather, since that were an imperfect simile, like a company of jolly comrades. Locks and keys were forbidden among them, as they are forbidden in ship's fo'c's'les to this day; for every man was expected to show that he put trust in his mates. A man caught thieving from his fellow was whipped about the ship by all hands with little whips of ropeyarn or of fibrous maho bark. His back was then pickled with some salt, after which he was discharged the company. If a man were in want of clothes, he had but to ask a shipmate to obtain all he required. They were not very curious in the rigging or cleansing of their ships; nor did they keep watch with any regularity. They set their Mosquito Indians in the tops to keep a good lookout; for the Indians were long-sighted folk, who could descry

a ship at sea at a greater distance than a white man.
They slept, as a rule, on "mats" upon the deck, in the
open air. Few of them used hammocks, nor did they
greatly care if the rain drenched them as they lay
asleep.

After the raids of Morgan, the buccaneers seem to
have been more humane to the Spaniards whom they
captured. They treated them as Drake treated them,
with all courtesy. They discovered that the cutting out
of prisoners' hearts, and eating of them raw without
salt, as had been the custom of one of the most famous
buccaneers, was far less profitable than the priming of
a prisoner with his own aqua-vitæ. The later buccaneers,
such as Dampier, were singularly zealous in the collection
of information of "the Towns within 20 leagues of the sea,
on all the coast from Trinidado down to La Vera Cruz ; and
are able to give a near guess of the strength and riches
of them." For, as Dampier says, "they make it their
business to examine all Prisoners that fall into their
hands, concerning the Country, Town, or City that they
belong to ; whether born there, or how long they have
known it ? how many families ? whether most Spaniards ?
or whether the major part are not Copper-colour'd,
as Mulattoes [people half white, half black], Mustesoes
[mestizos, or people half white, half Indian. These are
not the same as mustees, or octoroons], or Indians ? whether
rich, and what their riches do consist in ? and what their
chiefest mauufactures ? If fortified, how many Great
Guns, and what number of small Arms ? whether it is
possible to come undescried on them ? How many Look-
outs or Centinels ? for such the Spaniards always keep ;
and how the Look-outs are placed ? Whether possible to
avoid the Look-outs or take them ? If any River or
Creek comes near it, or where the best Landing ? or
numerous other such questions, which their curiosities

lead them to demand. And if they have had any former discourse of such places from other Prisoners, they compare one with the other ; then examine again, and enquire if he or any of them, are capable to be guides to conduct a party of men thither : if not, where and how any Prisoner may be taken that may do it, and from thence they afterwards lay their Schemes to prosecute whatever design they take in hand."

If, after such a careful questioning as that just mentioned, the rovers decided to attack a city on the Main at some little distance from the sea, they would debate among themselves the possibility of reaching the place by river. Nearly all the wealthy Spanish towns were on a river, if not on the sea ; and though the rivers were unwholesome, and often rapid, it was easier to ascend them in boats than to march upon their banks through jungle. If on inquiry it were found that the suggested town stood on a navigable river, the privateers would proceed to some island, such as St Andreas, where they could cut down cedar-trees to make them boats. St Andreas, like many West Indian islands, was of a stony, sandy soil, very favourable to the growth of cedar-trees. Having arrived at such an island, the men went ashore to cut timber. They were generally good lumbermen, for many buccaneers would go to cut logwood in Campeachy when trade was slack. As soon as a cedar had been felled, the limbs were lopped away, and the outside rudely fashioned to the likeness of a boat. If they were making a periagua, they left the stern "flat"—that is, cut off sharply without modelling ; if they were making a canoa, they pointed both ends as a Red Indian points his birch-bark. The bottom of the boat in either case was made flat, for convenience in hauling over shoals or up rapids. The inside of the boat was hollowed out by fire, with the help of the Indians, who were very expert at the management of the flame. For oars they had paddles made of ash or cedar plank, spliced to the tough and straight-growing lance wood, or to the less tough, but equally straight, white mangrove. Thwarts they made of cedar plank. Tholes or grummets for the oars they twisted out of manatee hide. Having equipped their canoes or periaguas they secured them to the stern of their ship, and set sail towards their quarry.

Authorities.—Captain James Burney: "Voyages and Discoveries in the South Sea"; "History of the Buccaneers." Père Charlevoix: "Histoire de l'Isle Espagnole"; "Histoire et description de la N. France." B. Edwards: "Historical Survey of the Island of San Domingo." Gage: "Histoire de l'Empire Mexicain"; "The English American." S. Hazard: "Santo Domingo, Past and Present." Justin: "Histoire Politique de l'Isle de Haïti." Cal. State Papers: "America and West Indies." Abbé Raynal: "History of the Settlements and Trades of the Europeans in the East and West Indies." A. O. Exquemeling: "History of the Buccaneers." A. de Herrera: "Description des Indes Occidentales (d'Espagnol)." J. de Acosta: "History of the Indies." Cieca de Leon: "Travels."

CHAPTER IX

BUCCANEER CUSTOMS

Mansvelt and Morgan—Morgan's raid on Cuba—Puerto del
Principe

THROUGHOUT the years of buccaneering, the buccaneers often put to sea in canoes and periaguas,[1]
just as Drake put to sea in his three pinnaces. Life
in an open boat is far from pleasant, but men who
passed their leisure cutting logwood at Campeachy, or
hoeing tobacco in Jamaica, or toiling over gramma grass
under a hot sun after cattle, were not disposed to make
the worst of things. They would sit contentedly upon
the oar bench, rowing with a long, slow stroke for hours
together without showing signs of fatigue. Nearly all
of them were men of more than ordinary strength, and
all of them were well accustomed to the climate. When
they had rowed their canoa to the Main they were able
to take it easy till a ship came by from one of the Spanish
ports. If she seemed a reasonable prey, without too
many guns, and not too high charged, or high built, the
privateers would load their muskets, and row down to
engage her. The best shots were sent into the bows,
and excused from rowing, lest the exercise should cause
their hands to tremble. A clever man was put to the
steering oar, and the musketeers were bidden to sing out
whenever the enemy yawed, so as to fire her guns. It
was in action, and in action only, that the captain had
command over his men. The steersman endeavoured

---

[1] Dampier and Exquemeling.

129

to keep the masts of the quarry in a line, and to approach her from astern. The marksmen from the bows kept up a continual fire at the vessel's helmsmen, if they could be seen, and at any gun-ports which happened to be open. If the helmsmen could not be seen from the sea, the canoas aimed to row in upon the vessel's quarters, where they could wedge up the rudder with wooden chocks or wedges. They then laid her aboard over the quarter, or by the after chains, and carried her with their knives and pistols. The first man to get aboard received some gift of money at the division of the spoil.

When the prize was taken, the prisoners were questioned, and despoiled. Often, indeed, they were stripped stark naked, and granted the privilege of seeing their finery on a pirate's back. Each buccaneer had the right to take a shift of clothes out of each prize captured. The cargo was then rummaged, and the state of the ship looked to, with an eye to using her as a cruiser. As a rule, the prisoners were put ashore on the first opportunity, but some buccaneers had a way of selling their captives into slavery. If the ship were old, leaky, valueless, in ballast, or with a cargo useless to the rovers, she was either robbed of her guns, and turned adrift with her crew, or run ashore in some snug cove, where she could be burnt for the sake of the iron-work. If the cargo were of value, and, as a rule, the ships they took had some rich thing aboard them, they sailed her to one of the Dutch, French, or English settlements, where they sold her freight for what they could get—some tenth or twentieth of its value. If the ship were a good one, in good condition, well found, swift, and not of too great draught (for they preferred to sail in small ships), they took her for their cruiser as soon as they had emptied out her freight. They sponged and loaded her guns, brought their stores aboard her, laid their mats upon her deck, secured the boats astern, and sailed

away in search of other plunder. They kept little discipline aboard their ships. What work had to be done
they did, but works of supererogation they despised and
rejected as a shade unholy. The night watches were
partly orgies. While some slept, the others fired guns
and drank to the health of their fellows. By the light of
the binnacle, or by the light of the slush lamps in the
cabin, the rovers played a hand at cards, or diced each
other at " seven and eleven," using a pannikin as dice-box.
While the gamblers cut and shuffled, and the dice rattled
in the tin, the musical sang songs, the fiddlers set their
music chuckling, and the sea-boots stamped approval.
The cunning dancers showed their science in the moonlight, avoiding the sleepers if they could. In this jolly
fashion were the nights made short. In the daytime, the
gambling continued with little intermission ; nor had the
captain any authority to stop it. One captain, in the
histories, was so bold as to throw the dice and cards
overboard, but, as a rule, the captain of a buccaneer cruiser
was chosen as an artist, or navigator, or as a lucky fighter.
He was not expected to spoil sport. The continual
gambling nearly always led to fights and quarrels. The
lucky dicers often won so much that the unlucky had to
part with all their booty. Sometimes a few men would
win all the plunder of the cruise, much to the disgust of
the majority, who clamoured for a redivision of the spoil.
If two buccaneers got into a quarrel they fought it out
on shore at the first opportunity, using knives, swords, or
pistols, according to taste. The usual way of fighting
was with pistols, the combatants standing back to back,
at a distance of ten or twelve paces, and turning round to
fire at the word of command. If both shots missed, the
question was decided with cutlasses, the man who drew
first blood being declared the winner. If a man were
proved to be a coward he was either tied to the mast, and

shot, or mutilated, and sent ashore.   No cruise came to an end until the company declared themselves satisfied with the amount of plunder taken.   The question, like all other important questions, was debated round the mast, and decided by vote.

At the conclusion of a successful cruise, they sailed for Port Royal, with the ship full of treasure, such as vicuna wool, packets of pearls from the Hatch, jars of civet or of ambergris, boxes of "marmalett" and spices, casks of strong drink, bales of silk, sacks of chocolate and vanilla, and rolls of green cloth and pale blue cotton which the Indians had woven in Peru, in some sandy village near the sea, in sight of the pelicans and the penguins. In addition to all these things, they usually had a number of the personal possessions of those they had taken on the seas.   Lying in the chests for subsequent division were swords, silver-mounted pistols, daggers chased and inlaid, watches from Spain, necklaces of uncut jewels, rings and bangles, heavy carved furniture, "cases of bottles" of delicately cut green glass, containing cordials distilled of precious mints, with packets of emeralds from Brazil, bezoar stones from Patagonia, paintings from Spain, and medicinal gums from Nicaragua.   All these things were divided by lot at the main-mast as soon as the anchor held.   As the ship, or ships, neared port, her men hung colours out—any colours they could find—to make their vessel gay.   A cup of drink was taken as they sailed slowly home to moorings, and as they drank they fired off the cannon, "bullets and all," again and yet again, rejoicing as the bullets struck the water.   Up in the bay, the ships in the harbour answered with salutes of cannon; flags were dipped and hoisted in salute; and so the anchor dropped in some safe reach, and the division of the spoil began.

After the division of the spoil in the beautiful Port

The fight between Lieutenant Maynard of the *Swallow* and Blackbeard. The latter was wounded twenty-five times before dying. *The Pirates' Own Book, 1842.*

Royal harbour, in sight of the palm-trees and the fort with the colours flying, the buccaneers packed their gear, and dropped over the side into a boat. They were pulled ashore by some grinning black man with a scarlet scarf about his head and the brand of a hot iron on his shoulders. At the jetty end, where the Indians lounged at their tobacco and the fishermen's canoas rocked, the sunburnt pirates put ashore. Among the noisy company which always gathers on a pier they met with their companions. A sort of Roman triumph followed, as the "happily returned" lounged swaggeringly towards the taverns. Eager hands helped them to carry in their plunder. In a few minutes the gang was entering the tavern, the long, cool room with barrels round the walls, where there were benches and a table and an old blind fiddler jerking his elbow at a jig. Noisily the party ranged about the table, and sat themselves upon the benches, while the drawers, or potboys, in their shirts, drew near to take the orders. I wonder if the reader has ever heard a sailor in the like circumstance, five minutes after he has touched his pay, address a company of parasites in an inn with the question : "What's it going to be?"

After the settlement of Jamaica by the English, the buccaneers became more enterprising. One buccaneer captain, the most remarkable of all of them, a man named Mansvelt, probably a Dutchman from Curaçoa, attempted to found a pirate settlement upon the island of Santa Katalina, or Old Providence. Mansvelt was a fortunate sea-captain, with considerable charm of manner. He was popular with the buccaneers, and had a name among them, for he was the first of them to cross the isthmus and to sail the South Sea. His South-Sea cruise had come to little, for provisions ran short, and his company had been too small to attempt a Spanish town. He had, therefore, retreated to the North Sea to his ships, and had then gone cruising northward along the Nicaragua coast as far as the Blewfields River. From this point he stood away to the island of Santa Katalina, or Old Providence—an island about six miles long, with an excellent harbour, which, he thought, might easily be fortified. A smaller island lies directly to the north of it, separated from it by a narrow channel of the sea. Twenty years before his visit it had been the haunt of an old captain of the name of Blewfields, who had made it his base while his men went logwood cutting on the mainland. Blewfields was now dead, either of rum or war, and the Spaniards had settled there, and had built themselves a fort or castle to command the harbour. Having examined the place, Mansvelt sailed away to Jamaica to equip a fleet to take it. He saw that the golden times which the buccaneers were then enjoying could not last for ever, and that their occupation might be wrecked by a single ill-considered treaty, dated from St James's or the Court of France. He thought that the islands should be seized as a general rendezvous for folk of that way of life. With a little trouble the harbour could be made impregnable. The land was good, and suited for the growing of maize or tobacco—the two products most in demand among them. The islands were near the Main, being only thirty-five leagues from the Chagres River, the stream from which the golden harvest floated from the cities of the south. They were close to the coast of Nicaragua, where the logwood grew in clumps, waiting for the axes of the lumbermen. With the islands in their hands, the buccaneers could drive the Spaniards off the isthmus—or so Mansvelt thought. It would at anyrate have been an easy matter for them to have wrecked the trade routes from Panama to Porto Bello, and from Porto Bello to Vera Cruz.

While Mansvelt lay at Port Royal, scraping and tallow-ing his ships, getting beef salted and boucanned, and drumming up his men from the taverns, a Welshman, of the name of Henry Morgan, came sailing up to moorings with half-a-dozen captured merchantmen. But a few weeks before, he had come home from a cruise with a little money in his pockets. He had clubbed together with some shipmates, and had purchased a small ship with the common fund. She was but meanly equipped, yet her first cruise to the westward, on the coast of Campeachy, was singularly lucky. Mansvelt at once saw his opportunity to win recruits. A captain so fortunate as Morgan would be sure to attract followers, for the buccaneers asked that their captains should be valorous and lucky. For other qualities, such as prudence and forethought, they did not particularly care. Mansvelt at once went aboard Morgan's ship to drink a cup of sack with him in the cabin. He asked him to act as vice-admiral to the fleet he was then equipping for Santa Katalina. To this Henry Morgan very readily consented, for he judged that a great company would be able to achieve great things. In a few days, the two set sail together from Port Royal, with a fleet of fifteen ships, manned by 500 buccaneers, many of whom were French and Dutch.

As soon as they arrived at Santa Katalina, they anchored, and sent their men ashore with some heavy guns. The Spanish garrison was strong, and the fortress well situated, but in a few days they forced it to surrender. They then crossed by a bridge of boats to the lesser island to the north, where they ravaged the plantations for fresh supplies. Having blown up all the fortifications save the castle, they sent the Spanish prisoners aboard the ships. They then chose out 100 trusty men to keep the island for them. They left these on the island, under the command of a Frenchman of the name of Le

Sieur Simon. They also left the Spanish slaves behind, to work the plantations, and to grow maize and sweet potatoes for the future victualling of the fleet. Mansvelt then sailed away towards Porto Bello, near which city he put his prisoners ashore. He cruised to the eastward for some weeks, snapping up provision ships and little trading vessels; but he learned that the Governor of Panama, a determined and very gallant soldier, was fitting out an army to encounter him, should he attempt to land. The news may have been false, but it showed the buccaneers that they were known to be upon the coast, and that their raid up " the river of Colla " to " rob and pillage " the little town of Nata, on the Bay of Panama, would be fruitless. The Spanish residents of little towns like Nata buried all their gold and silver, and then fled into the woods when rumours of the pirates came to them. To attack such a town some weeks after the townsfolk had received warning of their intentions would have been worse than useless.

Mansvelt, therefore, returned to Santa Katalina to see how the colony had prospered while he had been at sea. He found that Le Sieur Simon had put the harbour " in a very good posture of defence," having built a couple of batteries to command the anchorage. In these he had mounted his cannon upon platforms of plank, with due munitions of cannon-balls and powder. On the little island to the north he had laid out plantations of maize, sweet potatoes, plantains, and tobacco. The first-fruits of these green fields were now ripe, and " sufficient to revictual the whole fleet with provisions and fruits."

Mansvelt was so well satisfied with the prospects of the colony that he determined to hurry back to Jamaica to beg recruits and recognition from the English Governor. The islands had belonged to English subjects in the past, and of right belonged to England still. However, the

Jamaican Governor disliked the scheme. He feared that
by lending his support he would incur the wrath of the
English Government, while he could not weaken his
position in Jamaica by sending soldiers from his garrison.
Mansvelt, "seeing the unwillingness" of this un-English
Governor, at once made sail for Tortuga, where he hoped
the French might be less squeamish. He dropped anchor,
in the channel between Tortuga and Hispaniola early in
the summer of 1665. He seems to have gone ashore to
see the French authorities. Perhaps he drank too strong
a punch of rum and sugar—a drink very prejudicial in
such a climate to one not used to it. Perhaps he took the
yellow fever, or the coast cramp; the fact cannot now be
known. At any rate he sickened, and died there, " before
he could accomplish his desires "—" all things hereby remaining in suspense." One account, based on the hearsay
of a sea-captain, says that Mansvelt was taken by the
Spaniards, and brought to Porto Bello, and there put to
death by the troops.

Le Sieur Simon remained at his post, hoeing his tobacco
plants, and sending detachments to the Main to kill manatee,
or to cut logwood. He looked out anxiously for Mansvelt's
ships, for he had not men enough to stand a siege, and
greatly feared that the Spaniards would attack him. While
he stayed in this perplexity, wondering why he did not
hear from Mansvelt, he received a letter from Don John
Perez de Guzman, the Spanish captain-general, who bade
him "surrender the island to his Catholic Majesty," on
pain of severe punishment. To this Le Sieur Simon made
no answer, for he hoped that Mansvelt's fleet would soon
be in those waters to deliver him from danger. Don John,
who was a very energetic captain-general, determined to
retake the place. He left his residence at Panama, and
crossed the isthmus to Porto Bello, where he found a ship,
called the *St Vincent*, "that belonged to the Company of

the Negroes" (the Isthmian company of slavers), lying at anchor, waiting for a freight.   We are told that she was a good ship, "well mounted with guns."   He provisioned her for the sea, and manned her with about 400 men, mostly soldiers from the Porto Bello forts.   Among the company were seven master gunners and "twelve Indians very dexterous at shooting with bows and arrows."   The city of Cartagena furnished other ships and men, bringing the squadron to a total of four vessels and 500 men-at-arms.   With this force the Spanish commander arrived off Santa Katalina, coming to anchor in the port there on the evening of a windy day, the 10th of August 1665. As they dropped anchor they displayed their colours. As soon as the yellow silk blew clear, Le Sieur Simon discharged "three guns with bullets" at the ships, "the which were soon answered in the same coin."   The Spaniard then sent a boat ashore to summon the garrison, threatening death to all if the summons were refused.   To this Le Sieur Simon replied that the island was a possession of the English Crown, "and that, instead of surrendering it, they preferred to lose their lives."   As more than a fourth of the little garrison was at that time hunting on the Main, or at sea, the answer was heroic. Three days later, some negroes swam off to the ships to tell the Spaniards of the garrison's weakness.   After two more days of council, the boats were lowered from the ships, and manned with soldiers.   The guns on the gun-decks were loaded, and trained.   The drums beat to quarters both on the ships and in the batteries.   Under the cover of the warship's guns, the boats shoved off towards the landing-place, receiving a furious fire from the buccaneers.   The "weather was very calm and clear," so that the smoke from the guns did not blow away fast enough to allow the buccaneers to aim at the boats.   The landing force formed into three parties, two of which attacked the flanks, and the third the centre. The battle was very furious, though the buccaneers were out-numbered and had no chance of victory. They ran short of cannon-balls before they surrendered, but they made shift for a time with small shot and scraps of iron, "also the organs of the church," of which they fired " threescore pipes" at a shot. The fighting lasted most of the day, for it was not to the advantage of the Spaniards to come to push of pike. Towards sunset the buccaneers were beaten from their guns. They fought in the open for a few minutes, round " the gate called Costadura," but the Spaniards surrounded them, and they were forced to lay down their arms. The Spanish colours were set up, and two poor Spaniards who had joined the buccaneers were shot to death upon the Plaza. The English prisoners were sent aboard the ships, and carried into Porto Bello, where they were put to the building of a fortress—the Iron Castle, a place of great strength, which later on the English blew to pieces. Some of the men were sent to Panama "to work in the castle of St Jerome "—a wonderful, great castle, which was burned at the sack of Panama almost before the mortar dried.

While the guns were roaring over Santa Katalina, as Le Sieur Simon rammed his cannon full of organ pipes, Henry Morgan was in lodgings at Port Royal, greatly troubled at the news of Mansvelt's death. He was busily engaged at the time with letters to the merchants of New England. He was endeavouring to get their help towards the forti-fication of the island he had helped to capture. " His principal intent," writes one who did not love the man, " was to consecrate it as a refuge and sanctuary to the Pirates of those parts," making it " a convenient receptacle or store house of their preys and robberies." It is pleasant to speculate as to the reasons he urged to the devout New England Puritans. He must have chuckled to himself, and

shared many a laugh with his clerk, to think that perhaps
a Levite, or a Man of God, a deacon, or an elder, would
untie the purse-strings of the sealed if he did but agonise
about the Spanish Inquisition with sufficient earthquake
and eclipse.   He heard of the loss of the island before the
answers came to him, and the news, of course, "put him
upon new designs," though he did not abandon the scheme
in its entirety.   He had his little fleet at anchor in the
harbour, gradually fitting for the sea, and his own ship
was ready.   Having received his commission from the
Governor, he gave his captains orders to meet him on the
Cuban coast, at one of the many inlets affording safe
anchorage.   Here, after several weeks of cruising, he was
joined by "a fleet of twelve sail," some of them of several
hundred tons.   These were manned by 700 fighting men,
part French, part English.

At the council of war aboard the admiral's ship, it was
suggested that so large a company should venture on
Havana, which city, they thought, might easily be taken,
"especially if they could but take a few of the ecclesiastics."   Some of the pirates had been prisoners in the
Havana, and knew that a town of 30,000 inhabitants
would hardly yield to 700 men, however desperate.
"Nothing of consequence could be done there," they
pronounced, even with ecclesiastics, "unless with fifteen
hundred men."   One of the pirates then suggested
the town of Puerto del Principe, an inland town surrounded by tobacco fields, at some distance from the
sea.   It did a thriving trade with the Havana; and he
who suggested that it should be sacked, affirmed upon his
honour, like Boult over Maria, that it never yet "was
sacked by any Pirates."   Towards this virginal rich town
the buccaneers proceeded, keeping close along the coast
until they made the anchorage of Santa Maria.   Here they
dropped anchor for the night.

When the men were making merry over the punch, as they cleaned their arms, and packed their satchels, a Spanish prisoner "who had overheard their discourse, while they thought he did not understand the English tongue," slipped through a port-hole to the sea, and swam ashore. By some miracle he escaped the ground sharks, and contrived to get to Puerto del Principe some hours before the pirates left their ships. The Governor of the town, to whom he told his story, at once raised all his forces, "both freemen and slaves," to prejudice the enemy when he attacked. The forest ways were blocked with timber baulks, and several ambuscades were laid, with cannon in them, "to play upon them on their march." In all, he raised and armed 800 men, whom he disposed in order, either in the jungle at the ambuscades or in a wide expanse of grass which surrounded the town.

In due course Morgan sent his men ashore, and marched them through the wood towards the town. They found the woodland trackways blocked by the timber baulks, so they made a detour, hacking paths for themselves with their machetes, until they got clear of the wood. When they got out of the jungle they found themselves on an immense green field, covered with thick grass, which bowed and shivered in the wind. A few pale cattle grazed here and there on the savannah ; a few birds piped and twittered in the sunshine. In front of them, at some little distance, was the town they had come to pillage. It lay open to them—a cluster of houses, none of them very large, with warehouses and tobacco drying-rooms and churches with bells in them. Outside the town, some of them lying down, some standing so as to get a view of the enemy, were the planters and townsfolk, with their pikes and muskets, waiting for the battle to begin. Right in the pirates' front was a troop of horsemen armed with lances, swords, and pistols, drawn up in very good order, and ready to advance.   The pirates on their coming from the wood formed into a semicircle or half-moon shape, the bow outwards, the horns curving to prevent the cavalry from taking them in flank.   They had drums and colours in their ranks.   The drums beat out a bravery, the colours were displayed.   The men halted for a moment to get their breath and to reprime their guns.   Then they advanced slowly, to the drubbing of the drums, just as the Spanish horsemen trotted forward.   As the Spaniards sounded the charge, the buccaneers fired a volley of bullets at them, which brought a number of cavaliers out of their saddles.   Those horsemen who escaped the bullets dashed down upon the line, and fired their pistols at close quarters, afterwards wheeling round, and galloping back to reform. They charged again and again, "like valiant and courageous soldiers," but at every charge the pirates stood firm, and withered them with file-firing.   As they retired after each rush, the marksmen in the ranks picked them off one by one, killing the Governor, in his plumed hat, and strewing the grass with corpses.   They also manœuvred during this skirmish so as to cut off the horsemen from the town.   After four hours of battle the cavalry were broken and defeated, and in .no heart to fight further.   They made a last charge on their blown horses, but their ranks went to pieces at the muzzles of the pirates' guns.   They broke towards the cover of the woods, but the pirates charged them as they ran, and cut them down without pity.   Then the drums beat out a bravery, and the pirates rushed the town in the face of a smart fire.   The Spaniards fought in the streets, while some fired from the roofs and upper windows.   So hot was the tussle that the pirates had to fight from house to house.   The townsmen did not cease their fire, till the pirates were gathering wood to burn the town, in despair of taking it.

As soon as the firing ceased, the townsfolk were driven

to the churches, and there imprisoned under sentinels. Afterwards the pirates "searched the whole country round about the town, bringing in day by day many goods and prisoners, with much provision." The wine and spirits of the townsfolk were set on tap, and "with this they fell to banqueting among themselves, and making great cheer after their customary way." They feasted so merrily that they forgot their prisoners, "whereby the greatest part perished." Those who did not perish were examined in the Plaza, "to make them confess where they had hidden their goods." Those who would not tell where they had buried their gold were tortured very barbarously by burning matches, twisted cords, or lighted palm leaves. Finally, the starving wretches were ordered to find ransoms, "else they should be all transported to Jamaica" to be sold as slaves. The town was also laid under a heavy contribution, without which, they said, "they would turn every house into ashes."

It happened that, at this juncture, some buccaneers, who were raiding in the woods, made prisoner a negro carrying letters from the Governor of the Havana. The letters were written to the citizens, telling them to delay the payment of their ransoms as long as possible, for that he was fitting out some soldiers to relieve them. The letters warned Henry Morgan that he had better be away with the treasure he had found. He gave order for the plunder to be sent aboard in the carts of the townsfolk. He then called up the prisoners, and told them very sharply that their ransoms must be paid the next day, "forasmuch as he would not wait one moment longer, but reduce the whole town to ashes, in case they failed to perform the sum he demanded." As it was plainly impossible for the townsfolk to produce their ransoms at this short notice he graciously relieved their misery by adding that he would be contented with 500 beeves, "together with

sufficient salt wherewith to salt them." He insisted that
the cattle should be ready for him by the next morning,
and that the Spaniards should deliver them upon the
beach, where they could be shifted to the ships without
delay. Having made these terms, he marched his men
away towards the sea, taking with him six of the principal
prisoners "as pledges of what he intended." Early the
next morning the beach of Santa Maria bay was thronged
with cattle in charge of negroes and planters. Some of
the oxen had been yoked to carts to bring the necessary
salt. The Spaniards delivered the ransom, and demanded
the six hostages. Morgan was by this time in some anxiety
for his position. He was eager to set sail before the Havana
ships came round the headland, with their guns run out,
and matches lit, and all things ready for a fight. He
refused to release the prisoners until the vaqueros "had
helped his men to kill and salt the beeves." The work
of killing and salting was performed "in great haste," lest
the Havana ships should come upon them before the beef
was shipped. The hides were left upon the sands, there
being no time to dry them before sailing. A Spanish
cowboy can kill, skin, and cut up a steer in a few minutes.
The buccaneers were probably no whit less skilful. By
noon the work was done. The beach of Santa Maria was
strewn with mangled remnants, over which the seagulls
quarrelled. But before Morgan could proceed to sea, he
had to quell an uproar which was setting the French and
English by the ears. The parties had not come to blows,
but the French were clamouring for vengeance with drawn
weapons. A French sailor, who was working on the
beach, killing and pickling the meat, had been plundered
by an Englishman, who "took away the marrowbones he
had taken out of the ox." Marrow, "toute chaude," was a
favourite dish among these people. The Frenchman could
not brook an insult of a kind as hurtful to his dinner as to

his sense of honour. He challenged the thief to single combat: swords the weapon, the time then. The buccaneers knocked off their butcher's work to see the fight. As the poor Frenchman turned his back to make him ready, his adversary stabbed him from behind, running him quite through, so that "he suddenly fell dead upon the place." Instantly the beach was in an uproar. The Frenchmen pressed upon the English to attack the murderer and to avenge the death of their fellow. There had been bad blood between the parties ever since they mustered at the quays before the raid began. The quarrel now raging was an excuse to both sides. Morgan walked between the angry groups, telling them to put up their swords. At a word from him, the murderer was seized, set in irons, and sent aboard an English ship. Morgan then seems to have made a little speech to pacify the rioters, telling the French that the man should be hanged ("hanged immediately," as they said of Admiral Byng) as soon as the ships had anchored in Port Royal bay. To the English, he said that the criminal was worthy of punishment, "for although it was permitted him to challenge his adversary, yet it was not lawful to kill him treacherously, as he did." After a good deal of muttering, the mutineers returned aboard their ships, carrying with them the last of the newly salted beef. The hostages were freed, a gun was fired from the admiral's ship, and the fleet hove up their anchors, and sailed away from Cuba, to some small sandy quay with a spring of water in it, where the division of the plunder could be made. The plunder was heaped together in a single pile. It was valued by the captains, who knew by long experience what such goods would fetch in the Jamaican towns.

To the "resentment and grief" of all the 700 men these valuers could not bring the total up to 50,000 pieces of eight—say £12,000—"in money and goods."

All hands were disgusted at "such a small booty, which was not sufficient to pay their debts at Jamaica." Some cursed their fortune ; others cursed their captain. It does not seem to have occurred to them to blame themselves for talking business before their Spanish prisoners. Morgan told them to "think upon some other enterprize," for the ships were fit to keep the sea, and well provisioned. It would be an easy matter, he told them, to attack some town upon the Main "before they returned home," so that they should have a little money for the taverns, to buy them rum with, at the end of the cruise. But the French were still sore about the murder of their man : they raised objections to every scheme the English buccaneers proposed. Each proposition was received contemptuously, with angry bickerings and mutterings. At last the French captains intimated that they desired to part company. Captain Morgan endeavoured to dissuade them from this resolution by using every flattery his adroit nature could suggest. Finding that they would not listen to him, even though he swore by his honour that the murderer, then in chains, should be hanged as soon as they reached home, he brought out wine and glasses, and drank to their good fortune. The booty was then shared up among the adventurers. The Frenchmen got their shares aboard, and set sail for Tortuga to the sound of a salute of guns. The English held on for Port Royal, in great "resentment and grief." When they arrived there they caused the murderer to be hanged upon a gallows, which, we are told, "was all the satisfaction the French Pirates could expect."

[NOTE.

Note.—If we may believe Morgan's statement to Sir T. Modyford, then Governor of Jamaica, he brought with him from Cuba reliable evidence that the Spaniards were planning an attack upon that colony (see State Papers : West Indies and Colonial Series). If the statements of his prisoners were correct, the subsequent piratical raid upon the Main had some justification. Had the Spaniards matured their plans, and pushed the attack home, it is probable that we should have lost our West Indian possessions.

Authorities.—A. O. Exquemeling : " Bucaniers of America," eds. 1684-5 and 1699. Cal. State Papers : " West Indies."

CHAPTER X

THE SACK OF PORTO BELLO

The Gulf of Maracaibo—Morgan's escape from the Spaniards

IT was a melancholy home-coming. The men had little more than ten pounds apiece to spend in jollity. The merchants who enjoyed their custom were of those kinds least anxious to give credit. The ten pounds were but sufficient to stimulate desire. They did not allow the jolly mariner to enjoy himself with any thoroughness. In a day or two, the buccaneers were at the end of their gold, and had to haunt the street corners, within scent of the rum casks, thinking sadly of the pleasant liquor they could not afford to drink. Henry Morgan took this occasion to recruit for a new enterprise. He went ashore among the drinking-houses, telling all he met of golden towns he meant to capture. He always "communicated vigour with his words," for, being a Welshman, he had a certain fervour of address, not necessarily sincere, which touched his simplest phrase with passion. In a day or two, after a little talk and a little treating, every disconsolate drunkard in the town was "persuaded by his reasons, that the sole execution of his orders, would be a certain means of obtaining great riches." This persuasion, the writer adds, "had such influence upon their minds, that with inimitable courage they all resolved to follow him." Even "a certain Pirate of Campeachy," a shipowner of considerable repute, resolved to follow Morgan "to seek new fortunes and greater advantages than he had found before." The French might hold aloof,

Nicholls delin.   J. Basire sculp

Capt BARTHOLOMEW ROBERTS.

Captain Bartholomew Roberts (1682–1722) who is reputed to have captured
over 400 ships in his career. Roberts was killed when his ship was captured by
H.M.S. *Swallow*. Johnson

they all declared, but an Englishman was still the equal
of a Spaniard ; while after all a short life and a merry
one was better than work ashore or being a parson.
With this crude philosophy, they went aboard again to
the decks they had so lately left. The Campeachy pirate
brought in a ship or two, and some large canoas. In all
they had a fleet of nine sail, manned by "four hundred
and three score military men." With this force Captain
Morgan sailed for Costa Rica.

When they came within the sight of land, a council
was called, to which the captains of the vessels went.
Morgan told them that he meant to plunder Porto Bello
by a night attack, "being resolved" to sack the place,
"not the least corner escaping his diligence." He added
that the scheme had been held secret, so that "it would
not fail to succeed well." Besides, he thought it likely
that a city of such strength would be unprepared for
any sudden attack. The captains were staggered by
this resolution, for they thought themselves too weak
"to assault so strong and great a city." To this the
plucky Welshman answered : "If our number is small, our
hearts are great. And the fewer persons we are, the more
union and better shares we shall have in the spoil." This
answer, with the thought of "those vast riches they
promised themselves," convinced the captains that the
town could be attempted. It was a "dangerous voyage
and bold assault" but Morgan had been lucky in the past,
and the luck might still be with him. He knew the Porto
Bello country, having been there with a party (perhaps
Mansvelt's party) some years before. At any rate the
ships would be at hand in the event of a repulse.

It was something of a hazard, for the Spanish garrison
was formed of all the desperate criminals the colonial
police could catch. These men made excellent soldiers,
for after a battle they were given the plunder of the men

they had killed. Then Panama, with its great garrison, was perilously near at hand, being barely sixty miles away, or two days' journey. Lastly, the town was strongly fortified, with castles guarding it at all points. The garrison was comparatively small, mustering about three companies of foot. To these, however, the buccaneers had to add 300 townsfolk capable of bearing arms. Following John Ex-quemeling's plan, we add a brief description of this famous town, to help the reader to form a mental picture of it.

Porto Bello stands on the south-eastern side of a fine bay, " in the province of Costa Rica." At the time when Morgan captured it (in June 1668) it was one of the strongest cities in the possession of the King of Spain. It was neglected until 1584, when a royal mandate caused the traders of Nombre de Dios to migrate thither. It then became the port of the galleons,[1] where the treasures of the south were shipped for Spain. The city which Morgan sacked was built upon a strip of level ground planted with fruit-trees, at a little distance from the sea, but within a few yards of the bay. The westward half of the town was very stately, being graced with fine stone churches and the residence of the lieutenant-general. Most of the merchants' dwellings (and of these there may have been 100) were built of cedar wood. Some were of stone, a thing unusual in the Indies, and some were partly stone, with wooden upper storeys. There was a fine stone convent peopled by Sisters of Mercy, and a dirty, ruinous old hospital for " the sick men belonging to the ships of war." On the shore there was a quay, backed by a long stone custom-house. The main street ran along the shore behind this custom-house, with cross-streets leading to the two great squares. The eastward half of the city, through which the road to Panama ran, was called Guinea ; for there the slaves and negroes used to

---

[1] With reservations. See p. 13, *note.*

live, in huts and cottages of sugar-cane and palm leaves. There, too, was the slave mart, to which the cargoes of the Guinea ships were brought. A little river of clear water divided the two halves of the town. Another little river, bridged in two places, ran between the town and Castle Gloria. The place was strongly fortified. Ships entering the bay had to pass close to the "Iron Castle," built upon the western point. Directly they stood away towards the town they were exposed to the guns of Castle Gloria and Fort Jeronimo—the latter a strong castle built upon a sandbank off the Guinea town. The constant population was not large, though probably 300 white men lived there all the year round, in addition to the Spanish garrison. The native quarter was generally inhabited by several hundred negroes and mulattoes. When the galleons arrived there, and for some weeks before, the town was populous with merchants, who came across from Panama to buy and sell. Tents were pitched in the Grand Plaza, in front of the Governor's house, for the protection of perishable goods, like Jesuits'-bark. Gold and silver bars became as common to the sight as pebbles. Droves of mules came daily in from Panama, and ships arrived daily from all the seaports in the Indies. As soon as the galleons sailed for Spain, the city emptied as rapidly as it had filled. It was too unhealthy a place for white folk, who continued there "no longer than was needful to acquire a fortune."

Indeed, Porto Bello was one of the most pestilential cities ever built, "by reason of the unhealthiness of the Air, occasioned by certain Vapours that exhale from the Mountains." It was excessively hot, for it lay (as it still lies) in a well, surrounded by hills, "without any intervals to admit the refreshing gales." It was less marshy than Nombre de Dios, but "the sea, when it ebbs, leaves a vast quantity of black, stinking mud, from whence there exhales an intolerable noisome vapour." At every fair-time "a kind of pestilential fever" raged, so that at least 400 folk were buried there annually during the five or six weeks of the market. The complaint may have been yellow fever; (perhaps the cholera), perhaps pernicious fever, aggravated by the dirty habits of the thousands then packed within the town. The mortality was especially heavy among the sailors who worked aboard the galleons, hoisting in or out the bales of merchandise. These mariners drank brandy very freely "to recruit their spirits," and in other ways exposed themselves to the infection. The drinking water of the place was "too fine and active for the stomachs of the inhabitants," who died of dysentery if they presumed to drink of it. The town smoked in a continual steam of heat, unrelieved even by the torrents of rain which fall there every day. The woods are infested with poisonous snakes, and abound in a sort of large toad or frog which crawls into the city after rains. The tigers "often make incursions into the street," as at Nombre de Dios, to carry off children and domestic animals. There was good fishing in the bay, and the land was fertile "beyond wonder," so that the cost of living there, in the *tiempo muerto*, was very small. There is a hill behind the town called the Capiro, about which the streamers of the clouds wreathe whenever rain is coming. The town was taken by Sir Francis Drake in 1595, by Captain Parker in 1601, by Morgan in 1668, by Coxon in 1679, and by Admiral Vernon in 1740.

Having told his plans, the admiral bade his men make ready. During the afternoon he held towards the west of Porto Bello, at some distance from the land. The coast up to the Chagres River, and for some miles beyond, is low, so that there was not much risk of the ships being sighted from the shore. As it grew darker, he edged into the land, arriving "in the dusk of the evening" at a place called Puerto de Naos, or Port of Ships, a bay midway between Porto Bello and the Chagres, and about ten leagues from either place.

They sailed westward up the coast for a little distance to a place called Puerto Pontin, where they anchored. Here the pirates got their boats out, and took to the oars, "leaving in the ships only a few men to keep them, and conduct them the next day to the port." By the light of lamps and battle lanterns the boats rowed on through the darkness, till at midnight they had came to a station called Estera longa Lemos, a river-mouth a few miles from Porto Bello, "where they all went on shore." After priming their muskets, they set forth towards the city, under the guidance of an English buccaneer, who had been a prisoner at Porto Bello but a little while before. When they were within a mile or two of the town, they sent this Englishmen with three or four companions to take a solitary sentry posted at the city outskirts. If they could not take him, they were to kill him, but without giving the alarm to the inhabitants. By creeping quietly behind him, the party took the sentry, "with such cunning that he had no time to give warning with his musket, or make any other noise." A knife point pressing on his spine, and a gag of wood across his tongue, warned him to attempt no outcry. Some rope-yarn was passed about his wrists, and in this condition he was dragged to Captain Morgan. As soon as he was in the admiral's presence, he was questioned as to the number of soldiers then in the forts, "with many other circumstances." It must have been a most uncomfortable trial, for "after every question, they made him a thousand menaces to kill him, in case he declared not the truth." When they had examined him to their satisfaction, they recommenced their march, "carrying always the said sentry bound before them." Another mile brought them to an outlying fortress, which was built apparently between Porto Bello and the sea, to protect the coast road and a few outlying plantations. It was not yet light, so the pirates crept about the fort unseen, "so that no person could get either in or out." When they had taken up their, ground Morgan bade the captured sentry hail the garrison, charging them to surrender on pain of being cut to pieces. The garrison at once ran to their weapons, and opened a fierce fire on the unseen enemy, thus giving warning to the city that the pirates were attacking. Before they could reload, the buccaneers, "the noble Sparks of Venus," stormed in among them, taking them in their confusion, hardly knowing what was toward. Morgan was furious that the Spaniards had not surrendered at discretion on his challenge. The pirates were flushed with the excitement of the charge. Someone proposed that they "should be as good as their words, in putting the Spaniards to the sword, thereby to strike a terror into the rest of the city." They hustled the Spanish soldiers "into one room," officers and men together. The cellars of the fort were filled with powder barrels. Some ruffian took a handful of the powder, and spilled a train along the ground, telling his comrades to stand clear. His mates ran from the building applauding his device. In another moment the pirate blew upon his musket match to make the end red, and fired the train he had laid, "and blew up the whole castle into the air, with all the Spaniards that were within." "Much the better way of the two," says one of the chroniclers, who saw the explosion.

"This being done," says the calm historian, "they pursued the course of their victory" into the town. By this time, the streets were thronged with shrieking townsfolk. Men ran hither and thither with their poor belongings. Many flung their gold and jewels into wells and cisterns, or stamped them underground, "to excuse their being totally robbed." The bells were set clanging in the belfries; while, to increase the confusion, the Governor rode into the streets, calling on the citizens to rally and stand firm. As the dreadful panic did not cease, he rode out of the mob to one of the castles (Castle Gloria), where the troops were under arms. It was now nearly daybreak, or light enough for them to see their enemy. As the pirates came in sight among the fruit-trees, the Governor trained his heavy guns upon them, and opened a smart fire. Some lesser castles, or the outlying works of Castle Gloria, which formed the outer defences of the town, followed his example; nor could the pirates silence them. One party of buccaneers crept round the fortifications to the town, where they attacked the monastery and the convent, breaking into both with little trouble, and capturing a number of monks and nuns. With these they retired to the pirates' lines.

For several hours, the pirates got no farther, though the fire did not slacken on either side. The pirates lay among the scrub, hidden in the bushes, in little knots of two and three. They watched the castle embrasures after each discharge of cannon, for the Spaniards could not reload without exposing themselves as they sponged or rammed. Directly a Spaniard appeared, he was picked off from the bushes with such precision that they lost "one or two men every time they charged each gun anew." The losses on the English side were fully as severe; for, sheltered though they were, the buccaneers lost heavily. The lying still under a hot sun was galling to the pirates' temper. They made several attempts to storm, but failed in each attempt owing to the extreme gallantry of the defence. Towards noon they made a furious attack, carrying fire-balls, or cans filled with powder and resin, in their hands "designing, if possible, to burn the doors of the castle." As they came beneath the walls, the Spaniards rolled down stones upon them, with "earthen pots full of powder" and iron shells filled full of chain-shot, "which forced them to desist from that attempt." Morgan's party was driven back with heavy loss. It seemed to Morgan at this crisis that the victory was with the Spanish. He wavered for some minutes, uncertain whether to call off his men. "Many faint and calm meditations came into his mind" seeing so many of his best hands dead and the Spanish fire still so furious. As he debated "he was suddenly animated to continue the assault, by seeing the English colours put forth at one of the lesser castles, then entered by his men." A few minutes later the conquerors came swaggering up to join him, "proclaiming victory with loud shouts of joy."

Leaving his musketeers to fire at the Spanish gunners, Morgan turned aside to reconnoitre. Making the capture of the lesser fort his excuse, he sent a trumpet, with a white flag, to summon the main castle, where the Governor had flown the Spanish standard. While the herald was gone upon his errand, Morgan set some buccaneers to make a dozen scaling ladders, "so broad that three or four men at once might ascend by them." By the time they were finished, the trumpeter returned, bearing the Governor's answer that "he would never surrender himself alive." When the message had been given, Captain Morgan formed his soldiers into companies, and bade the monks and nuns whom he had taken, to place the ladders against the walls of the chief castle. He thought that the Spanish Governor would hardly shoot down these religious persons, even though they bore the ladders for the scaling parties. In this he was very much mistaken. The Governor was there to hold the castle for his Catholic Majesty, and, like "a brave and courageous soldier," he "refused not to use his utmost endeavours to destroy whoever came near the walls." As the wretched monks and nuns came tottering forward with the ladders, they begged of him, "by all the Saints of Heaven," to haul his colours down, to the saving of their lives. Behind them were the pirates, pricking them forward with their pikes and knives. In front of them were the cannon of their friends, so near that they could see the matches burning in the hands of the gunners. "They ceased not to cry to him," says the narrative; but they could not "prevail with the obstinacy and fierceness that had possessed the Governor's mind"—"the Governor valuing his honour before the lives of the Mass-mumblers." As they drew near to the walls, they quickened their steps, hoping, no doubt, to get below the cannon muzzles out of range. When they were but a few yards from the walls, the cannon fired at them, while the soldiers pelted them with a fiery hail of hand-grenades. "Many of the religious men and nuns were killed before they could fix the ladders"; in fact, the poor folk were butchered there in heaps, before the ladders caught against the parapet. Directly the ladders held, the pirates stormed up with a shout, in great swarms, like a ship's crew going aloft to make the sails fast. They had "fireballs in their hands and earthen pots full of powder," which "they kindled and cast in among the Spaniards" from the summits of the walls. In the midst of the smoke and flame which filled the fort the Spanish Governor stood fighting gallantly. His wife and child were present in that house of death, among the blood and smell, trying to urge him to surrender. The men were running from their guns, and the hand-grenades were bursting all about him, but this Spanish Governor refused to leave his post. The buccaneers who came about him called upon him to surrender, but he answered that he would rather die like a brave soldier than be hanged as a coward for deserting his command, "so that they were enforc'd to kill him, nothwithstanding the cries of his Wife and Daughter."

The sun was setting over Iron Castle before the firing came to an end with the capture of the Castle Gloria. The pirates used the last of the light for the securing of their many prisoners. They drove them to some dungeon in the castle, where they shut them up under a guard. The wounded "were put into a certain apartment by itself," without medicaments or doctors, "to the intent their own complaints might be the cure of their diseases." In the dungeons of the castle's lower battery they found eleven English prisoners chained hand and foot. They were the survivors of the garrison of Providence, which the Spaniards treacherously took two years before. Their backs were scarred with many floggings, for they had been forced to work like slaves at the laying of the quay piles in the hot sun, under Spanish overseers. They were released at once, and tenderly treated, nor were they denied a share of the plunder of the town.

"Having finish'd this Jobb" the pirates sought out the "recreations of Heroick toil." "They fell to eating and drinking" of the provisions stored within the city, "committing in both these things all manner of debauchery and excess." They tapped the casks of wine and brandy, and "drank about" till they were roaring drunk. In this condition they ran about the town, like cowboys on a spree, "and never examined whether it were Adultery or Fornication which they committed." By midnight they were in such a state of drunken disorder that "if there had been found only fifty courageous men, they might easily have retaken the City, and killed the Pirats." The next day they gathered plunder, partly by routing through the houses, partly by torturing the townsfolk. They seem to have been no less brutal here than they had been in Cuba, though the Porto Bello houses yielded a more golden spoil than had been won at Puerto Principe. They racked one or two poor men until they died. Others they slowly cut to pieces, or treated to the punishment called "woolding," by which the eyes were forced from their sockets under the pressure of a twisted cord. Some were tortured with burning matches "and such like slight torments." A woman was roasted to death "upon a baking stone"—a sin for which one buccaneer ("as he lay sick") was subsequently sorry.

While they were indulging these barbarities, they drank and swaggered and laid waste. They stayed within the town for fifteen days, sacking it utterly, to the last ryal. They were too drunk and too greedy to care much about the fever, which presently attacked them, and killed a number, as they lay in drunken stupor in the kennels. News of their riot being brought across the isthmus, the Governor of Panama resolved to send a troop of soldiers, to attempt to retake the city, but he had great difficulty in equipping a sufficient force. Before his men were fit to march, some messengers came in from the imprisoned townsfolk, bringing word from Captain Morgan that he wanted a ransom for the city, "or else he would by fire consume it to ashes." The pirate ships were by this time lying off the town, in Porto Bello bay. They were taking in fresh victuals for the passage home. The ransom asked was 100,000 pieces of eight, or £25,000. If it had not been paid the pirates could have put their threat in force without the slightest trouble. Morgan made all ready to ensure his retreat in the event of an attack from Panama. He placed an outpost of 100 "well-arm'd" men in a narrow part of the passage over the isthmus. All the plunder of the town was sent on board the ships. In this condition he awaited the answer of the President.

As soon as that soldier had sufficient musketeers in arms, he marched them across the isthmus to relieve the city. They attempted the pass which Morgan had secured, but lost very heavily in the attempt. The buccaneers charged, and completely routed them, driving back the entire company along the road to Panama. The President had "to retire for that time," but he sent a blustering note to Captain Morgan, threatening him and his with death "when he should take them, as he hoped soon to do." To this Morgan replied that he would not deliver the castles till he had the money, and that if the money did not come, the castles should be blown to pieces, with the prisoners inside them. We are told that "the Governor of Panama perceived by this answer that no means would serve to mollify the hearts of the Pirates, nor reduce them to reason." He decided to let the townsfolk make what terms they could. In a few days more these wretched folk contrived to scrape together the required sum of money, which they paid over as their ransom.

Before the expedition sailed away, a messenger arrived from Panama with a letter from the Governor to Captain Morgan. It made no attempt to mollify his heart nor to reduce him to reason, but it expressed a wonder at the pirates' success. He asked, as a special favour, that Captain Morgan would send him "some small patterns" of the arms with which the city had been taken. He thought it passing marvellous that a town so strongly fortified should have been won by men without great guns. Morgan treated the messenger to a cup of drink, and gave him a pistol and some leaden bullets "to carry back to the President, his Master." "He desired him to accept that pattern of the arms wherewith he had taken Porto Bello." He requested him to keep them for a twelve-month, "after which time he promised to come to

Panama and fetch them away." The Spaniard returned the gift to Captain Morgan, "giving him thanks for lending him such weapons as he needed not." He also sent a ring of gold, with the warning "not to give himself the trouble of coming to Panama," for "he should not speed so well there" as he had sped at Porto Bello.

"After these transactions" Captain Morgan loosed his top-sail, as a signal to unmoor. His ships were fully victualled for the voyage, and the loot was safely under hatches. As a precaution, he took with him the best brass cannon from the fortress. The iron guns were securely spiked with soft metal nails, which were snapped off flush with the touch-holes. The anchors were weighed to the music of the fiddlers, a salute of guns was fired, and the fleet stood out of Porto Bello bay along the wet, green coast, passing not very far from the fort which they had blown to pieces. In a few days' time they raised the Keys of Cuba, their favourite haven, where "with all quiet and repose" they made their dividend. "They found in ready money two hundred and fifty thousand pieces of eight, besides all other merchandises, as cloth, linen, silks and other goods." The spoil was amicably shared about the mast before a course was shaped for their "common rendezvous"—Port Royal.

A godly person in Jamaica, writing at this juncture in some distress, expressed himself as follows :—"There is not now resident upon this place ten men to every [licensed] house that selleth strong liquors . . . besides sugar and rum works that sell without license." When Captain Morgan's ships came flaunting into harbour, with their colours fluttering and the guns thundering salutes, there was a rustle and a stir in the heart of every publican. "All the Tavern doors stood open, as they do at London, on Sundays, in the afternoon." Within those tavern doors, "in all sorts of vices and debauchery," the pirates spent their plunder "with huge prodigality," not caring what might happen on the morrow.

Shortly after the return from Porto Bello, Morgan organised another expedition with which he sailed into the Gulf of Maracaibo. His ships could not proceed far on account of the shallowness of the water, but by placing his men in the canoes he penetrated to the end of the Gulf. On the way he sacked Maracaibo, a town which had been sacked on two previous occasions—the last time by L'Ollonais only a couple of years before. Morgan's men tortured the inhabitants, according to their custom, either by "woolding" them or by placing burning matches between their toes. They then set sail for Gibraltar, a small town strongly fortified, at the south-east corner of the Gulf. The town was empty, for the inhabitants had fled into the hills with "all their goods and riches." But the pirates sent out search parties, who brought in many prisoners. These were examined, with the usual cruelties, being racked, pressed, hung up by the heels, burnt with palm leaves, tied to stakes, suspended by the thumbs and toes, flogged with rattans, or roasted at the camp fires. Some were crucified, and burnt between the fingers as they hung on the crosses ; "others had their feet put into the fire."

When they had extracted the last ryal from the sufferers they shipped themselves aboard some Spanish vessels lying in the port. They were probably cedar-built ships, of small tonnage, built at the Gibraltar yards. In these they sailed towards Maracaibo, where they found "a poor distressed old man, who was sick." This old man told them that the Castle de la Barra, which guarded the entrance to the Gulf, had been mounted with great guns and manned by a strong garrison. Outside the channel were three Spanish men-of-war with their guns run out and decks cleared for battle.

The truth of these assertions was confirmed by a scouting party the same day. In order to gain a little time Morgan sent a Spaniard to the admiral of the men-of-war, demanding a ransom "for not putting Maracaibo to the flame." The answer reached him in a day or two, warning him to surrender all his plunder, and telling him that if he did not, he should be destroyed by the sword. There was no immediate cause for haste, because the Spanish admiral could not cross the sandbanks into the Gulf until he had obtained flat-bottomed boats from Caracas. Morgan read the letter to his men "in the market-place of Maracaibo," "both in French and English," and then asked them would they give up all their spoil, and pass unharmed, or fight for its possession. They agreed with one voice to fight, "to the very last drop of blood," rather than surrender the booty they had risked their skins to get. One of the men undertook to rig a fireship to destroy the Spanish admiral's flagship. He proposed to fill her decks with logs of wood "standing with hats and Montera caps," like gunners standing at their guns. At the port-holes they would place other wooden logs to resemble cannon. The ship should then hang out the English colours, the Jack or the red St George's cross, so that the enemy should deem her "one of our best men of war that goes to fight them." The scheme pleased everyone, but there was yet much anxiety among the pirates. Morgan sent another letter to the Spanish admiral, offering to spare Maracaibo without ransom ; to release his prisoners, with one half of the captured slaves ; and to send home the hostages he brought away from Gibraltar, if he might be granted leave to pass the entry. The Spaniard rejected all these terms, with a curt intimation that, if the pirates did not surrender within two more days, they should be compelled to do so at the sword's point. Morgan received the Spaniard's answer angrily, resolving to attempt the passage "without surrendering anything." He ordered his men to tie the slaves and prisoners, so that there should be no chance of their attempting to rise. They then rummaged Maracaibo for brimstone, pitch, and tar, with which to make their fire-ship. They strewed her deck with fireworks and with dried palm leaves soaked in tar. They cut her outworks down, so that the fire might more quickly spread to the enemy's ship at the moment of explosion. They broke open some new gun-ports, in which they placed small drums, "of which the negroes make use." "Finally, the decks were handsomely beset with many pieces of wood dressed up in the shape of men with hats or monteras, and like-wise armed with swords, muskets, and bandoliers." The plunder was then divided among the other vessels of the squadron. A guard of musketeers was placed over the prisoners, and the pirates then set sail towards the passage. The fireship went in advance, with orders to fall foul of the *Spanish Admiral*, a ship of forty guns.

When it grew dark they anchored for the night, with sentinels on each ship keeping vigilant watch. They were close to the entry, almost within shot of the Spaniards; and they half expected to be boarded in the darkness. At dawn they got their anchors, and set sail towards the Spaniards, who at once unmoored, and beat to quarters. In a few minutes the fireship ran into the man-of-war, "and grappled to her sides" with kedges thrown into her shrouds. The Spaniards left their guns, and strove to thrust her away, but the fire spread so rapidly that they could not do so. The flames caught the warship's sails, and ran along her sides with such fury that her men had hardly time to get away from her before she blew her bows out, and went to the bottom. The second ship made no attempt to engage: her crew ran her ashore, and deserted, leaving her bilged in shallow water. As the

Bartholomew Roberts doodgebleeven.

Another portrait of Roberts showing his crimson damask coat and breeches that he was wearing at the time of his death. *Johnson.*

pirates rowed towards the wreck some of the deserters hurried back to fire her. The third ship struck her colours without fighting.

Seeing their advantage a number of the pirates landed to attack the castle, where the shipwrecked Spaniards were rallying. A great skirmish followed, in which the pirates lost more men than had been lost at Porto Bello. They were driven off with heavy loss, though they continued to annoy the fort with musket fire till the evening. As it grew dark they returned to Maracaibo, leaving one of their ships to watch the fortress and to recover treasure from the sunken flagship. Morgan now wrote to the Spanish admiral, demanding a ransom for the town. The citizens were anxious to get rid of him at any cost, so they compounded with him, seeing that the admiral disdained to treat, for the sum of 20,000 pieces of eight and 500 cattle. The gold was paid, and the cattle duly counted over, killed, and salted; but Morgan did not purpose to release his prisoners until his ship was safely past the fort. He told the Maracaibo citizens that they would not be sent ashore until the danger of the passage was removed. With this word he again set sail to attempt to pass the narrows. He found his ship still anchored near the wreck, but in more prosperous sort than he had left her. Her men had brought up 15,000 pieces of eight, with a lot of gold and silver plate, "as hilts of swords and other things," besides "great quantity of pieces of eight" which had "melted and run together" in the burning of the vessel.

Morgan now made a last appeal to the Spanish admiral, telling him that he would hang his prisoners if the fortress fired on him as he sailed past. The Spanish admiral sent an answer to the prisoners, who had begged him to relent, informing them that he would do his duty, as he wished they had done theirs. Morgan heard the answer, and realised that he would have to use some stratagem to escape the threatened danger. He made a dividend of the plunder before he proceeded farther, for he feared that some of the fleet might never win to sea, and that the captains of those which escaped might be tempted to run away with their ships. The spoils amounted to 250,000 pieces of eight, as at Porto Bello, though in addition to this gold there were numbers of slaves and heaps of costly merchandise.

When the booty had been shared he put in use his stratagem. He embarked his men in the canoes, and bade them row towards the shore " as if they designed to land." When they reached the shore they hid under the overhanging boughs "till they had laid themselves down along in the boats." Then one or two men rowed the boats back to the ships, with the crews concealed under the thwarts. The Spaniards in the fortress watched the going and returning of the boats. They could not see the stratagem, for the boats were too far distant, but they judged that the pirates were landing for a night attack. The boats plied to and from the shore at intervals during the day. The anxious Spaniards resolved to prepare for the assault by placing their great guns on the landward side of the fortress. They cleared away the scrub on that side, in order to give their gunners a clear view of the attacking force when the sun set. They posted sentries, and stood to their arms, expecting to be attacked.

As soon as night had fallen the buccaneers weighed anchor. A bright moon was shining, and by the moonlight the ships steered seaward under bare poles. As they came abreast of the castle on the gentle current of the ebb, they loosed their sails to a fair wind blowing seaward. At the same moment, while the top-sails were yet slatting, Captain Morgan fired seven great guns "with bullets" as a last defiance. The Spaniards dragged their cannon across the fortress, "and began to fire very furiously," without much success. The wind freshened, and as the ships drew clear of the narrows they felt its force, and began to slip through the water. One or two shots took effect upon them before they drew out of range, but "the Pirates lost not many of their men, nor received any considerable damage in their ships." They hove to at a distance of a mile from the fort in order to send a boat in with a number of the prisoners. They then squared their yards, and stood away towards Jamaica, where they arrived safely, after very heavy weather, a few days later. Here they went ashore in their stolen velvets and silks to spend their silver dollars in the Port Royal rum shops. Some mates of theirs were ashore at that time after an unlucky cruise. It was their pleasure "to mock and jeer" these unsuccessful pirates, "often telling them: Let us see what money you brought from Comana, and if it be as good silver as that which we bring from Maracaibo."

Note.—On his return from Maracaibo, Morgan gave out that he had met with further information of an intended Spanish attack on Jamaica. He may have made the claim to justify his actions on the Main, which were considerably in excess of the commission Modyford had given him. On the other hand, a Spanish attack may have been preparing, as he stated; but the preparations could not have gone far, for had the Spaniards been prepared for such an expedition Morgan's Panama raid could never have succeeded.

Authorities.—Exquemeling's "History of The Bucaniers of America"; Exquemeling's "History" (the Malthus edition), 1684. Cal. State Papers: West Indian and Colonial Series.

For my account of Porto Bello I am indebted to various brief accounts in Hakluyt, and to a book entitled "A Description of the Spanish Islands," by a "Gentleman long resident in those parts." I have also consulted the brief notices in Dampier's Voyages, Wafer's Voyages, various gazetteers, and some maps and pamphlets relating to Admiral Vernon's attack in 1739-40. There is a capital description of the place as it was in its decadence, *circa* 1820, in Michael Scott's "Tom Cringle's Log."

CHAPTER XI

MORGAN'S GREAT RAID

Chagres castle—Across the isthmus—Sufferings of the buccaneers
—Venta Cruz—Old Panama

SOME months later Henry Morgan found his pirates
in all the miseries of poverty. They had wasted all
their silver dollars, and longed for something "to expend
anew in wine" before they were sold as slaves to pay
their creditors. He thought that he would save them
from their misery by going a new cruise. There was
no need for him to drum up recruits in the rum shops,
for his name was glorious throughout the Indies. He
had but to mention that "he intended for the Main" to
get more men than he could ship. He "assigned the
south side of the Isle of Tortuga" for his rendezvous,
and he sent out letters to the "ancient and expert
Pirates" and to the planters and hunters in Hispaniola,
asking them, in the American general's phrase, "to come
and dip their spoons in a platter of glory." Long before
the appointed day the rendezvous was crowded, for ships,
canoes, and small boats came thronging to the anchorage
with all the ruffians of the Indies. Many marched to
the rendezvous across the breadth of Hispaniola "with
no small difficulties." The muster brought together a
grand variety of rascaldom, from Campeachy in the west
to Trinidad in the east. Hunters, planters, logwood
cutters, Indians, and half-breeds came flocking from their
huts and inns to go upon the grand account. Lastly,
Henry Morgan came in his fine Spanish ship, with the

brass and iron guns. At the firing of a gun the assembled captains came on board to him for a pirates' council, over the punch-bowl, in the admiral's cabin.

It was decided at this council to send a large party to the Main, to the de la Hacha River, "to assault a small village" of the name of La Rancheria—the chief granary in all the "Terra Firma." The pirates were to seize as much maize there as they could find—enough, if possible, to load the ships of the expedition. While they were away their fellows at Tortuga were to clean and rig the assembled ships to fit them for the coming cruise. Another large party was detailed to hunt in the woods for hogs and cattle.

In about five weeks' time the ships returned from Rio de la Hacha, after much buffeting at sea. They brought with them a grain ship they had taken in the port, and several thousand sacks of corn which the Spaniards had paid them as "a ransom for not burning the town." They had also won a lot of silver, "with all other things they could rob"—such as pearls from the local pearl beds. The hunters had killed and salted an incredible quantity of beef and pork, the ships were scraped and tallowed, and nothing more was to be done save to divide the victuals among all the buccaneers. This division did not take much time. Within a couple of days the admiral loosed his top-sail. The pirates fired off their guns and hove their anchors up. They sailed out of Port Couillon with a fair wind, in a great bravery of flags, towards the rendezvous at Cape Tiburon, to the south-west of the island Hispaniola. When they reached Cape Tiburon, where there is a good anchorage, they brought aboard a store of oranges, to save them from the scurvy. While the men were busy in the orange groves Henry Morgan "gave letters patent, or commissions," to all his captains, "to act all manner of hostility against the Spanish nation." For this act he had the sealed authority of the Council of Jamaica. He was no longer a pirate or buccaneer, but an admiral leading a national enterprise. As we have said, he had heard, on the Main, of an intended Spanish attack upon Jamaica; indeed, it is probable that his capture of Porto Bello prevented the ripening of the project. There is no need to whitewash Morgan, but we may at least regard him at this juncture as the saviour of our West Indian colonies. After the serving out of these commissions, and their due sealing, the captains were required to sign the customary articles, allotting the shares of the prospective plunder. The articles allotted very liberal compensation to the wounded; they also expressly stated the reward to be given for bravery in battle. Fifty pieces of eight were allotted to him who should haul a Spanish colour down and hoist the English flag in its place. Surgeons received 200 pieces of eight "for their chests of medicaments." Carpenters received one half of that sum. Henry Morgan, the admiral of the fleet, was to receive one-hundredth part of all the plunder taken. His vice-admiral's share is not stated. As a stimulus to the pirates, it was published through the fleet that any captain and crew who ventured on, and took, a Spanish ship should receive a tenth part of her value as a reward to themselves for their bravery. When the contracts had been signed Morgan asked his captains which town they should attempt. They had thirty-seven ships, carrying at least 500 cannon. They had 2000 musketeers, "besides mariners and boys," while they possessed "great quantity of ammunition, and fire balls, with other inventions of powder." With such an armament, he said, they could attack the proudest of the Spanish cities. They could sack La Vera Cruz, where the gold from Manila was put aboard the galleons, as they lay alongside the quays

moored to the iron ring-bolts; or they could go eastward to the town of Cartagena to pillage our Lady's
golden altar in the church there; or they could row up
the Chagres River, and keep the promise Morgan had
made to the Governor of Panama. The captains pronounced for Panama, but they added, as a rider, that it
would be well to go to Santa Katalina to obtain guides.
The Santa Katalina fort was still in the possession of
the Spaniards, who now used it as a convict settlement,
sending thither all the outlaws of the "Terra Firma." It
would be well, they said, to visit Santa Katalina to select
a few choice cut-throats to guide them over the isthmus.
With this resolution they set sail for Santa Katalina,
where they anchored on the fourth day, "before sunrise,"
in a bay called the Aguada Grande.

Some of the buccaneers had been there under Mansvelt,
and these now acted as guides to the men who went
ashore in the fighting party. A day of hard fighting
followed, rather to the advantage of the Spaniards, for
the pirates won none of the batteries, and had to sleep
in the open, very wet and hungry. The next day Morgan
threatened the garrison with death if they did not yield
"within few hours." The Governor was not a very gallant
man, like the Governor at Porto Bello. Perhaps he was
afraid of his soldiers, the convicts from the "Terra Firma."
At anyrate he consented to surrender, but he asked that
the pirates would have the kindness to pretend to attack
him, "for the saving of his honesty." Morgan agreed
very gladly to this proposition, for he saw little chance
of taking the fort by storm. When the night fell, he
followed the Governor's direction, and began a furious
bombardment, "but without bullets, or at least into the
air." The castles answered in the like manner, burning
a large quantity of powder. Then the pirates stormed
into the castles in a dramatic way; while the Spaniards

retreated to the church, and hung out the white flag.

Early the next morning the pirates sacked the place, and made great havoc in the poultry-yards and cattle-pens. They pulled down a number of wooden houses to supply their camp fires. The guns they nailed or sent aboard. The powder they saved for their own use, but some proportion of it went to the destruction of the forts, which, with one exception, they blew up. For some days they stayed there, doing nothing but "roast and eat, and make good cheer," sending the Spaniards to the fields to rout out fresh provisions. While they lay there, Morgan asked "if any banditti were there from Panama," as he had not yet found his guides. Three scoundrels came before him, saying that they knew the road across the isthmus, and that they would act as guides if such action were made profitable. Morgan promised them "equal shares in all they should pillage and rob," and told them that they should come with him to Jamaica at the end of the cruise. These terms suited the three robbers very well. One of them, "a wicked fellow," "the greatest rogue, thief and assassin among them," who had deserved rather "to be broken alive upon a wheel than punished with serving in a garrison," was the spokesman of the trio. He was the Dubosc of that society, "and could domineer and command over them," "they not daring to refuse obedience." This truculent ruffian, with his oaths and his knives and his black moustachios, was elected head guide.

After several days of ease upon the island Morgan sent a squadron to the Main, with 400 men, four ships, and a canoa, "to go and take the Castle of Chagre," at the entrance to the Chagres River. He would not send a larger company, though the fort was strong, for he feared "lest the Spaniards should be jealous of his designs upon

Panama "—lest they should be warned, that is, by re-
fugees from Chagres before he tried to cross the isthmus.
Neither would he go himself, for he was still bent upon
establishing a settlement at Santa Katalina. He chose
out an old buccaneer, of the name of Brodely or Bradly,
who had sailed with Mansvelt, to command the expedition. He was famous in his way this Captain Brodely,
for he had been in all the raids, and had smelt a quantity
of powder. He was as brave as a lion, resourceful as a
sailor, and, for a buccaneer, most prudent. Ordering his
men aboard, he sailed for the Chagres River, where, three
days later, he arrived. He stood in towards the river's
mouth ; but the guns of the castle opened on him, making
that anchorage impossible. But about a league from the
castle there is a small bay, and here Captain Brodely
brought his ships to anchor, and sent his men to their
blankets, warning them to stand by for an early call.

The castle of San Lorenzo, which guarded the Chagres
River's mouth, was built on the right bank of that river, on
a high hill of great steepness. The hill has two peaks,
with a sort of natural ditch some thirty feet in depth
between them. The castle was built upon the seaward
peak, and a narrow drawbridge crossed the gulley to the
other summit, which was barren and open to the sight.
The river swept round the northern side of the hill with
considerable force. To the south the hill was precipitous,
and of such "infinite asperity," that no man could climb
it. To the east was the bridged gully connecting the
garrison with the isthmus. To the west, in a crook of
the land, was the little port of Chagres, where ships
might anchor in seven or eight fathoms, "being very
fit for small vessels." Not far from the foot of the hill,
facing the river's mouth, there was a battery of eight great
guns commanding the approach. A little way beneath
were two more batteries, each with six great guns, to

supplement the one above.   A path led from these lower batteries to the protected harbour.   A steep flight of stairs, "hewed out of the rock," allowed the soldiers to pass from the water to the summit of the castle.   The defences at the top of the hill were reinforced with palisadoes.   The keep, or inner castle, was hedged about with a double fence of plank—the fences being six or seven feet apart, and the interstices filled in with earth, like gabions.   On one side of the castle were the store-sheds for merchandise and ammunition.   On the other, and within the palisadoes everywhere, were soldiers' huts, built of mud and wattle, thatched with palm leaves, "after the manner of the Indians."   Lastly, as a sort of outer defence, a great submerged rock prevented boats from coming too near the seaward side.

Early in the morning Captain Bradly turned his hands up by the boatswain's pipe, and bade them breakfast off their beef and parched corn.   Maize and charqui were packed into knapsacks for the march, and the pirates rowed ashore to open the campaign.   The ruffians from Santa Katalina took their stations at the head of the leading company, with trusty pirates just behind them ready to pistol them if they played false.   In good spirits they set forth from the beach, marching in the cool of the morning before the sun had risen.   The way led through mangrove swamps, where the men sank to their knees in rotting grasses or plunged to their waists in slime.   Those who have seen a tropical swamp will know how fierce the toil was.   They were marching in a dank world belonging to an earlier age than ours.   They were in the age of the coal strata, among wet, green things, in a silence only broken by the sound of dropping or by the bellow of an alligator.   They were there in the filth, in the heat haze, in a mist of miasma and mosquitoes.   In all probability they were swearing at themselves for coming thither.

At two o'clock in the afternoon the buccaneers pushed through a thicket of liane and green cane, and debouched quite suddenly upon the barren hilltop facing San Lorenzo Castle. As they formed up, they were met with a thundering volley, which threw them into some confusion. They retreated to the cover of the jungle to debate a plan of battle, greatly fearing that a fort so strongly placed would be impregnable without great guns to batter it. However, they were a reckless company, careless of their lives, and hot with the tramping through the swamp. Give it up they could not, for fear of the mockery of their mates. The desperate course was the one course open to them. They lit the fireballs, or grenades, they had carried through the marsh; they drew their swords, and "Come on!" they cried. "Have at all!" And forward they stormed, cursing as they ran. A company in reserve remained behind in cover, firing over the storming party with their muskets.

As the pirates threw themselves into the gully, the walls of San Lorenzo burst into a flame of gun fire. The Spaniards fought their cannon furiously—as fast as they could fire and reload—while the musketeers picked off the leaders from the loopholes. "Come on, ye English dogs!" they cried. "Come on, ye heretics! ye cuckolds! Let your skulking mates behind there come on too! You'll not get to Panama this bout." "Come on" the pirates did, with great gallantry. They flung themselves down into the ditch, and stormed up the opposite slope to the wooden palings. Here they made a desperate attempt to scale, but the foothold was too precarious and the pales too high. In a few roaring minutes the attack was at an end: it had withered away before the Spanish fire. The buccaneers were retreating in knots of one or two, leaving some seventy of their number on the sun-bleached rocks of the gully.

When they got back to the jungle they lay down to rest, and slept there quietly while the daylight lasted, though the Spaniards still sent shots in their direction. As soon as it was dark, they made another furious assault, flinging their fireballs against the palings in order to burst the planks apart. While they were struggling in the ditch, a pirate ran across the gully with his body bent, as is natural to a running man. As he ran, an arrow took him in the back, and pierced him through to the side. He paused a moment, drew the arrow from the wound, wrapped the shaft of it with cotton as a wad, and fired it back over the paling with his musket. The cotton he had used caught fire from the powder, and it chanced that this blazing shaft drove home into a palm thatch. In the hurry and confusion the flame was not noticed, though it spread rapidly across the huts till it reached some powder casks. There was a violent explosion just within the palisadoes, and stones and blazing sticks came rattling down about the Spaniards' ears. The inner castle roared up in a blaze, calling the Spaniards from their guns to quench the fire—no easy task so high above the water. While the guns were deserted, the pirates ran along the bottom of the ditch, thrusting their fireballs under the palisadoes, which now began to burn in many places. As the flames spread, the planking warped, and fell. The outer planks inclined slightly outward, like the futtocks of a ship, so that, when they weakened in the fire, the inner weight of earth broke them through. The pirates now stood back from the fort, in the long black shadows, to avoid the showers of earth—"great heaps of earth"—which were falling down into the ditch. Presently the slope from the bottom of the gully was piled with earth, so that the pirates could rush up to the breaches, and hurl their firepots across the broken woodwork. The San Lorenzo fort was now a spiring red flame of fire—a beacon to the ships at sea. Before midnight the wooden walls were burnt away to charcoal ; the inner fort was on fire in many places ; yet the Spaniards still held the earthen ramparts, casting down "many flaming pots," and calling on the English dogs to attack them. The pirates lay close in the shadows, picking off the Spaniards as they moved in the red firelight, so that many poor fellows came toppling into the gully from the mounds.

When day dawned, the castle lay open to the pirates. The walls were all burnt, and fallen down, but in the breaches stood the Spanish soldiers, manning their guns as though the walls still protected them. The fight began as furiously as it had raged the day before. By noon most of the Spanish gunners had been shot down by the picked musketeers ; while a storming party ran across the ditch, and rushed a breach. As the pirates gained the inside of the fort, the Spanish Governor charged home upon them with twenty-five soldiers armed with pikes, clubbed muskets, swords, or stones from the ruin. For some minutes these men mixed in a last desperate struggle ; then the Spaniards were driven back by the increasing numbers of the enemy. Fighting hard, they retreated to the inner castle, cheered by their Governor, who still called on them to keep their flag aloft. The inner castle was a ruin, but the yellow flag still flew there, guarded by some sorely wounded soldiers and a couple of guns. Here the last stand was made, and here the gallant captain was hit by a bullet, "which pierced his skull into the brain." The little band of brave men now went to pieces before the rush of pirates. Some of them fell back, still fighting, to the wall, over which they flung themselves "into the sea," dying thus honourably rather than surrender. About thirty of them, "whereof scarce ten were not wounded," surrendered in the ruins of the

inner fortress. These thirty hurt and weary men were
the survivors of 314 who had stood to arms the day
before. All the rest were dead, save "eight or nine," who
had crept away by boat up the Chagres to take the news to
Panama. No officer remained alive, nor was any powder
left ; the Spaniards were true soldiers. The pirates lost
"above one hundred killed" and over seventy wounded,
or rather more than half of the men engaged. While the
few remaining Spaniards dug trenches in the sand for
the burial of the many dead, the pirates questioned them
as to their knowledge of Morgan's enterprise. They knew
all about it, they said, for a deserter from the pirate ships
which raided the Rio de la Hacha (for grain) had spoken
of the scheme to the Governor at Cartagena. That
captain had reinforced the Chagres garrison, and had
sent a warning over the isthmus to the Governor at
Panama. The Chagres was now well lined with ambuscades. Panama was full of soldiers, and the whole Spanish
population was ready to take up arms to drive the pirates
to their ships, so they knew what they might look to
get in case they persisted in their plan. This information was sent to Henry Morgan at the Santa Katalina fort, with news of the reduction of the Chagres
castle. Before he received it, Captain Joseph Bradly
died in the castle, of a wound he had received in the
fighting.

When Morgan received the news that San Lorenzo had
been stormed, he began to send aboard the meat, maize,
and cassava he had collected in Santa Katalina. He had
already blown the Spanish forts to pieces, with the one
exception of the fort of St Teresa. He now took all the
captured Spanish guns, and flung them into the sea, where
they lie still, among the scarlet coral sprays. The Spanish
town was then burnt, and the Spanish prisoners placed
aboard the ships. It was Morgan's intention to return to

the island after sacking Panama, and to leave there a strong garrison to hold it in the interests of the buccaneers. When he had made these preparations he weighed his anchors, and sailed for the Chagres River under the English colours.

Eight days later they came sailing slowly up towards the river's mouth. Their joy was so great "when they saw the English colours upon the castle, that they minded not their way into the river," being gathered at the rum cask instead of at the lead, and calling healths instead of soundings. As a consequence, four ships of the fleet, including the admiral's flagship, ran foul of the ledge of rocks at the river's entry. Several men were drowned, but the goods and ships' stores were saved, though with some difficulty. As they got out warps to bring the ships off, the north wind freshened. In shallow water, such as that, a sea rises very quickly. In a few hours a regular "norther" had set in, and the ships beat to pieces on the ledge before the end of the day.

As Morgan came ashore at the port, the guns were fired in salute, and the pirates lined the quay and the castle walls to give him a triumphant welcome. He examined the castle, questioned the lieutenants, and at once took steps to repair the damage done by the fire. The thirty survivors of the garrison and all the prisoners from Santa Katalina, were set to work to drive in new palisadoes in the place of those burnt in the attack. The huts were rethatched and the whole place reordered. There were some Spanish ships in the port whose crews had been pressed into the Spanish garrison at the time of the storm. They were comparatively small, of the kind known as chatas, or chatten, a sort of coast boat of slight draught, used for river work and for the conveyance of goods from the Chagres to the cities on the Main. They had iron and brass guns aboard them, which were hoisted out, and mounted in the fort. Captain Morgan then picked a garrison of 500 buccaneers to hold the fort, under a buccaneer named Norman. He placed 150 more in the ships in the anchorage, and embarked the remainder in flat-bottomed boats for the voyage up the Chagres.

It was the dry season, so that the river, at times so turbulent, was dwindled to a tenth of its volume. In order that the hard work of hauling boats over shallows might not be made still harder, Morgan gave orders that the men should take but scanty stock of provisions. A few maize cobs and a strip or two of charqui was all the travelling store in the scrips his pilgrims carried. They hoped that they would find fresh food in the Spanish strongholds, or ambuscades, which guarded the passage over the isthmus.

The company set sail from San Lorenzo on the morning of the 12th (one says the 18th) of January 1671. They numbered in all 1200 men, packed into thirty-two canoas and the five chatas they had taken in the port. His guides went on ahead in one of the chatas, with her guns aboard her and the matches lit, and one Robert Delander, a buccaneer captain, in command. The first day's sailing against a gentle current was pleasant enough. In spite of the heat and the overcrowding of the boats, they made six leagues between dawn and sunset, and anchored at a place called De los Bracos. Here a number of the pirates went ashore to sleep " and stretch their limbs, they being almost crippled with lying too much crowded in the boats." They also foraged up and down for food in the plantations ; but the Spaniards had fled with all their stores. It was the first day of the journey over the isthmus, yet many of the men had already come to an end of their provisions. " The greatest part of them " ate nothing all day, nor enjoyed " any other refreshment " than a pipe of tobacco. The next day,

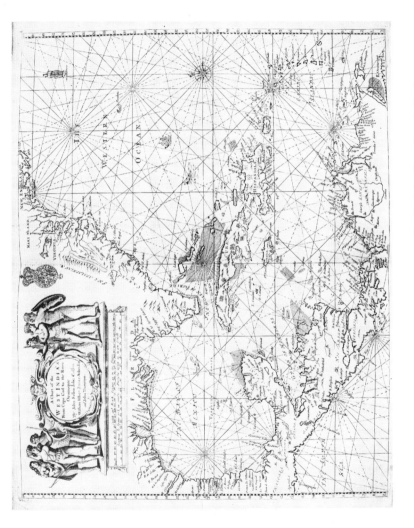

Chart of the West Indies. John Seller's : *The English Pilot. Fourth Book....*
London; 1713

"very early in the morning," before the sun rose, they
shoved off from the mooring-place. They rowed all
day, suffering much from the mosquitoes, but made little
progress. The river was fallen very low, so that they
were rowing or poling over a series of pools joined by
shallow rapids. To each side of them were stretches of
black, alluvial mud, already springing green with shrubs
and water-plants. Every now and then, as they rowed
on, on the dim, sluggish, silent, steaming river, they butted
a sleeping alligator as he sunned in the shallows, or were
stopped by a fallen tree, brought by the summer floods
and left to rot there. At twilight, when the crying of
the birds became more intense and the monkeys gathered
to their screaming in the treetops, the boats drew up
to the bank at a planter's station, or wayside shrine, known
as Cruz de Juan Gallego. Here they went ashore to
sleep, still gnawed with famine, and faint with the hard
day's rowing. The guides told Henry Morgan that after
another two leagues they might leave the boats, and push
through the woods on foot.

Early the next morning the admiral decided to leave
the boats, for with his men so faint from hunger he
thought it dangerous to tax them with a labour so
severe as rowing. He left 160 men to protect the fleet,
giving them the strictest orders to remain aboard. "No
man," he commanded, "upon any pretext whatsoever,
should dare to leave the boats and go ashore." The
woods there were so dark and thick that a Spanish
garrison might have lain within 100 yards of the
fleet, and cut off any stragglers who landed. Having
given his orders, he chose out a gang of macheteros, or
men carrying the sharp sword-like machetes, to march
ahead of the main body, to cut a trackway in the pulpy
green stuff. They then set forward through the forest,
over their ankles in swampy mud, up to their knees some-

times in rotting leaves, clambering over giant tree trunks, wading through stagnant brooks, staggering and slipping and swearing, faint with famine; a very desperate gang of cut-throats. As they marched, the things called gara-patadas, or wood-ticks, of which some six sorts flourish there, dropped down upon them in scores, to add their burning bites to the venom of the mosquitoes. In a moist atmosphere of at least 90°, with heavy arms to carry, that march must have been terrible. Even the buccaneers, men hardened to the climate, could not endure it: they straggled back to the boats, and re-embarked.

With a great deal of trouble the pirates dragged the boats "to a place farther up the river, called Cedro Bueno," where they halted for the stragglers, who drifted in during the evening. Here they went ashore to a wretched bivouac, to lie about the camp fires, with their belts drawn tight, chewing grass or aromatic leaves to allay their hunger. After Cedro Bueno the river narrowed, so that there was rather more water to float the canoas. The land, too, was less densely wooded, and easier for the men to march upon. On the fourth day "the greatest part of the Pirates marched by land, being led by one of the guides." Another guide led the rest of them in the canoes; two boats going ahead of the main fleet, one on each side of the river, to discover "the ambuscades of the Spaniards." The Spaniards had lined the river-banks at intervals with Indian spies, who were so "very dexterous" that they brought intelligence of the coming of the pirates "six hours at least before they came to any place." About noon on this day, as the boats neared Torna Cavallos, one of the guides cried out that he saw an ambuscade. "His voice caused infinite joy to all the Pirates," who made sure that the fastness would be well provisioned, and that at last they might "afford something to the ferment of their stomachs, which now was grown

so sharp that it did gnaw their very bowels." The place
was carried with a rush ; but the reboubt was empty. The
Spaniards had all fled away some hours before, when
their spies had come in from down the river. There had
been 500 Spaniards there standing to arms behind the
barricade of tree trunks. They had marched away with
all their gear, save only a few leather bags, "all empty,"
and a few crusts and bread crumbs "upon the ground
where they had eaten." There were a few shelter huts,
thatched with palm leaves, within the barricade. These
the pirates tore to pieces in the fury of their disappointment. They fell upon the leather bags like hungry dogs
quarrelling for a bone. They fought and wrangled for
the scraps of leather, and ate them greedily, "with frequent
gulps of water." Had they taken any Spaniards there
"they would certainly in that occasion [or want] have
roasted or boiled" them "to satisfy their famine."

Somewhat relieved by the scraps of leather, they
marched on along the river-bank to "another post called
Torna Munni." Here they found a second wall of tree
trunks, loopholed for musketry, "but as barren and
desert as the former." They sought about in the woods
for fruits or roots, but could find nothing—"the Spaniards
having been so provident as not to leave behind them
anywhere the least crumb of sustenance." There was
nothing for them but "those pieces of leather, so hard
and dry," a few of which had been saved "for supper"
by the more provident. He who had a little scrap of hide,
would slice it into strips, "and beat it between two stones,
and rub it, often dipping it in the water of the river, to
render it by these means supple and tender." Lastly, the
hair was scraped off, and the piece "roasted or broiled"
at the camp fire upon a spit of lance wood. "And being
thus cooked they cut it into small morsels, and eat it,"
chewing each bit for several minutes as though loth to

lose it, and helping it down "with frequent gulps of water."
There was plenty of fish in the Chagres, but perhaps they
had no lines. It seems strange, however, that they made
no attempt to kill some of the myriads of birds and
monkeys in the trees, or the edible snakes which swarm
in the grass, or, as a last resource, the alligators in the
river.

Gaunt with hunger, they took the trail again after a
night of misery at Torna Munni. The going was slightly
better, but there was still the wood-ticks, the intense,
damp heat, and the lust for food to fight against. About
noon they staggered in to Barbacoas, now a station on the
Isthmian Railway. There were a few huts at Barbacoas,
for the place was of some small importance. A native
swinging bridge, made of bejuco cane, was slung across
the river there for the benefit of travellers going to
Porto Bello. An ambush had been laid at Barbacoas,
but the Spaniards had left the place, after sweeping it
as bare as Torna Munni. The land was in tillage near
the huts, but the plantations were barren. " They searched
very narrowly, but could not find any person, animal or
other thing that was capable of relieving their extreme
and ravenous hunger." After a long search they chanced
upon a sort of cupboard in the rocks, "in which they
found two sacks of meal, wheat, and like things, with two
great jars of wine, and certain fruits called Platanos,"
or large bananas. Morgan very firmly refused to allow
the buccaneers to use this food. He reserved it strictly
for those who were in greatest want, thereby saving a
number of lives. The dying men were given a little
meal and wine, and placed in the canoas, "and those
commanded to land that were in them before." They
then marched on "with greater courage than ever," till
late into the night, when they lay down in a plundered
bean patch.

"On the sixth day" they were nearly at the end of their tether. They dragged along slowly, some in boats, some in the woods, halting every now and then in despair of going farther, and then staggering on again, careless if they lived or died. Their lips were scummy with a sort of green froth, caused by their eating grass and the leaves of trees. In this condition they came at noon to a plantation, "where they found a barn full of maize." They beat the door in in a few minutes, "and fell to eating of it dry," till they were gorged with it. There was enough for all, and plenty left to take away, so they distributed a great quantity, "giving to every man a good allowance." With their knapsacks full of corn cobs they marched on again, in happier case than they had been in for several days. They soon came to "an ambuscade of Indians," but no Indians stayed within it to impeach their passage. On catching sight of the barricade many buccaneers flung away their corn cobs, with the merry improvidence of their kind, "with the sudden hopes they conceived of finding all things in abundance." But the larder was as bare as it had been in the other strongholds: it contained "neither Indians, nor victuals, nor anything else." On the other side of the river, however, there were many Indians, "a troop of a hundred," armed with bows, "who escaped away through the agility of their feet." Some of the pirates "leapt into the river" to attack these Indians, and to bring them into camp as prisoners. They did not speed in their attempt, but two or three of them were shot through the heart as they waded. Their corpses drifted downstream, to catch in the oars of the canoas, a horrible feast for the caymans. The others returned to their comrades on the right or northern bank of the river among the howls of the Indians: "Hey, you dogs, you, go on to the savannah; go on to the savannah, to find out what's in pickle for you."

They could go no farther towards the savannah for that time, as they wished to cross the river, and did not care to do so, in the presence of an enemy, without due rest. They camped about big fires of wood, according to their custom, but they slept badly, for the hunger and toil had made them mutinous. The growling went up and down the camp till it came to Morgan's ears. Most of the pirates were disgusted with their admiral's "conduct," or leadership, and urged a speedy return to Port Royal. Others, no less disgusted, swore savagely that they would see the job through. Some, who had eaten more burnt leather than the others, "did laugh and joke at all their discourses," and so laid a last straw upon their burden. "In the meanwhile" the ruffian guide, "the rogue, thief, and assassin," who had merited to die upon a wheel, was a great comfort to them. "It would not be long," he kept saying, "before they met with folk, when they would come to their own, and forget these hungry times." So the night passed, round the red wood logs in the clearing, among the steaming jungle.

Early in the morning of the seventh day they cleaned their arms, wiping away the rust and fungus which had grown upon them. "Every one discharged his pistol or musket, without bullet, to examine the security of their firelocks." They then loaded with ball, and crossed the river in the canoes. At midday they sighted Venta Cruz, the village, or little town, which Drake had taken. The smoke was going up to heaven from the Venta Cruz chimneys—a sight very cheering to these pirates. They had "great joy and hopes of finding people in the town . . . and plenty of good cheer." They went on merrily, "making several arguments to one another [like the grave-diggers in *Hamlet*] upon those external signs"—saying that there could be no smoke without a fire, and no fire in such a climate save to cook by, and that, therefore, Venta

Cruz would be full of roast and boiled by the time they marched into its Plaza. Thus did they cheer the march and the heavy labour at the oars as far as the Venta Cruz jetty.

As they entered Venta Cruz at the double, " all sweating and panting" with the hurry of their advance, they found the town deserted and in a blaze of fire. There was nothing eatable there, for the place had been swept clean, and then fired, by the retreating Spaniards. The only houses not alight were "the store-houses and stables belonging the King." These, being of stone, and Government property, had not been kindled. The storehouses and stables were, however, empty. Not a horse nor a mule nor an ass was in its stall. "They had not left behind them any beast whatsoever, either alive or dead." Venta Cruz was as profitless a booty as all the other stations. A few pariah dogs and cats were in the street, as was perhaps natural, even at that date, in a Central-American town. These were at once killed, and eaten half raw, "with great appetite." Before they were de-spatched, a pirate lighted on a treasure in a recess of the King's stables. He found there a stock of wine, some fifteen or sixteen jars, or demijohns, of good Peruvian wine, "and a leather sack full of bread." "But no sooner had they begun to drink of the said wine when they fell sick, almost every man." Several hundreds had had a cup or two of the drink, and these now judged themselves poisoned, and "irrecoverably lost." They were not poisoned, as it happened, but they had gone hungry for several days, living on "manifold sorts of trash." The sudden use of wine and bread caused a very natural sickness, such as comes to all who eat or drink greedily after a bout of starving. The sickness upset them for the day, so that the force remained there, at bivouac in the village, until the next morning. During the halt Morgan landed all his men ("though never so weak")

from the canoas. He retained only one boat, which he
hid, for use as an advice boat, "to carry intelligence" to
those down the river. The rest of the canoas were sent
downstream to the anchorage at Bueno Cedro, where the
chatas lay moored under a guard. He gave strict orders
to the rest of the pirates that they were not to leave
the village save in companies of 100 together. "One
party of English soldiers stickled not to contravene these
commands, being tempted with the desire of finding victuals." While they straggled in the tilled ground outside
Venta Cruz they were attacked "with great fury" by a
number of Spaniards and Indians, "who snatched up" one
of them, and carried him off. What was done to this one
so snatched up we are not told. Probably he was tortured
to give information of the pirates' strength, and then
hanged up to a tree.

On the eighth day, in the early morning, the sick
men being recovered, Morgan thought they might proceed. He chose out an advance-guard of 200 of the
strongest of his men, and sent them forward, with their
matches lighted, to clear the road. The road was a very
narrow one, but paved with cobble stones, and easy to the
feet after the quagmires of the previous week. The men
went forward at a good pace, beating the thickets on each
side of the road. When they had marched some seven or
eight miles they were shot at from some Indian ambush.
A shower of arrows fell among them, but they could not
see a trace of the enemy, till the Indians, who had shot the
arrows, broke from cover and ran to a second fastness.
A few stood firm, about a chief or cacique, "with full
design to fight and defend themselves." They fought very
gallantly for a few moments ; but the pirates stormed their
poor defence, and pistolled the cacique, losing eight men
killed and ten wounded before the Indians broke. Shortly
after this skirmish, the advance-guard left the wood,

coming to open, green grass-land "full of variegated meadows." On a hill at a little distance they saw a number of Indians gathered, watching their advance. They sent out a troop to capture some of these, but the Indians escaped again, "through the agility of their feet," to reappear a little later with their howls of scorn : " Hey, you dogs, you English dogs, you. Get on to the savannah, you dogs, you cuckolds. On to the savannah, and see what's coming to you." " While these things passed the ten pirates that were wounded were dressed and plastered up."

In a little while the pirates seized a hilltop facing a ridge of hill which shut them from the sight of Panama. In the valley between the two hills was a thick little wood, where Morgan looked to find an ambush. He sent his advance-guard of 200 men to search the thicket. As they entered, some Spaniards and Indians entered from the opposite side, but no powder was burnt, for the Spaniards stole away by a bypath, "and were seen no more." That night a drenching shower of rain fell, blotting out the landscape in a roaring grey film. It sent the pirates running hither and thither to find some shelter "to preserve their arms from being wet." Nearly all the huts and houses in the district had been fired by the Indians, but the pirates found a few lonely shepherds' shealings, big enough to hold all the weapons of the army and a few of the men. Those who could not find a place among the muskets were constrained to lie shivering in the open, enduring much hardship, for the rain did not slacken till dawn.

At daybreak Morgan ordered them to march " while the fresh air of the morning lasted "; for they were now in open country, on the green savannah, where they would have no treetops to screen them from the terrible sun. During their morning march they saw a troop of Spanish

horse, armed with spears, watching the advance at a safe
distance, and retiring as the pirates drew nearer.   Shortly
after this they topped a steep rise, and lo! the smoke
of Panama, and the blue Pacific, with her sky-line
trembling gently, and a ship under sail, with five boats,
going towards some emerald specks of islands.   The clouds
were being blown across the sky.   The sun was glorious
over all that glorious picture, over all the pasture, so green
and fresh from the rain.   There were the snowy Andes
in the distance, their peaks sharply notched on the clear
sky.   Directly below them, in all her beauty, was the
royal city of Panama, only hidden from sight by a roll of
green savannah.

Just at the foot of the rise, in a wealth of fat pasture,
were numbers of grazing cattle, horses, and asses—the
droves of the citizens.   The pirates crept down, and shot
a number of these, "chiefly asses," which they promptly
flayed, while some of their number gathered firewood.
As soon as the fires were lit the meat was blackened
in the flame, and then greedily swallowed in "convenient
pieces or gobbets."   "They more resembled cannibals
than Europeans at this banquet," for the blood ran down
the beards of many, so hungry were they for meat after
the long agony of the march.   What they could not eat
they packed in their satchels.   After a long midday rest
they fell in again for the march, sending fifty men ahead
to take prisoners "if possibly they could," for in all the
nine days' tramp they had taken no one to give them
information of the Spaniards' strength.   Towards sunset
they saw a troop of Spaniards spying on them, who
hallooed at them, but at such a distance that they could
not distinguish what was said.   As the sun set "they
came the first time within sight of the highest steeple
of Panama."

This was a stirring cordial to the way-weary men

limping down the savannah. The sight of the sea was
not more cheering to the Greeks than the sight of the
great gilt weathercock, shifting on the spire, to these
haggard ruffians with the blood not yet dry upon their
beards. They flung their hats into the air, and danced
and shouted. All their trumpets shouted a levity, their
drums beat, and their colours were displayed. They
camped there, with songs and laughter, in sight of that
steeple, "waiting with impatience," like the French
knights in the play, for the slowly coming dawn. Their
drums and trumpets made a merry music to their singing,
and they caroused so noisily that a troop of horsemen
rode out from Panama to see what was the matter. "They
came almost within musket-shot of the army, being pre-
ceded by a trumpet that sounded marvellously well."
They rode up "almost within musket-shot," but made
no attempt to draw the pirates' fire. They "hallooed
aloud to the Pirates, and threatened them," with "Hey,
ye dogs, we shall meet ye," in the manner of the Indians.
Seven or eight of them stayed "hovering thereabouts,"
riding along the camp until the day broke, to watch the
pirates' movements. As soon as their main body reached
the town, and reported what they had seen, the Governor
ordered the city guns to open on the pirates' camp. The
biggest guns at once began a heavy fire, from which one
or two spent balls rolled slowly to the outposts without
doing any damage. At the same time, a strong party
took up a position to the rear of the camp, as though
to cut off the retreat.

Morgan placed his sentries, and sent his men to supper.
They feasted merrily on their "pieces of bulls' and horses'
flesh," and then lay down on the grass to smoke a pipe
of tobacco before turning in. That last night's camp
was peaceful and beautiful: the men were fed and near
their quarry, the sun had dried their wet clothes ; the

night was fine, the stars shone, the Panama guns were harmless. They slept "with great repose and huge satisfaction," careless of the chance of battle, and anxious for the fight to begin.

PANAMA

Old Panama, the chief Spanish city in South America, with the one exception of Cartagena, was built along the sea-beach, fronting the bay of Panama, between the rivers Gallinero and Matasnillos. It was founded between 1518 and 1520 by Pedrarias Davila, a poor adventurer, who came to the Spanish Indies to supersede Balboa, having at that time "nothing but a sword and buckler." Davila gave it the name of an Indian village then standing on the site. The name means "abounding in fish." It soon became the chief commercial city in those parts, for all the gold and silver and precious merchandise of Peru and Chili were collected there for transport to Porto Bello. At the time of Morgan's attack upon it, it contained some 7000 houses, with a number of huts and hovels for the slaves. The population, counting these latter, may have been as great as 30,000. Many of the houses were of extreme beauty, being built of an aromatic rose wood, or "native cedar," ingeniously carved. Many were built of stone in a Moorish fashion, with projecting upper storeys. It had several stone monasteries and convents, and a great cathedral, dedicated to St Anastasius, which was the most glorious building in Spanish America. Its tower still stands as a landmark to sailors, visible many miles to sea. The stones of it are decorated with defaced carvings. Inside it, within the ruined walls, are palm and cedar trees, green and beautiful, over the roots of which swarm the scarlet-spotted coral snakes. The old town was never properly fortified. The

isthmus was accounted a sufficient protection to it, and
the defences were consequently weak. It was a town
of merchants, who "thought only of becoming rich, and
cared little for the public good." They lived a very stately
life there, in houses hung with silk, stamped leather,
and Spanish paintings, drinking Peruvian wines out of
cups of gold and silver. The Genoese Company, a company of slavers trading with Guinea, had a "stately house"
there, with a spacious slave market, where the blacks were
sold over the morning glass. The Spanish King had
some long stone stables in the town, tended by a number
of slaves. Here the horses and mules for the recuas were
stabled in long lines, like the stables of a cavalry barrack.
Near these were the royal storehouses, built of stone, for
the storage of the gold from the King's mines. There were
also 200 merchants' warehouses, built in one storey, round
which the slaves slept, under pent roofs.

Outside the city was the beautiful green savannah,
a rolling sea of grass, with islands of trees, cedar and
palm, thickly tangled with the many-coloured bindweeds.
To one side of it, an arm of the sea crept inland, to
a small salt lagoon, which rippled at high tide, at the
back of the city. The creek was bridged to allow the
Porto Bello carriers to enter the town, and a small
gatehouse or porter's lodge protected the way. The
bridge is a neat stone arch, still standing. The streets
ran east and west, "so that when the sun rises no one can
walk in any of the streets, because there is no shade
whatever; and this is felt very much as the heat is intense; and the sun is so prejudicial to health, that if a
man is exposed to its rays for a few hours, he will be
attacked with a fatal illness [pernicious fever], and this has
happened to many." The port was bad for shipping,
because of the great rise and fall of the tides. The bay
is shallow, and ships could only come close in at high

water. At low water the town looked out upon a strip
of sand and a mile or more of very wet black mud. " At
full moon, the waves frequently reach the houses and enter
those on that side of the town." The roadstead afforded
safe anchorage for the great ships coming up from Lima.
Loading and unloading was performed by launches, at
high water, on days when the surf was moderate. Small
ships sailed close in at high tide, and beached themselves.

To landward there were many gardens and farms, where
the Spaniards had " planted many trees from Spain "—such
as oranges, lemons, and figs. There were also plantain
walks, and a great plenty of pines, guavas, onions, lettuces,
and "alligator pears." Over the savannah roamed herds
of fat cattle. On the seashore, "close to the houses of
the city," were "quantities of very small mussels." The
presence of these mussel beds determined the site of the
town, "because the Spaniards felt themselves safe from
hunger on account of these mussels."

The town is all gone now, saving the cathedral tower,
where the sweet Spanish bells once chimed, and the
little stone bridge, worn by so many mules' hoofs.
There is dense tropical forest over the site of it, though
the foundations of several houses may be traced, and
two or three walls still stand, with brilliant creepers
covering up the carved work. It is not an easy place
to reach, for it is some six miles from new Panama, and
the way lies through such a tangle of creepers, over such
swampy ground, poisonous with so many snakes, that
it is little visited. It can be reached by sea on a fine
day at high tide if the surf be not too boisterous. To
landward of the present Panama there is a fine hill, called
Mount Ançon. A little to the east of this there is a roll
of high land, now a fruitful market-garden, or farm of
orchards. This high land, some five or six miles from
the ruins, is known as Buccaneers' Hill. It was from the

summit of this high land that the pirates first saw the city steeple. Local tradition points out a few old Spanish guns of small size, brass and iron, at the near-by village of El Moro, as having been left by Morgan's men. At the island of Taboga, in the bay of Panama, they point with pride to a cave, the haunt of squid and crabs, as the hiding-place of Spanish treasure. In the blackness there, they say, are the golden sacramental vessels and jewelled vestments of the great church of St Anastasius. They were hidden there at the time of the raid, so effectually that they could never be recovered. We can learn of no other local tradition concerning the sack and burning.

What old Panama was like we do not know, for we can trace no picture of it. It was said to be the peer of Venice, "the painted city," at a time when Venice was yet the "incomparable Queene." It could hardly have been a second Venice, though its situation on that beautiful blue bay, with the Andes snowy in the distance, and the islands, like great green gems, to seaward, is lovely beyond words. It was filled with glorious houses, carved and scented, and beautiful with costly things. The merchants lived a languorous, luxurious life there, waited on by slaves, whom they could burn or torture at their pleasure. It was "the greatest mart for gold and silver in the whole world." There were pearl fisheries up and down the bay, yielding the finest of pearls; and "golden Potosi"—the tangible Eldorado, was not far off. The merchants of old Panama were, perhaps, as stately fellows and as sumptuous in their ways of life as any "on the Rialto." Their city is now a tangle of weeds and a heap of sun-cracked limestone; their market-place is a swamp; their haven is a stretch of surf-shaken mud, over which the pelicans go quarrelling for the bodies of fish.

Authorities.—Exquemeling's "History"; "The Bucaniers of America." Don Guzman's Account, printed in the "Voyages and Adventures of Captain Bartholomew Sharp." Cal. State Papers: West Indies and Colonial Series. "Present State of Jamaica," 1683. "New History of Jamaica," 1740.

For my account of Chagres I am indebted to friends long resident on the isthmus, and to Dampier's and Wafer's Voyages.

Captain Roberts' two ships the *Royal Fortune* and *Ranger,* capturing 11 ships in Whydah Road, on the coast of Guinea. *Johnson.*

CHAPTER XII

THE SACK OF PANAMA

The burning of the city—Buccaneer excesses—An abortive mutiny
—Home—Morgan's defection

" ON the tenth day, betimes in the morning," while the
black and white monkeys were at their dawn song,
or early screaming, the pirates fell in for the march, with
their red flags flying and the drums and trumpets making
a battle music. They set out gallantly towards the city
by the road they had followed from Venta Cruz. Before
they came under fire, one of the guides advised Morgan
to attack from another point. The Spaniards, he said,
had placed their heavy guns in position along the probable line of their advance. Every clump of trees near
the trackway would be filled with Spanish sharpshooters,
while they might expect earth-works or trenches nearer
to the city. He advised Morgan to make a circuit, so
as to approach the city through the forest—over the
ground on which new Panama was built, a year or
two later. Morgan, therefore, turned rather to the west
of the highway, through some tropical woodland, where
the going was very irksome. As they left the woodland,
after a march of several hours, they again entered the
savannah, at a distance of about a mile and a half from
the town. The ground here was in sweeping folds, so
that they had a little hill to climb before the town lay
open to them, at the edge of the sea, to the eastward
of the salt lagoon. When they topped this rise they

saw before them "the forces of the people of Panama, extended in battle array," between them and the quarry.

The Spanish strength on this occasion, according to the narrative, was as follows :—400 horse, of the finest horsemen in the world ; twenty-four companies of foot, each company mustering a full 100 men ; and "sixty Indians and some negroes." These last were "to drive two thousand wild bulls and cause them to run over the English camp, and thus, by breaking their files, put them into a total disorder and confusion." Morgan gives the numbers as 2100 foot and 600 horse, with "two Droves of Cattel of 1500 apiece," one for each flank or for the angles of the rear. The Spanish Governor, who had been "lately blooded 3 times for an Erysipelas," had not done as well as he could have wished in the preparation of an army of defence. He says that he had brought together 1400 coloured men, armed with "Carbins, Harque-busses, and Fowling Pieces," the muskets having been lost at Chagres. He gives the number of cavalry as 200, "mounted on the same tired Horses which had brought them thither." He admits that there were "50 cow-keepers" and an advance-guard of 300 foot. He had also five field-guns "covered with leather." To these forces may be added the townsfolk capable of bearing arms. These were not very numerous, for most of the inhabitants, as we have seen, "thought only of getting rich and cared little for the public good." They were now, however, in a cold sweat of fear at the sight of the ragged battalion trooping down from the hilltop. They had dug trenches for themselves within the city and had raised batteries to sweep the important streets. They had also mounted cannon on the little stone fort, or watchman's lodge, at the town end of the bridge across the creek.

The sight of so many troops drawn out in order "sur-

prised" the pirates "with great fear." The droves of
"wild bulls" pasturing on the savannah grass were new
to their experience; the cavalry they had met before
in Cuba and did not fear, nor did they reckon themselves
much worse than the Spanish foot; but they saw that
the Spaniards outnumbered them by more than two to
one, and they recognised the advantage they had in
having a defensible city to fall back upon. The buccaneers were worn with the long march, and in poor
case for fighting. They halted at this point, while Morgan
formed them into a tertia, or division of three battalions
or troops, of which he commanded the right wing. The
sight of so many Spaniards halted below them set them
grumbling in the ranks. "Yea few or none there were
but wished themselves at home, or at least free from
the obligation of that Engagement." There was, however,
nothing else for it. A "wavering condition of Mind" could
not help them. They had no alternative but "to fight
resolutely, or die." They might not look to get quarter
"from an Enemy against whom they had committed so
many Cruelties."

Morgan formed his men in order, and sent out skirmishers to annoy the Spanish troops, and to draw them
from their position. A few shots were exchanged; but the
Spaniards were not to be tempted, nor was the ground
over which the skirmishers advanced at all suitable for
moving troops. Morgan, therefore, edged his men away
to the left, to a little hill beyond a dry gut or water-
course—a position which the Spaniards could not attack
from more than one side owing to the nature of the
ground, which was boggy. Before they could form upon
the lower slopes of the hill the Spanish horse rode softly
forward, shouting: "Viva el Rey!" ("Long live the King"),
with a great display of courage. "But the field being full
of quaggs, and very soft under foot, they could not ply

to and fro, and wheel about, as they desired." When they had come to a little beyond musket-shot "one Francisco Detarro," the colonel of the cavalry, called out to his troopers to charge home upon the English van. The horses at once broke into a gallop, and charged in "so furiously" that Morgan had to strengthen his ranks to receive them, "we having no Pikes" with which to gall the horses. As the men galloped forward, the line of buccaneers made ready to fire. Each musketeer put one knee to the ground, and touched off his piece, blasting the Spanish regiment almost out of action at the one discharge. The charge had been pressed so nearly home that the powder corns burnt the leading horses. Those who survived the shock of the volley swung off to the right to re-form, while the foot came on in their tracks "to try their Fortunes." They were received with such a terrible fire that they never came to handystrokes. They disputed the point for some hours, gradually falling into disorder as their losses became more and more heavy. The cavalry re-formed, and charged a second and a third time, with the result that after two hours' fighting "the Spanish Horse was ruined, and almost all killed." During the engagement of the foot, the Indians and negroes tried their stratagem of the bulls. They drove the herds round the flanking parties to the rear, and endeavoured to force them through the English lines. " But the greatest part of that wild cattle ran away, being frighted with the noise of the Battle. And some few, that broke through the English Companies, did no other harm than to tear the Colours in pieces ; whereas the Buccaneers shooting them dead, left not one to Trouble them thereabouts."

Seeing the Spanish foot in some disorder, with many of their officers killed and few of the men firing, Morgan plied them with shot and sent his left wing forward as they fell back. The horse made one last gallant attempt to break the English line, but the attempt caused their complete destruction. At the same moment Morgan stormed down upon the foot with all his strength. The Spaniards fired "the Shot they had in their Muskets," and flung their weapons down, not caring to come to handystrokes. They ran "everyone which way he could run"—an utter rout of broken soldiers. The pirates were too fatigued to follow, but they picked them off as they ran till they were out of musket-shot.

The buccaneers apparently then cleared away the stragglers, by pistolling them wherever they could find them. In this employment they beat through the shrubs by the sea, where many poor citizens had hidden themselves after the final routing of the troops. Some monks who were brought in to Captain Morgan were treated in the same manner, "for he, being deaf to their Cries, commanded them to be instantly pistolled," which order was obeyed there and then. A captain or colonel of troops was soon afterwards taken, and held to ransom after a strict examination. He told Morgan that he might look to have great trouble in winning the city, for the streets were all dug about with trenches and mounted with heavy brass guns. He added that the main entrance to the place was strongly fortified, and protected by a half company of fifty men with eight brass demi-cannon.

Morgan now bade his men rest themselves and take food before pushing on to the town. He held a review of his army before he marched, and found that he had lost heavily—perhaps 200 men—while the Spaniards had lost about three times that number. "The Pirates," we read, "were nothing discouraged, seeing their number so much diminished but rather filled with greater pride than before." The comparative heaviness of the Spanish loss must have been very comforting. After they had rested and eaten they set out towards the town, "plighting their Oaths to one another in general, they would fight till never a man were left alive." A few prisoners, who seemed rich enough to be held to ransom, were marched with them under a guard of musketeers.

Long before they trod the streets of Panama, they were under fire from the batteries, "some of which were charged with small pieces of iron, and others with musket-bullets."

They lost men at every step; but their ranks kept steady, and street by street the town was won. The main agony of the fight took place between two and three o'clock, in the heat of the day, when the last Spanish gunners were cut to pieces at their guns. After the last gun was taken, a few Spaniards fired from street corners or from upper windows, but these were promptly pistolled or knocked on the head. The town was in the hands of the pirates by the time the bells chimed three that afternoon.

As Morgan rested with his captains in the Plaza, after the heat of the battle, word was brought to him that the city was on fire in several places. Many have supposed that the town was fired by his orders, or by some careless and drunken musketeer of his. It was not the buccaneer custom to fire cities before they had sacked them, nor is it in the least likely that Morgan would have burnt so glorious a town before he had offered it to ransom. The Spaniards have always charged Morgan with the crime, but it seems more probable that the Spanish Governor was the guilty one. It is yet more probable that the fire was accidental. Most of the Spanish houses were of wood, and at that season of the year the timber would have been of extreme dryness, so that a lighted wad or match end might have caused the conflagration. At the time when the fire was first noticed, the pirates were raging through the town in search of plunder. They may well have flung

away their lighted matches to gather up the spoils they
found, and thus set fire to the place unwittingly.

Hearing that the town was burning, Morgan caused his
trumpeters to sound the assembly in the Plaza. When
the pirates mustered, Morgan at once told off men to
quench the fire " by blowing up houses by gunpowder, and
pulling down others to stop its progress." He ordered
strong guards to patrol the streets and to stand sentry
without the city. Lastly, he forbade any member of the
army " to dare to drink or taste any wine," giving out that
it had all been poisoned beforehand by the Spaniards.
He feared that his men would get drunk unless he frightened them by some such tale. With a drunken army
rolling in the streets he could hardly hope to hold the
town against an enemy so lightly beaten as the Spaniards.
He also sent some sailors down to the beach to seize " a
great boat which had stuck in the mud of the port."

For all that the pirates could do, the fire spread rapidly,
for the dry cedar beams burned furiously. The warehouses full of merchandise, such as silks, velvets, and fine
linen, were not burned, but all the grand houses of the
merchants, where the life had been so stately, were utterly
gutted—all the Spanish pictures and coloured tapestries
going up in a blaze. The splendid house of the Genoese,
where so many black men had been bought and sold, was
burned to the ground. The chief streets were ruined
before midnight, and the fire was not wholly extinguished
a month later when the pirates marched away. It continued to burn and smoulder long after they had gone.

Having checked the riot among his army, Morgan sent
a company of 150 men back to the garrison at the mouth
of the Chagres with news of his success. Two other companies, of the same strength, he sent into the woods, " being
all very stout soldiers and well-armed," giving them orders
to bring in prisoners to hold to ransom. A third company

was sent to sea under a Captain Searles to capture a Spanish galleon which had left the port, laden with gold and silver and the jewels of the churches, a day or two before. The rest of his men camped out of doors, in the green fields without the city, ready for any attack the Spaniards might make upon them. Search parties rummaged all day among the burning ruins, "especially in wells and cisterns," which yielded up many jewels and fine gold plates. The warehouses were sacked, and many pirates made themselves coats of silk and velvet to replace the rags they came in. It is probable that they committed many excesses in the heat of the first taking of the town, but one who was there has testified to the comparative gentleness of their comportment when "the heat of the blood" had cooled. "As to their women," he writes, "I know [not] or ever heard of anything offered beyond their wills ; something I know was cruelly executed by Captain Collier [commander of one of the ships and one of the chief officers of the army] in killing a Frier in the field after quarter given ; but for the Admiral he was noble enough to the vanquished enemy." In fact, the

> "Want of rest and victual
> Had made them chaste—they ravished very little"

—which matter must be laid to their credit.

A day or two was passed by the pirates in rummaging among the ruins, eating and drinking, and watching the Spaniards as they moved in the savannahs. Troops of Spaniards prowled there under arms, looking at their burning houses and the grey smoke ever going upward. They did not attack the pirates ; they did not even fire at them from a distance. They were broken men without a leader, only thankful to be allowed to watch their blazing city. A number of them submitted to the armed men sent out to bring in prisoners. A number lingered in the

near-by forests in great misery, living on grass and
alligator eggs, the latter tasting "like half-rotten musk"—
a poor diet after "pheasants" and Peruvian wine.

Morgan soon received word from Chagres castle that
all was very well with the garrison. Captain Norman,
who had remained in charge, under oath to keep the
"bloody flag," or red pirates' banner, flying, "had sent forth
to sea two boats, to exercise piracy." These had hoisted
Spanish colours, and set to sea, meeting with a fine
Spanish merchantman that very same day. They chased
this ship into the Chagres River, where "the poor
Spaniards" were caught in a snare under the guns of the
fort. Her cargo "consisted in victuals and provisions,
that were all eatable things," unlike the victuals given
usually to sailors. Such a prize came very opportunely,
for the castle stores were running out, while the ship's
crew proved useful in the bitter work of earth carrying
then going on daily on the ramparts for the repairing of
the palisado. Hearing that the Chagres garrison was in
such good case, and so well able to exercise piracy without
further help, Admiral Morgan resolved to make a longer
stay in the ruins of old Panama. He arranged "to send forth
daily parties of two hundred men" to roam the country-
side, beating the thickets for prisoners, and the prisoners for
gold. These parties ranged the country very thoroughly,
gathering "in a short time, a huge quantity of riches, and
no less number of prisoners." These poor creatures were
shut up under a guard, to be brought out one by one for
examination. If they would not confess where they had
hidden their gold, nor where the gold of their neighbours
lay, the pirates used them as they had used their prisoners
at Porto Bello. "Woolding," burning with palm leaves,
and racking out the arm-joints, seem to have been the
most popular tortures. Many who had no gold were
brutally ill treated, and then thrust through with a lance.

Among these diversions Admiral Morgan fell in love with a beautiful Spanish lady, who appears to have been something of a paragon. The story is not worth repeating, nor does it read quite sincerely, but it is very probably true.   John Exquemeling, who had no great love for Morgan, declares that he was an eye-witness of the love-making, "and could never have judged such constancy of mind and virtuous chastity to be found in the world." The fiery Welshman did not win the lady, but we gather from the evidence that he could have had the satisfaction of Matthew Arnold's American, who consoled himself, in similar circumstances, with saying: "Well, I guess I lowered her moral tone some."

During the first week of their stay in Panama, the ship they had sent to sea returned with a booty of three small coast boats. Captain Searles had sailed her over Panama Bay to the beautiful island of Taboga, in order to fill fresh water and rob the inhabitants.   Here they took "the boatswain and most of the crew "[1] of the *Trinity*, a Spanish galleon, "on board which were the Friers and Nuns, with all the old gentlemen and Matrons of the Town, to the number of 1500 souls, besides an immense Treasure in Silver and Gold."   This galleon had seven small guns and ten or twelve muskets for her whole defence.   She was without provisions, and desperately short of water, and she had "no more sails than the uppermost sails of the mainmast."   Her captain was "an old and stout Spaniard, a native of Andalusia, in Spain, named Don Francisco de Peralta."   She was "very richly laden with all the King's Plate and great quantity of riches of gold, pearl, jewels, and other most precious goods, of all the best and richest merchants of Panama.   On board of this galleon were also the religious women, belonging to the nunnery of the said city, who had embarked with them all

[1] They had come ashore to get water.

the ornaments of their church, consisting in great quantity of gold, plate, and other things of great value." This most royal prize was even then slowly dipping past Taboga, with her sea-sick holy folk praying heartily for the return of the water casks. She could have made no possible defence against the pirates had they gone at once in pursuit of her. But this the pirates did not do. In the village at Taboga there was a wealthy merchant's summer-house, with a cellar full of "several sorts of rich wines." A bird in the hand is worth two in the bush, or as a bibulous wit once said to the present writer: "A bottle now is worth a bath of it to-morrow." Captain Searles and his men chose to drink a quiet bowl in the cabin rather than go sail the blue seas after the golden galleon. They made a rare brew of punch, of which they drank "logwood-cutters' measure," or a gallon and a half a man. After this they knocked out their tobacco pipes, and slept very pleasantly till the morning. They woke "repenting of their negligence" and "totally wearied of the vices and debaucheries aforesaid." With eyes red with drink they blinked at the empty punch-bowls. Then with savage "morning-tempers" they damned each other for a lot of lunkheads, and put to sea (in one of the Taboga prizes) "to pursue the said galleon" with all speed. However, by this time Don Peralta, a most gallant and resourceful captain, had brought the golden *Trinity* to a place of safety. Had she been taken, she would have yielded a spoil hardly smaller than that taken by Cavendish in the *Madre de Dios* or that which Anson won in the Manila galleon. Several waggon loads of golden chalices and candlesticks, with ropes of pearls, bags of emeralds and bezoars, and bar upon bar of silver in the crude, were thus bartered away for a sup of punch and a drunken chorus in the cabin. Poor Captain Searles never prospered after. He went logwood cutting a year or two later, and as a logwood cutter he arrived at the Rio Summasenta, where he careened his ship at a sandy key, since known as Searles Key. He was killed a few days afterwards, "in the western lagune" there, "by one of his Company as they were cutting Logwood together." That was the end of Captain Searles.

Morgan was very angry when he heard of the escape of the galleon. He at once remanned the four prizes, and sent them out, with orders to scour the seas till they found her. They cruised for more than a week, examining every creek and inlet, beating up many a sluggish river, under many leafy branches, but finding no trace of the *Trinity*. They gave up the chase at last, and rested at Taboga, where, perhaps, some "rich wines" were still in bin. They found a Payta ship at anchor at Taboga, "laden with cloth, soap, sugar and biscuit, with twenty thousand pieces of eight in ready money." She was "a reasonable good ship,", but the cargo, saving the money, was not much to their taste. They took the best of it, and loaded it aboard her longboat, making the Taboga negroes act as stevedores. They then set the negroes aboard the prize, and carried her home to Panama, "some thing better satisfied of their voyage, yet withal much discontented they could not meet with the galleon." It was at Taboga, it seems, that the lady who so inflamed Sir Henry was made prisoner.

At the end of three weeks of "woolding" and rummaging, Admiral Morgan began to prepare for the journey home. He sent his men to look for mules and horses on which to carry the plunder to the hidden canoas in the river. He learned at this juncture that a number of the pirates intended to leave him "by taking a ship that was in the port," and going to "rob upon the South Sea." They had made all things ready, it seems, having hidden "great quantity of provisions," powder, bullets, and water casks,

with which to store their ship. They had even packed
the good brass guns of the city, "where with they designed
not only to equip the said vessel but also to fortify themselves and raise batteries in some island or other, which
might serve them for a place of refuge." The scheme
was fascinating, and a very golden life they would have
had of it, those lucky mutineers, had not some spoil-sport
come sneaking privily to Morgan with a tale of what
was toward. They might have seized Cocos Island or
Juan Fernandez, or "some other island," such as one of
the Enchanted, or Gallapagos, Islands, where the goddesses
were thought to dwell. That would have been a happier
life than cutting logwood, up to the knees in mud, in
some drowned savannah of Campeachy.

However, just as the wine-bowl spoiled the project of
the galleon, so did the treachery of a lickspittle, surely
one of the meanest of created things, put an end to the
mutiny. Morgan was not there to colonise Pacific Oceans,
but to sack Panama. He had no intention of losing half
his army for an imperial idea. He promptly discouraged
the scheme by burning all the boats in the roads. The
ship or chata, which would have been the flagship of the
mutineers, was dismasted, and the masts and rigging
were added to the general bonfire. All the brass cannon
they had taken were nailed and spiked. Wooden bars
were driven down their muzzles as firmly as possible, and
the wood was then watered to make it swell. There was
then no more talk of going a-cruising to found republics.

Morgan thought it wise to leave Panama as soon as
possible, before a second heresy arose among his merry
men. He had heard that the Governor of Panama was
busily laying ambuscades "in the way by which he ought
to pass at his return." He, therefore, picked out a strong
company of men, including many of the mutineers, and
sent them out into the woods to find out the truth of the

matter.   They found that the report was false, for a few
Spanish prisoners, whom they captured, were able to tell
them how the scheme had failed.   The Governor, it was
true, had planned to make " some opposition by the way,"
but none of the men remaining with him would consent
to " undertake any such enterprize."   With this news the
troops marched back to Panama.   While they were away,
the poor prisoners made every effort to raise money for
their ransoms, but many were unable to raise enough to
satisfy their captors.   Morgan had no wish to wait till
they could gather more, for by this time, no doubt, he
had satisfied himself that he had bled the country of all
the gold it contained.   Nor did he care to wait till the
Spaniards had plucked up heart, and planted some
musketeers along the banks of the Chagres.   He had
horses and mules enough to carry the enormous heaps of
plunder to the river.   It was plainly foolish to stay longer,
for at any time a force might attack him (by sea) from
Lima or (by land) from Porto Bello.   He, therefore, gave
the word for the army to prepare to march.   He passed
his last evening in Panama (as we suppose) with the
female paragon from Taboga.   The army had one last
debauch over the punch-bowls round the camp fires, and
then fell in to muster, thinking rapturously of the inns
and brothels which waited for their custom at Port Royal.

"On the 24th of February, of the year 1671, Captain
Morgan departed from the city of Panama, or rather from
the place where the said city of Panama did stand ; of the
spoils whereof he carried with him one hundred and seventy-
five beasts of carriage, laden with silver, gold and other
precious things, besides six hundred prisoners more or less,
between men, women, children and slaves."   Thus they
marched out of the ruined capital, over the green savannah,
towards the river, where a halt was called to order the army
for the march to Venta Cruz.   A troop of picked marksmen

was sent ahead to act as a scouting party; the rest of the
company marched in hollow square, with the prisoners in
the hollow.   In this array they set forward towards Venta
Cruz to the sound of drums and trumpets, amid "lamentations, cries, shrieks and doleful sighs" from the wretched
women and children.   Most of these poor creatures were
fainting with thirst and hunger, for it had been Morgan's
policy to starve them, in order "to excite them more
earnestly to seek for money wherewith to ransom themselves." "Many of the women," says the narrative, "begged
of Captain Morgan upon their knees, with infinite sighs
and tears, he would permit them to return to Panama,
there to live in company of their dear husbands and
children, in little huts of straw which they would erect,
seeing they had no houses until the rebuilding of the
city.   But his answer was: he came not thither to hear
lamentations and cries, but rather to seek money.   Therefore they ought to seek out for that in the first place,
wherever it were to be had, and bring it to him, otherwise
he would assuredly transport them all to such places
whither they cared not to go."   With this answer they had
to remain content, as they lay in camp, under strict guard,
on the banks of the Rio Grande.

Early the next morning, "when the march began,"
"those lamentable cries and shrieks were renewed, in so
much as it would have caused compassion in the hardest
heart to hear them.   But Captain Morgan, a man little
given to mercy, was not moved therewith in the least."
They marched in the same order as before, but on this
day, we read, the Spaniards "were punched and thrust
in their backs and sides, with the blunt end of [the pirates']
arms, to make them march the faster."   The "beautiful
and virtuous lady" "was led prisoner by herself, between
two Pirates," both of whom, no doubt, wished the other dear
charmer away.   She, poor lady, was crying out that she

had asked two monks to fetch her ransom from a certain hiding-place.   They had taken the money, she cried, according to her instruction, but they had used it to ransom certain "of their own and particular friends." This evil deed "was discovered by a slave, who brought a letter to the said lady."   In time, her words were reported to Captain Morgan, who held a court of inquiry there and then, to probe into the truth of the matter. The monks made no denial of the fact, "though under some frivolous excuses, of having diverted the money but for a day or two, within which time they expected more sums to repay it."   The reply angered Morgan into releasing the poor woman, "detaining the said religious men as prisoners in her place," and "using them according to the deserts of their incompassionate intrigues." Probably they were forced to run the gauntlet between two rows of pirates armed with withes of bejuco.

A day's hard marching brought them to the ruins of Venta Cruz, on the banks of the river, where the canoas lay waiting for them under a merry boat guard.   The army rested at Venta Cruz for three days, while maize and rice were collected for the victualling of the boats. Many prisoners succeeded in raising their ransoms during this three days' halt.   Those who failed, were carried down the river to San Lorenzo.   On the 5th of March the plunder was safely shipped, the army went aboard the canoas, the prisoners (including some from Venta Cruz) were thrust into the bottoms of the boats, and the homeward voyage began.   The two monks who had embezzled the lady's money escaped translation at this time, being ransomed by their friends before the sailing of the fleet. The canoas dropped down the river swiftly, with songs and cheers from the pirates, till they came to some opening in the woods, half way across the isthmus, where the banks were free enough from brush to allow them to

FRANCIS LOLONOIS.

Part. 2. Page. 1.

an-David Nau, better known as Francis L'Ollonais. Notorious for his cruelty to prisoners, L'Ollonais met a violent death at the hands of Carib Indians. *Exquemeling.*

camp. Here they mustered in order, as though for a review, each man in his place with his sword and firelock. Here Captain Morgan caused each man to raise his right hand, and to swear solemnly that he had concealed nothing privately, "even not so much as the value of sixpence." Captain Morgan, a Welshman by birth, "having had some experience that those lewd fellows would not much stickle to swear falsely in points of interest, commanded every one to be searched very strictly, both in their clothes and satchels and everywhere it might be presumed they had reserved anything. Yea, to the intent this order might not be ill-taken by his companions, he permitted himself to be searched, even to the very soles of his shoes." One man out of each company was chosen to act as searcher to his fellows, and a very strict search was made. "The French Pirates were not well satisfied with this new custom of searching," but there were not very many of them, and "they were forced to submit to it." When the search was over, they re-embarked, and soon afterwards the current caught them, and spun them down swiftly to the lion-like rock at the river's mouth. They came safely to moorings below San Lorenzo on the 9th of March. They found that most of the wounded they had left there had died of fever, but the rest of the garrison was in good case, having "exercised piracy" with profit all the time the army had been plundering. There was "joy, and a full punch-bowl," in the castle rooms that night.

Morgan now sent his Santa Katalina prisoners to Porto Bello in "a great boat," demanding a ransom for Chagres castle, "threatening otherwise" to blast it to pieces. "Those of Porto Bello," who needed all their money to repair their own walls, replied that "They would not give one farthing towards the ransom of the said castle, and that the English might do with it as they pleased"—a sufficiently

bold answer, which sealed the fate of San Lorenzo. When
the answer came, the men were again mustered, and " the
dividend was made of all the spoil they had purchased
in that voyage."   Each man received his due share, " or
rather what part thereof Captain Morgan was pleased
to give."   There was general dissatisfaction with " his
proceedings in this particular," and many shaggy ruffians
" feared not to tell him openly " that he had " reserved the best jewels to himself."   They " judged it
impossible " that the share per man should be but
a paltry 200 pieces of eight, or £50, after " so many
valuable booties and robberies."   Why, they said, it is
less than we won at Porto Bello.   Many swore fiercely
that, if they had known how small the booty was
to prove, they would have seen Henry Morgan in gaol
before they 'listed.   Why they did not tear him piece-
meal, and heave him into the sea, must remain a mystery.
They contented themselves with damning him to his face
for a rogue and a thief, at the same time praying that a
red-hot hell might be his everlasting portion.   " But
Captain Morgan," says the narrative, " was deaf to all
these, and many other complaints of this kind, having
designed in his mind to cheat them of as much as he
could."

Deaf though he was, and callous, he had a fine regard
for his own skin. The oaths and curses which were shouted
after him as he walked in the castle made him " to fear
the consequence thereof."   He " thought it unsafe to
remain any longer time at Chagre," so he planned a
master stroke to defeat his enemies. The castle guns
were dismounted, and hoisted aboard his flagship. The
castle walls were then blasted into pieces, the lower
batteries thrown down, and the houses burnt. When
these things had been done " he went secretly on board
his own ship, without giving any notice of his departure

to his companions, nor calling any council, as he used to do. Thus he set sail, and put out to sea, not bidding anybody adieu, being only followed by three or four vessels of the fleet." The captains of these ships, it was believed, had shared with him in the concealed plunder.

There was great fury among the buccaneers when Morgan's escape was known. The French pirates were for putting to sea in pursuit, to blow his ships out of the water, but Morgan had been sufficiently astute to escape in the provision ships. The pirates left behind had not food enough to stock their ships, and could not put to sea till more had been gathered. While they cursed and raged at Chagres, Morgan sailed slowly to Port Royal, where he furled his sails, and dropped anchor, after a highly profitable cruise. The Governor received his percentage of the profits, and Morgan at once began to levy recruits for the settling of Santa Katalina.

As for his men, they stayed for some days in considerable misery at San Lorenzo. They then set sail in companies, some for one place, some for another, hoping to find food enough to bring them home. Some went to the eastward, raiding the coast for food, and snapping up small coasting vessels. Some went to the bay of Campeachy to cut logwood and to drink rum punch. Others went along the Costa Rican coast to find turtle to salt for victuals, and to careen their barnacled and wormy ships. One strong company went to Cuba, where they sacked the Town of the Keys, and won a good booty. Most of them came home, in time, but to those who returned that home-coming was bitter.

Shortly after Morgan's return to Jamaica, a new Governor arrived from England with orders to suppress the gangs of privateers. He had instructions to proclaim a general pardon for all those buccaneers who cared to take advantage of the proclamation within a given time. Those who wished to leave "their naughty way of life" were to be encouraged by grants of land (thirty-five acres apiece), so that they might not starve when they forsook piracy. But this generous offer was merely a lure or bait to bring the buccaneers to port, in order that the Governor might mulct them "the tenths and fifteenths of their booty as the dues of the Crown for granting them commissions." The news of the intended taxation spread abroad among the pirates. They heard, too, that in future they would find no rest in Port Royal; for this new Governor was earnest and diligent in his governorship. They, therefore, kept away from Port Royal, and made Tortuga their rendezvous, gradually allying themselves with the French buccaneers, who had their stronghold there. Some of them, who returned to Port Royal, were brought before the magistrate, and hanged as pirates. Their old captain, Henry Morgan, left his former way of life, and soon afterwards become Governor of Jamaica. He was so very zealous in "discouraging" the buccaneers that the profession gradually lost its standing. The best of its members took to logwood cutting or to planting; the worst kept the seas, like water-Ishmaelites, plundering the ships of all nations save their own. They haunted Tortuga, the keys of Cuba, the creeks and inlets of the coast, and the bays at the western end of Jamaica. They were able to do a great deal of mischief; for there were many of them, and the English Colonial governors could not spare many men-of-war to police the seas. Often the pirates combined and made descents upon the coast as in the past. Henry Morgan's defection did but drive them from their own pleasant haunt, Port Royal. The "free-trade" of buccaneering throve as it had always thriven. But about the time of Morgan's consulship we read of British men-of-war helping to discourage the trade, and thenceforward the buccaneers were without the support of the Colonial Government. Those who sailed the seas after Morgan's time were public enemies, sailing under the shadow of the gallows.

Authorities.—W. Nelson: "Five Years at Panama." P. Mimande: "Souvenirs d'un Echappé de Panama." A. Reclus: "Panama et Darien." A. Radford: "Jottings on Panama." J. de Acosta: "Voyages." S. de Champlain: "Narrative." Cieça de Leon: "Travels." Exquemeling: "Bucaniers of America." Don Perez de la Guzman: "Account of the Sack of Panama."

I am also indebted to friends long resident in the present city of Panama.

CHAPTER XIII

CAPTAIN DAMPIER

Campeachy—Logwood cutting—The march to Santa Maria

WILLIAM DAMPIER, a Somersetshire man, who had a taste for roving, went to the West Indies for the first time in 1674, about three years after the sack of Panama. He was "then about twenty-two years old," with several years of sea-service behind him. He had been to the north and to the east, and had smelt powder in a King's ship during the Dutch wars. He came to the West Indies to manage a plantation, working his way "as a Seaman" aboard the ship of one Captain Kent. Planting sugar or cocoa on Sixteen-Mile Walk in an island so full of jolly sinners proved to be but dull work. Dampier tried it for some weeks, and then slipped away to sea with a Port Royal trader, who plied about the coast, fetching the planters' goods to town, and carrying European things, such as cloth, iron, powder, or the like, to the planters' jetties along the coast. That was a more pleasant life, for it took the young man all round the island, to quiet plantings where old buccaneers were at work. These were kindly fellows, always ready for a yarn with the shipmen who brought their goods from Port Royal. They treated the young man well, giving him yams, plantains, and sweet potatoes, with leave to wander through their houses. "But after six or seven Months" Dampier "left that Employ," for he had heard strange tales of the logwood cutters in Campeachy Bay, and longed to see something of them.

He, therefore, slipped aboard a small Jamaica vessel which was going to the bay "to load logwood," with two other ships in company. The cargo of his ship "was rum and sugar; a very good Commodity for the Log-wood Cutters, who were then about 250 Men, most English." When they anchored off One Bush Key, by the oyster banks and "low Mangrovy Land," these lumbermen came aboard for drink, buying rum by the gallon or firkin, besides some which had been brewed into punch. They stayed aboard, drinking, till the casks gave out, firing off their small-arms with every health, and making a dreadful racket in that still lagoon, where the silence was seldom so violently broken. The logwood began to come aboard a day or two later; and Dampier sometimes went ashore with the boat for it, on which occasions he visited the huts of the woodmen, and ate some merry meals with them, "with Pork and Pease, or Beef and Dough-boys," not to mention "Drams or Punch."

On the voyage home he was chased by Spaniards, who "fired a Gun" at the ketch, but could not fetch her alongside.

It was an easy life aboard that little ketch; for every morning they fished for their suppers, and at no time was any work done unless the ship was actually in peril of wreck. While they were lazying slowly eastward, "tumbling like an Egg-shell in the Sea," her captain ran her on the Alcranes, a collection of sandy little islands, where they stayed for some days before they found a passage out to sea. They spent the days in fishing, or flinging pebbles at the rats, or killing boobies, and then set sail again, arriving after some days' sailing, at the Isles of Pines.

Here they landed to fill fresh water at the brooks, among the sprays of red mangrove, which grew thickly at the water's edge. They also took ashore their "two

bad Fowling-pieces," with intent to kill a wild hog
or cow, being then in want of food, for the ship's
provisions had given out. They did not kill any meat
for all their hunting, nor did they catch much fish.
Their ill success tempted the sailors to make for the
Cuban keys, where they thought they would find great
abundance, "either Fish or Flesh." The Cuban keys
were favourite haunts of the buccaneers, but it was
dangerous for a small ship like the ketch to venture
in among them. On Cape Corientes there was a Spanish
garrison of forty soldiers, chiefly mulattoes and caribs,
who owned a swift periagua, fitted with oars and sails.
They kept sentinels always upon the Cape, and whenever a ship hove in sight they would "launch out," and
seize her, and cut the throats of all on board, "for fear
of telling Tales." Fear of this garrison, and the prudent
suggestion of Dampier—that "it was as probable that
we might get as little Food in the South Keys, as we
did at Pines, where, though there was plenty of Beefs
and Hogs, yet we could not to tell how to get any—" at
last prevailed upon the seamen to try for Jamaica. They
were without food of any kind, save a little flour from
the bottoms of the casks, and two "Barrels of Beef,"
which they had taken west to sell, "but 'twas so bad
that none would buy it." On a porridge of this meat,
chopped up with mouldy flour, they contrived to keep
alive, "jogging on" towards the east till they made
Jamaica. They arrived off Blewfield's Point thirteen
weeks after leaving Campeachy, and, as Dampier says:
"I think never any vessel before nor since made such
Traverses . . . as we did. . . . We got as much Experience as if we had been sent out on a Design."
However, they dropped their anchor "at Nigrill" "about
three a Clock in the Afternoon," and sent in the boat
for fruit and poultry. One or two sea-captains, whose

ketches were at anchor there, came out to welcome the
new arrival. In the little "Cabbin," where the lamp
swung in gimbals, the sailors "were very busie, going
to drink a Bowl of Punch, . . . after our long Fatigue
and Fasting." The thirsty sea-captains, bronzed by the
sun, came stumping down the ladder to bear a hand.
One captain, "Mr John Hooker," said that he was under
"Oath to drink but three Draughts of Strong Liquor
a Day." The bowl, which had not been touched, lay
with him, with six quarts of good rum punch inside
it. This Mr Hooker, "putting the Bowl to his Head,
turn'd it off at one Draught"—he being under oath,
and, doubtless, thirsty. "And so, making himself drunk,
disappointed us of our Expectations, till we made
another Bowl." Thus with good cheer did they recruit
themselves in that hot climate after long sailing of the
seas.

Dampier passed the next few weeks in Port Royal,
thinking of the jolly life at One Bush Key, and of the
little huts, so snugly thatched, and of the camp fires,
when the embers glowed so redly at night before the
moon rose. The thought of the logwood cutters passing
to and fro about those camp fires, to the brandy barrel
or the smoking barbecue, was pleasant to him. He felt
inclined "to spend some Time at the Logwood Trade,"
much as a young gentleman of that age would have
spent "some Time" on the grand tour with a tutor.
He had a little gold laid by, so that he was able to
lay in a stock of necessaries for the trade—such as
"Hatchets, Axes, Long Knives, Saws, Wedges, etc., a
Pavillion to sleep in, a Gun with Powder and Shot, etc."
When all was ready, he went aboard a New England
ship, and sailed for Campeachy, where he settled "in
the West Creek of the West Lagoon" with some old
logwood cutters who knew the trade.

Logwood cutting was then a very profitable business, for the wood fetched from £70 to £100 a ton in the European markets. The wood is very dense, and so heavy that it sinks in water. The work of cutting it, and bringing it to the ships, in the rough Campeachy country, where there were no roads, was very hard. The logwood cutters were, therefore, men of muscle, fond of violent work. Nearly all of them in Dampier's time were buccaneers who had lost their old trade. They were "sturdy, strong Fellows," able to carry "Burthens of three or four hundred Weight," and "contented to labour very hard." Their hands and arms were always dyed a fine scarlet with the continuous rubbing of the wood, and their clothes always smelt of the little yellow logwood flowers, which smell very sweet and strong, at most seasons of the year. The life lived by the lumbermen was wild, rough, and merry. They had each of them a tent, or a strongly thatched hut, to live in, and most of them had an Indian woman or a negress to cook their food. Some of them had white wives, which they bought at Jamaica for about thirty pounds apiece, or five pounds more than the cost of a black woman. As a rule, they lived close to the lips of the creeks, "for the benefit of the Sea-Breezes," in little villages of twenty or thirty together. They slept in hammocks, or in Indian cots, raised some three or four feet from the ground, to allow for any sudden flood which the heavy rains might raise. They cooked their food on a sort of barbecue strewn with earth. For chairs they used logs of wood or stout rails supported on crutches. On the Saturday in each week they left their saws and axes and tramped out into the woods to kill beef for the following week. In the wet seasons, when the savannahs were flooded, they hunted the cattle in canoas by rowing near to the higher grass-lands where the beasts were at graze. Sometimes a wounded steer would charge the canoa, and spill the huntsmen in the water, where the alligators nipped them. In the dry months, the hunters went on foot. When they killed a steer they cut the body into four, flung away the bones, and cut a big hole in each quarter. Each of the four men of the hunting party then thrust his head through the hole in one of the quarters, and put "it on like a Frock," and so trudged home. If the sun were hot, and the beef heavy, the wearer cut some off, and flung it away. This weekly hunting was "a Diversion pleasant enough" after the five days' hacking at the red wood near the lagoon-banks. The meat, when brought to camp, was boucanned or jerked—that is, dried crisp in the sun. A quarter of a steer a man was the week's meat allowance. If a man wanted fish or game, in addition, he had to obtain it for himself. This diet was supplemented by the local fruits, and by stores purchased from the ships—such as dried pease, or flour to make doughboys.

Men who worked hard under a tropical sun, in woods sometimes flooded to a depth of two feet, could hardly be expected to take a pride in their personal appearance. One little vanity they had, and apparently one only —they were fond of perfumes. They used to kill the alligator for his musk-sacs, which they thought "as good civet as any in the world." Each logwood cutter carried a musk-sac in his hat to diffuse scent about him, "sweet as Arabian winds when fruits are ripe," wheresoever his business led him.

The logwood cutters usually formed into little companies of from four to twelve men each. The actual "cutters" had less to do than the other members, for they merely felled the trees. Others sawed and hacked the tree trunks into logs. The boss, or chief man in the gang, then chipped away the white sappy rind surrounding the scarlet heart with its crystals of brilliant red. If the tree were very big (and some were six feet round) they split the bole by gunpowder. The red hearts alone were exported, as it is the scarlet crystal (which dries to a dull black after cutting) which gives the wood its value in dyeing. When the timber had been properly cut and trimmed it was dragged to the water's edge, and stacked there ready for the merchants. The chips burnt very well, "making a clear strong fire, and very lasting," in which the rovers used to harden "the Steels of their Fire Arms when they were faulty."

When a ship arrived at One Bush Key the logwood cutters went aboard her for rum and sugar. It was the custom for the ship's captain to give them free drinks on the day of his arrival, "and every Man will pay honestly for what he drinks afterwards." If the captain did not set the rum punch flowing with sufficient liberality they would "pay him with their worst Wood," and "commonly" they "had a stock of such" ready for the niggard when he came. Often, indeed, they would give such a one a load of hollow logs "filled with dirt in the middle, and both ends plugg'd up with a piece of the same." But if the captain commanding were "true steel, an old bold blade, one of the old buccaneers, a hearty brave toss-pot, a trump, a true twopenny"—why, then, they would spend thirty or forty pounds apiece in a drinking bout aboard his ship, "carousing and firing of Guns three or four days together." They were a careless company, concerned rather in "the squandering of life away" than in its preservation. Drink and song, and the firing of guns, and a week's work chipping blood-wood, and then another drunkenness, was the story of their life there. Any "sober men" who came thither were soon "debauched" by "the old Standards," and took to "Wickedness" and "careless Rioting." Those who found the work too hard used to go hunting in the woods. Often enough they marched to the woods in companies, to sack the Indian villages, to bring away women for their solace, and men slaves to sell at Jamaica. They also robbed the Indians' huts of honey, cocoa, and maize, but then the Indians were "very melancholy and thoughtful" and plainly designed by God as game for logwood cutters.

In the end the Spaniards fell upon the logwood men and carried them away to Mexico and Vera Cruz, sending some to the silver mines, and selling the others to tradesmen. As slaves they passed the next few years, till they escaped to the coast. One of those who escaped told how he saw a Captain Buckenham, once a famous man at those old drinking bouts, and owner of a sugar ship, working as a slave in the city of Mexico. "He saw Captain Buckenham, with a Log chained to his Leg, and a Basket at his Back, crying Bread about the Streets for a Baker his Master."

In this society of logwood cutters Dampier served a brief apprenticeship. He must have heard many strange tales, and jolly songs, around the camp fires of his mates, but none of them, apparently, were fit to print. He went hunting cattle, and got himself "bushed," or marooned— that is, lost—and had a narrow escape from dying in the woods. He helped at the cutting and trimming of the red wood, and at the curing of the hides of the slaughtered steers. When ships arrived he took his sup of rum, and fired his pistol, with the best of them. Had he stayed there any length of time he would have become a master logwood merchant, and so "gotten an Estate"; but luck was against him.

In June 1676, when he was recovering from a guinea-worm, a creature which nests in one's ankle, and causes great torment, a storm, or "South," reduced the logwood cutters of those parts to misery. The South was "long foretold," by the coming in of many sea-birds to the shore's shelter, but the lumbermen "believed it was a certain Token of the Arrival of Ships," and took no precautions against tempest. Two days later the wind broke upon them furiously, scattering their huts like scraps of paper. The creek began to rise "faster than I ever saw it do in the greatest Spring Tide," so that, by noon, the poor wretches, huddled as they were in a hut, without fire, were fain to make ready a canoa to save themselves from drowning. The trees in the woods were torn up by the roots, "and tumbled down strangely across each other." The ships in the creek were blown from their anchors. Two of them were driven off to sea, dipping their bows clean under, and making shocking weather of it. One of them was lost in the bay, being whelmed by a green sea.

The storm destroyed all the tools and provisions of the lumbermen, and left Dampier destitute. His illness, with the poisonous worm in his leg, had kept him from work for some weeks, so that he had no cords of red wood ready cut, "as the old Standards had," to buy him new tools and new stores. Many of the men were in the same case, so they agreed with the captains of two pirate ketches which called at the creek at that time, to go a cruise to the west to seek their fortunes. They cruised up and down the bay "and made many Descents into the country," "where we got Indian Corn to eat with the Beef, and other Flesh, that we got by the way." They also attacked Alvarado, a little, protected city on the river of that name, but they lost heavily in the attack. Of the sixty pirates engaged, ten or eleven were killed or desperately wounded. The fort was not surrendered for four or five hours, by which time the citizens had put their treasure into boats, and rowed it upstream to safety. It was dark by the time the pirates won the fort, so that pursuit was out of the question. They rested there that night, and spent the next day foraging. They killed and salted a number of beeves, and routed out much salt fish and Indian corn, "as much as we could stow away." They also took a number of poultry, which the Spaniards were fattening in coops ; and nearly a hundred tame parrots, "yellow and red," which "would prate very prettily." In short they heaped their decks with hen-coops, parrot-cages, quarters of beef, casks of salt fish, and baskets full of maize. In this state, the ships lay at anchor, with their men loafing on deck with their tobacco, bidding the "yellow and red" parrots to say "Damn," or "Pretty Polly," or other ribaldry. But before any parrot could have lost his Spanish accent, the pirates were called from their lessons by the sight of seven Spanish warships, under all sail, coming up to the river-bar from La Vera Cruz. Their ports were up, and their guns were run out, and they were not a mile away when the pirates first saw them. As it happened, the River Alvarado was full of water, so that these great vessels "could scarce stem the current." This piece of luck saved the pirates, for it gave them time to make sail, and to clear the bar before the Spaniards entered the river. As they dropped down the stream, they hove the clutter from the decks. Many a Pretty Polly there quenched her blasphemy in water, and many a lump of beef went to the mud to gorge the alligators. The litter was all overboard, and the men stripped to fight the guns, by the time the tide had swept them over the bar. At this moment they came within range of the Spanish flagship, the *Toro*, of ten guns and 100 men. She was to windward of them, and perilously close aboard, and her guns sent some cannon-balls into them, without doing any serious harm. Dampier was in the leading ship, which stood to the eastward, followed by her consort, as soon as she was over the bar. After her came the *Toro*, followed by a ship of four guns, and by five smaller vessels manned with musketeers, "and the Vessels

barricadoed round with Bull-hides Breast high." The *Toro*
ranged up on the quarter of Dampier's ship, "designing to
board" her. The pirates dragged their cannon aft, and
fired at her repeatedly, "in hopes to have lamed either
Mast or Yard." As they failed to carry away her spars,
they waited till "she was shearing aboard," when they
rammed the helm hard up, "gave her a good Volley," and
wore ship. As soon as she was round on the other tack,
she stood to the westward, passing down the Spanish line
under a heavy fire. The *Toro* held to her course, after the
second pirate ship, with the six ships of the fleet following
in her wake. The second pirate ship was much galled
by the fleet's fire, and ran great risk of being taken.
Dampier's ship held to the westward, till she was about
a mile to windward of the other ships. She then tacked,
and ran down to assist her consort, "who was hard put to
it." As she ran down, she opened fire on the *Toro*, "who
fell off, and shook her ears," edging in to the shore, to
escape, with her fleet after her. They made no fight of it,
but tacked and hauled to the wind "and stood away for
Alvarado." The pirates were very glad to see the last of
them ; "and we, glad of the Deliverance, went away to the
Eastward." On the way, they visited all the sandy bays
of the coast to look for "munjack," "a sort of Pitch or
Bitumen which we find in Lumps." When corrected with
oil or tallow this natural pitch served very well for the
paying of the seams "both of Ships and Canoas."

After this adventure, Dampier returned to the lumber
camp, and passed about a year there, cutting wood. Then,
for some reason, he determined to leave the Indies, and to
visit England ; and though he had planned to return to
Campeachy, after he had been home, he never did so. It
seems that he was afraid of living in that undefended
place, among those drunken mates of his. They were at
all times at the mercy of a Spanish man-of-war, and

Edward Thatch alias Zwartbaard doodgebleeven.

Captain Edward Teach, more commonly known as 'Blackbeard'. Teach took up piracy in 1716 and became one of the most feared men on the Spanish Main. He was killed in 1718 when his ship was attacked by H.M.S. *Swallow. Johnson.*

Dampier "always feared" that a Spanish prison would be his lot if he stayed there. It was the lot of his imprudent mates, "the old Standards," a few months after he had sailed for the Thames.

After a short stay in England, Dampier sailed for Jamaica with a general cargo. He sold his goods at Port Royal, but did not follow his original plan of buying rum and sugar, and going west as a logwood merchant. About Christmas 1679 he bought a small estate in Dorsetshire, "of one whose Title to it" he was "well assured of." He was ready to sail for England, to take charge of this estate, and to settle down as a farmer, when he met "one Mr Hobby," at a tavern, who asked him to go "a short trading voyage to the Country of the Moskito's." Dampier, who was a little short of gold at the moment, was very willing to fill his purse before sailing north. He therefore consented to go with Mr Hobby, whose ship was then ready for the sea. He "went on board Mr Hobby," and a fair wind blew them clear of Port Royal. A day or two of easy sailing brought them to Negril Bay, "at the West End of Jamaica," where Dampier had anchored before, when the valorous captain drained the punch-bowl. The bay was full of shipping, for Captains Coxon, Sawkins, Sharp, and other buccaneers, were lying there filling their water casks. They had the red wheft flying, for they were bound on the account, to raid the Main. The boats alongside them were full of meat and barrels. Mr Hobby's men did not wait to learn more than the fact that the ships were going cruising. They dumped their chests into the dinghy, and rowed aboard of them, and 'listed themselves among the sunburnt ruffians who were hoisting out the water breakers. Dampier and Mr Hobby were left alone on their ship, within hearing of the buccaneers, who sang, and danced to the fiddle, and clinked the cannikin, till the moon had set. For three or four

days they stayed there, hearing the merriment of the
rovers, but at the end of the fourth day Dampier wearied
of Mr Hobby, and joined the buccaneers, who were glad to
have him.

A day or two after Christmas 1679 they got their
anchors and set sail. They shaped their course for Porto
Bello, which had recovered something of its old wealth and
beauty, in the years of peace it had enjoyed since Morgan
sacked it. They landed 200 men to the eastward of
the town, "at such a distance" that the march "occupied
them three nights." During the day they lay in ambush
in the woods. As they "came to the town" a negro saw
them, and ran to set the bells ringing, to call out the
troops. The buccaneers followed him so closely that
the town was theirs before the troops could muster. They
stayed there forty-eight hours gathering plunder, and then
marched back to their ships staggering under a great weight
of gold. They shared thirty or forty pounds a man from
this raid. Afterwards they harried the coast, east and
west, and made many rich captures. Sawkins, it seems,
was particularly lucky, for he made a haul of 1000 chests
of indigo. Warrants were out for all these pirates, and
had they been taken they would most surely have been
hanged.

After these adventures, the squadron made for "a place
called Boco del Toro," "an opening between two islands
between Chagres and Veragua," where "the general
rendezvous of the fleet" had been arranged. The ships
anchored here, with one or two new-comers, including a
French ship commanded by a Captain Bournano, who
had been raiding on the isthmus, "near the South Sea,"
but a few days before. At the council aboard Captain
Sawkins' ship, it was given out, to all the assembled
buccaneers, that the Spaniards had made peace with the
Darien Indians. This was bad news; but Captain

Bournano was able to assure the company "that since the conclusion of the said peace, they had been already tried, and found very faithful"; for they had been of service to him in his late foray. He added that they had offered to guide him "to a great and very rich place called Tocamora," and that he had promised to come to them "with more ships and men," in three months' time. The buccaneers thought that Tocamora, apart from the beauty of the name, appeared to promise gold, so they decided to go thither as soon as they had careened and refitted. Boca del Toro, the anchorage in which they lay, was full of " green tortoise " for ships short of food. There were handy creeks, among the islands, for the ships to careen in, when their hulls were foul. The pirates hauled their ships into the creeks, and there hove them down, while their Moskito allies speared the tortoise, and the manatee, along the coast, and afterwards salted the flesh for sea-provision.

As soon as the squadron was ready, they mustered at Water Key, and set sail for Golden Island, where they meant to hold a final council. On the way to the eastward they put in at the Samballoes, or islands of San Blas, to fill fresh water, and to buy fruit from the Indians. When the anchors held, the Indians came aboard with fruit, venison, and native cloth, to exchange for edged iron tools, and red and green beads. They were tall men, smeared with black paint (the women used red, much as in Europe), and each Indian's nose was hung with a plate of gold or silver. Among the women were a few albinos, who were said to see better in the dark than in the light. "These Indians misliked our design for Tocamora," because the way thither was mountainous and barren and certain to be uninhabited. A force going thither would be sure to starve on the road, they said, but it would be an easy matter to march to Panama, as Drake had marched.

New Panama was already a rich city, so that they would not "fail of making a good voyage by going thither." This advice of the Indians impressed the buccaneers. They determined to abandon the Tocamora project as too dangerous. Most of them were in favour of going to sack Panama. But Captain Bournano, and Captain Row, who commanded about a hundred Frenchmen between them, refused to take their men on "a long march by land." Perhaps they remembered how Morgan had treated the French buccaneers after his Panama raid, nine years before. They therefore remained at anchor when the squadron parted company. An Indian chief, Captain Andreas, came aboard the English flagship. The bloody colours were hoisted, and a gun fired in farewell. The English ships then loosed their top-sails and stood away for Golden Island, to an anchorage they knew of, where a final muster could be held. They dropped anchor there, "being in all seven sail," on 3rd April 1680.

Their strength at the Samballoes had been as follows :—

		Tons	Guns	Men
Captain Coxon in a ship of		80	8	97
Captain Harris	„	150	25	107
Captain Sawkins	„	16	1	35
Captain Sharp	„	25	2	40
Captain Cook	„	35	0	43
Captain Alleston	„	18	0	24
Captain Macket	„	14	0	20

but of these 366 buccaneers a few had remained behind with the Frenchmen.

While they lay at Golden Island, the Indians brought them word of "a town called Santa Maria," on the Rio Santa Maria, near the Gulf of San Miguel, on the Pacific coast. It was a garrison town, with four companies of musketeers in its fort, for there were gold mines in the hills behind it. The gold caravans went from it, once a month in the dry seasons, to Panama. If the place failed to yield them a booty, the buccaneers were determined to attack new Panama. Had they done so they would probably have destroyed the place, for though the new city was something stronger than the old, the garrison was in the interior fighting the Indians. The design on Santa Maria was popular. On the matter being put to the vote it was carried without protest. The buccaneers passed the 4th of April in arranging details, and picking a party to protect the ships during their absence. They arranged that Captains Alleston and Macket, with about twenty-five or thirty seamen, should remain in the anchorage as a ship's guard. The remainder of the buccaneers, numbering 331 able-bodied men (seven of whom were French), were to march with the colours the next morning.

On the 5th of April 1680, these 331 adventurers dropped across the channel from Golden Island, and landed on the isthmus, somewhere near Drake's old anchorage. Captain Bartholomew Sharp, of "the dangerous voyage and bold assaults," came first, with some Indian guides, one of whom helped the Captain, who was sick and faint with a fever. This vanguard "had a red flag, with a bunch of white and green ribbons." The second company, or main battle, was led by the admiral, Richard Sawkins, who "had a red flag striped with yellow." The third and fourth companies, which were under one captain (Captain Peter Harris), had two green flags. The fifth and sixth companies, under Captain John Coxon, "had each of them a red flag." A few of Alleston's and Macket's men carried arms under Coxon in these companies. The rear-guard was led by Captain Edmund Cook, "with red colours striped with yellow, with a hand and sword for his device." " All or most" of the men who landed, "were armed with a French fuzee" (or musket), a pistol and hanger, with two pounds of powder and "proportionable bullet." Each of them carried a scrip or satchel containing "three or four cakes of bread," or doughboys, weighing half-a-pound apiece, with some modicum of turtle flesh. "For drink, the rivers afforded enough."

Among the men who went ashore in that company were William Dampier, the author of the best books of voyages in the language; Lionel Wafer, the chirurgeon of the party, who wrote a description of the isthmus; Mr Basil Ringrose, who kept an intimate record of the foray; and Captain Bartholomew Sharp, who also kept a journal, but whose writings are less reliable than those of the other three. It is not often that three historians of such supreme merit as Dampier, Wafer, and Ringrose, are associated in a collaboration so charming, as a piratical raid. Wafer had been a surgeon in Port Royal, but Edmund Cook had shown him the delights of roving, and the cruise he had made to Cartagena had confirmed him in that way of life. Basil Ringrose had but lately arrived at the Indies, and it is not known what induced him to go buccaneering. He was a good cartographer, and had as strong a bent towards the description of natural phenomena, as Dampier had. He probably followed the pirates in order to see the world, and to get some money, and to extend his knowledge. Sharp had been a pirate for some years, and there was a warrant out for him at Jamaica for his share in the sack of Porto Bello. With Dampier's history the reader has been made acquainted.

The Indians, under Captain Andreas, led the buccaneers from the landing-place "through a small skirt of wood," beyond which was a league of sandy beach. "After that, we went two leagues directly up a woody valley, where we saw here and there an old plantation, and had a very good path to march in." By dusk they had arrived at a river-bank, beneath which the water lay in pools, joined by trickles and little runlets, which babbled over sun-bleached pebbles. They built themselves huts in this place, about a great Indian hut which stood upon the river-bank. They slept there that night, " having nothing but the cold Earth for their Beds," in much discouragement " with the going back of some of the Men." The buccaneers who had been some weeks at sea, were not in marching trim, and it seems that the long day's tramp in the sun had sickened many of them. While they rested in their lodges, an Indian king, whom they called " Captain Antonio," came in to see them. He said that he had sent word to one of his tributaries, farther to the south, to prepare food and lodgings for the buccaneers " against their Arrival." As for himself, he wished very much that he could come with them to lead their guides, but unfortunately " his child lay very sick." However, it comforted him to think that the child would be dead by the next day, at latest, " and then he would most certainly follow and overtake " them. He warned the company not to lie in the grass, " for fear of monstrous adders "; and so bowed himself out of camp, and returned home. The kingly prayers seem to have been effectual, for Captain Antonio was in camp again by sunrise next morning, with no family tie to keep him from marching.

As the men sluiced themselves in the river before taking to the road, they noticed that the pebbles shone " with sparks of gold " when broken across. They did not stay to wash the river-mud, for gold dust and golden pellets, but fell in for the march, and climbed from dawn till nearly dusk. They went over " a steep Mountain " which was parched and burnt and waterless. Four of the buccaneers refused to go farther than the foot of this hill, so they returned to the ships. The others, under the guidance of Antonio, contrived to cross the mountain " to an Hollow of Water," at which they drank very greedily. Six miles farther on they halted for the night, beside a

stream. They slept there, "under the Canopy of Heaven,"
suffering much discomfort from some drenching showers.
After some days of climbing, wading, and suffering, the army
reached the house of King Golden Cap, an Indian king.
The King came out to meet them in his robes, with a
little reed crown on his head, lined with red silk, and
covered with a thin plate of gold. He had a golden ring
in his nose, and a white cotton frock over his shoulders.
His queen wore a red blanket, and a blouse "like our old-
fashioned striped hangings." This royal couple bade the
army welcome, and ordered food to be brought for them.
The buccaneers passed a couple of days in King Golden
Cap's city, trading their coloured beads, and scraps of iron,
for fresh fruit and meat. They found the Indians "very
cunning" in bargaining, which means, we suppose, that
they thought a twopenny whittle a poor return for a hog
or a sack of maize.

When the men had rested themselves, and had dried
their muddy clothes, they set out again, with Captain
Sawkins in the vanguard. As they marched out of the
town "the King ordered us each man to have three
plantains, with sugar-canes to suck, by way of a present."
They breakfasted on these fruits, as they marched. The
road led them "along a very bad Path" continually inter-
sected by a river, which they had to wade some fifty or
sixty times, to their great misery. They passed a few
Indian huts on the way, and at each hut door stood an
Indian to give "as we passed by, to every one of us, a
ripe plantain, or some sweet cassava-root." Some of the
Indians counted the army "by dropping a grain of corn
for each man that passed before them," for without
counters they could not reckon beyond twenty. The
army had by this time been swelled by an Indian con-
tingent, of about 150 men, "armed with Bows, Arrows and
Lances." The Indians dropping their corn grains must

have dropped nearly 500 before the last man passed them. That night, which was clear and fine, they rested in three large Indian huts, where King Golden Cap's men had stored up food and drink, and a number of canoas, for the voyage south. The river went brawling past their bivouac at a little distance, and some of the men caught fish, and broiled them in the coals for their suppers.

At daylight next morning, while they were getting the canoas to the water, Captain Coxon had "some Words" with Captain Harris (of the green flags). The words ran into oaths, for the two men were surly with the discomforts of turning out. Coxon whipped up a gun and fired at Peter Harris, "which he was [naturally] ready to return." Sharp knocked his gun up before he could fire, "and brought him to be quiet; so that we proceeded on our Journey." They had no further opportunities for fighting, for Sawkins gave the word a moment later for seventy of the buccaneers to embark in the canoas. There were fourteen of these boats, all of them of small size. Sharp, Coxon, and Cook were placed in charge of them. Captain Harris was told off to travel with the land party, with Sawkins, King Golden Cap, and the other men. Don Andreas, with twenty-eight other Indians (two to a canoa) acted as boatmen, or pilots, to the flotilla.

Basil Ringrose, who was one of the boat party, has told us of the miseries of the "glide down the stream." The river was low, and full of rotting tree trunks, so that "at the distance of almost every stone's cast," they had to leave the boats "and haul them over either sands or rocks, and at other times over trees." Sharp, who was of tougher fibre, merely says that they "paddled all Day down the Falls and Currents of the River, and at Night took up our Quarters upon a Green Bank by the Riverside, where we had Wild Fowl and Plantanes for Supper: But our Beds were made upon the cold Earth, and our Coverings were the Heavens, and green Trees we found there." The next day they went downstream again, over many more snags and shallows, which set them wading in the mud till their boots rotted off their feet. Ringrose was too tired to make a note in his journal, save that, that night, "a tiger" came out and looked at them as they sat round the camp fires. Sharp says that the labour "was a Pleasure," because "of that great Unity there was then amongst us," and because the men were eager "to see the fair South Sea." They lodged that night "upon a green Bank of the River," and ate "a good sort of a Wild Beast like unto our English Hog." The third day, according to Ringrose, was the worst day of all. The river was as full of snags as it had been higher up, but the last reach of it was clear water, so that they gained the rendezvous "about Four in the Afternoon." To their very great alarm they found that the land party had not arrived. They at once suspected that the Indians had set upon them treacherously, and cut them off in the woods. But Don Andreas sent out scouts "in Search of them," who returned "about an Hour before Sun-set," with "some of their Number," and a message that the rest would join company in the morning.

A little after daybreak the land force marched in, and pitched their huts near the river, "at a beachy point of land," perhaps the very one where Oxenham's pinnace had been beached. They passed the whole day there resting, and cleaning weapons, for they were now but "a Day and a Night's Journey" from the town they had planned to attack. Many more Indians joined them at this last camp of theirs, so that the army had little difficulty in obtaining enough canoes to carry them to Santa Maria. They set out early the next morning, in sixty-eight canoes, being in all "327 of us Englishmen, and 50 Indians." Until that day the canoes had been

" poled " as a punt is poled, but now they cut oars and paddles " to make what speed we could." All that day they rowed, and late into the night, rowing " with all haste imaginable," and snapping up one or two passing Indian boats which were laden with plantains. It was after midnight, and about " Two Hours before Day Light," when they ran into a mud bank, about a mile from the town, and stepped ashore, upon a causeway of oars and paddles. They had to cut themselves a path through jungle, as soon as they had crossed the mud, for the town was walled about with tropical forest. They " lay still in the Woods, till the Light appeared," when they " heard the Spaniard discharge his Watch at his Fort by Beat of Drum, and a Volley of Shot." It was the Spanish way of changing guard, at daybreak. It was also the signal for the " Forlorn " of the buccaneers to march to the battle, under Sawkins. This company consisted of seventy buccaneers. As they debouched from the forest, upon open ground, the Spaniards caught sight of them and beat to arms. The men in the fort at once opened fire " very briskly," but the advance-guard ran in upon them, tore down some of the stockade, and " entered the fort incontinently." A moment or two of wild firing passed inside the palisades, and then the Spanish colours were dowsed. The buccaneers in this storm lost two men wounded, of the fifty who attacked. The Spanish loss was twenty-six killed, and sixteen wounded, out of 300 under arms. About fifty more, of the Spanish prisoners, were promptly killed by the Indians, who took them into the woods and stabbed them " to death " with their lances. It seems that one of that garrison, a man named Josef Gabriele, had raped King Golden Cap's daughter who was then with child by him. (Gabriele, as it chanced, was not speared, but saved to pilot the pirates to Panama.) This was the sole action of the Indians in that engagement. During the

battle they lay "in a small hollow," "in great consterna-
tion" at "the noise of the guns."

Though the buccaneers had taken the place easily, they
had little cause for rejoicing. The town was "a little
pitiful Place," with a few thatched huts, or "wild houses
made of Cane," and "but one Church in it." The fort
"was only Stockadoes," designed merely as a frontier
post "to keep in subjection the Indians" or as a lodging
for men employed in the gold mines. There was no more
provision in store there than would serve their turn for
a week. As for the gold, they had missed it by three
days. Three hundredweight of gold had been sent to
Panama while they were struggling downstream. News
of their coming had been brought to the fort in time,
and "all their treasure of gold," "that huge booty of gold"
they had expected to win, had been shipped westward.
Nor had they any prisoners to hold to ransom. The
Governor, the town priest, and the chief citizens, had slipped
out of the town in boats, and were now some miles away.
Richard Sawkins manned a canoa, and went in chase of
them, but they got clear off, to give advice to Panama
that pirates were come across the isthmus. The only
pillage they could find, after torturing their prisoners
"severely," amounted to "twenty pounds' weight of gold,
and a small quantity of silver." To this may be added a
few personal belongings, such as weapons or trinkets, from
the chests of the garrison.

When the booty, such as it was, had been gathered, the
captains held a meeting "to discuss what were best to
be done." Some were for going to the South Sea, to
cruise ; but John Coxon, who had taken Porto Bello, and
hated to be second to Sawkins, was for going back to the
ships. The general vote was for going to Panama, "that
city being the receptacle of all the plate, jewels, and gold
that is dug out of the mines of all Potosi and Peru."

However, they could not venture on Panama without Coxon, and Coxon's company; so they made Coxon their admiral, "Coxon seeming to be well satisfied." Before starting, they sent their booty back to Golden Island, under a guard of twelve men. Most of the Indians fell off at this time, for they had "got from us what knives, scissors, axes, needles and beads they could." Old King Golden Cap, and his son, were less mercenary, and stayed with the colours, being "resolved to go to Panama, out of the desire they had to see that place taken and sacked." They may have followed the buccaneers in order to kill the Spaniard who had raped the princess, for that worthy was still alive, under guard. He had promised to lead the pirates "even to the very bed-chamber door of the governor of Panama."

With the vision of this bed-chamber door before them, the pirates embarked at Santa Maria "in thirty-five canoes" and a ship they had found at anchor in the river. As they "sailed, or rather rowed" downstream, with the ebb, the Spanish prisoners prayed to be taken aboard, lest the Indians should take them and torture them all to death. "We had much ado to find a sufficient number of boats for ourselves," says Ringrose, for the Indians had carried many of the canoas away. Yet the terror of their situation so wrought upon the Spaniards that they climbed on to logs, or crude rafts, or into old canoas, "and by that means shifted so . . . as to come along with us." The island Chepillo, off the mouth of the Cheapo River, had been named as the general rendezvous, but most of the buccaneers were to spend several miserable days before they anchored there. One canoa containing ten Frenchmen, was capsized, to the great peril of the Frenchmen, who lost all their weapons. Ringrose was separated from the company, drenched to the skin, half starved, and very nearly lynched by some Spaniards. His 19th of April was sufficiently stirring to have tired him of going a-roving till his death. He put out "wet and cold," at dawn; was shipwrecked at ten; saved the lives of five Spaniards at noon; "took a survey," or drew a sketch of the coast, an hour later; set sail again by four, was taken by the Spaniards and condemned to death at nine; was pardoned at ten; sent away "in God's name," "vaya ustad con Dios," at eleven; and was at sea again "wet and cold," by midnight. Sharp's party was the most fortunate, for as they entered the bay of Panama they came to an island "a very pleasant green Place," off which a barque of thirty tons came to anchor, "not long before it was dark." The island had a high hummock of land upon it with a little hut, and a stack for a bonfire, at the top. A watchman, an old man, lived in this hut, looking out over the sea for pirates, with orders to fire his beacon, to warn the men on the Main if a strange sail appeared. The pirates caught this watchman before the fire was lit. They learned from him that those at Panama had not yet heard of their coming. Shortly after they had captured the watchman, the little barque aforesaid, came to anchor, and furled her sails. Two of Sharp's canoas crept out, "under the shore," and laid her aboard "just as it began to be duskish." She proved to be a Panama boat, in use as a troop transport. She had just landed some soldiers on the Main, to quell some Indians, who had been raiding on the frontier. Her crew were negroes, Indians, and mulattoes. Most of the buccaneers, especially those in the small canoas, "endeavoured to get into" this ship, to stretch their legs, and to have the advantage of a shelter. More than 130 contrived to stow themselves in her 'tween decks, under "that sea-artist, and valiant commander" (the words are probably his own) "Captain Bartholomew Sharp." They put to sea in her the next day, followed by the canoas. During the morning they took another small barque, in which Captain Harris placed thirty men, and hoisted the green flag. The wind fell calm after the skirmish, but the canoes rowed on to Chepillo, to the rendezvous, where they found provisions such as "two fat hogs," and some plantains, and a spring of water.

A little after dawn, on the day following, while the ships were trying to make the anchorage, Captain Coxon, and Captain Sawkins, rowed out from Chepillo to board a barque which was going past the island under a press of sail. The wind was so light that the canoes overhauled her, but before they could hook to her chains "a young breeze, freshening at that instant," swept her clear of danger. Her men fired a volley into Coxon's boat, which the pirates returned. "They had for their Breakfast a small fight," says Sharp. One of the pirates—a Mr Bull—was killed with an iron slug. The Spaniards got clear away without any loss, "for the Wind blew both fresh and fair" for them. Three or four pirates were grazed with shot, and some bullets went through the canoes. The worst of the matter was that the Spaniards got safely to Panama, "to give intelligence of our coming."

As they could no longer hope to take the city by surprise, "while the Governor was in his bed-chamber," they determined to give the citizens as little time for preparation as was possible. They were still twenty miles from Panama, but the canoes could pass those twenty miles in a few hours' easy rowing. They set out at four o'clock in the evening, after they had delivered their Spanish prisoners "for certain reasons" (which Ringrose "could not dive into") into the hands of the Indians. This act of barbarity was accompanied with the order that the Indians were "to fight, or rather to murder and slay the said prisoners upon the shore, and that in view of the whole fleet." However, the Spaniards rushed the Indians, broke through them, and got away to the woods with the loss of but one soldier.

After they had watched the scuffle, the pirates rowed away merrily towards Panama, "though many showers of rain ceased not to fall." Sharp's vessel, with her crew of more than 130 men, made off for the Pearl Islands, ostensibly to fill fresh water, but really, no doubt, to rob the pearl fisheries. He found a woman (who was "very young and handsome"), and "a Case or two of Wines," at these islands, together with some poultry. He made a feast there, and stayed at anchor that night, and did not set sail again till noon of the day following, by which time the battle of Panama had been fought and won.

Authorities. — Dampier's Voyages.   Wafer's Voyages.   Ringrose's Journal.   "The Dangerous Voyage and Bold Assaults of Captain Bartholomew Sharp"; "The Voyages and Adventures of Captain Bartholomew Sharp" (four or five different editions).   Ringrose's MSS., Sharp's MSS., in the Sloane MSS.

Black Beard fighting with Capt. Maynard.

Victorian artist's impression of the fight between Blackbeard and
Lieutenant Maynard. From the 1839 edition of *Johnson*.

CHAPTER XIV

THE BATTLE OF PERICO

Arica—The South Sea cruise

ON 23rd April 1680, "that day being dedicated to St George, our Patron of England," the canoas arrived off Panama. "We came," says Ringrose, "before sunrise within view of the city of Panama, which makes a pleasant show to the vessels that are at sea." They were within sight of the old cathedral church, "the beautiful building whereof" made a landmark for them, reminding one of the buccaneers "of St Paul's in London," a church at that time little more than a ruin. The new city was not quite finished, but the walls of it were built, and there were several splendid churches, with scaffolding about them rising high, here and there, over the roofs of the houses The townspeople were in a state of panic at the news of the pirates' coming. Many of them had fled into the savannahs; for it chanced that, at that time, many of the troops in garrison, were up the country, at war with a tribe of Indians. The best of the citizens, under Don Jacinto de Baronha, the admiral of those seas, had manned the ships in the bay. Old Don Peralta, who had saved the golden galleon ten years before, had 'listed a number of negroes, and manned one or two barques with them. With the troops still in barracks, and these volunteers and pressed men, they had manned, in all "five great ships, and three pretty big barks." Their force may have numbered 280 men. One account gives the number, definitely, as 228. The buccaneer force

has been variously stated, but it appears certain that
the canoas, and periaguas, which took part in the fight,
contained only sixty-eight of their company. Sharp, as
we have seen, had gone with his company to the Pearl Islands. The remaining 117 men were probably becalmed,
in their barques and canoas, some miles from the vanguard.

When the buccaneers caught sight of Panama, they
were probably between that city and the islands of
Perico and Tobagilla. They were in great disorder, and
the men were utterly weary with the long night of rowing
in the rain, with the wind ahead. They were strung out
over several miles of sea, with five light canoas, containing six or seven men apiece, a mile or two in advance.
After these came two lumbering periaguas, with sixteen
men in each. King Golden Cap was in one of these
latter. Dampier and Wafer were probably not engaged
in this action. Ringrose was in the vanguard, in a small
canoa.

A few minutes after they had sighted the roofs of
Panama, they made out the ships at anchor off the Isle
of Perico. There were "five great ships and three pretty
big barks," manned, as we have said, by soldiers, negroes,
and citizens. The men aboard this fleet were in the rigging of their ships, keeping a strict lookout. As they
caught sight of the pirates the three barques "instantly
weighed anchor," and bore down to engage, under all
the sail they could crowd. The great ships had not
sufficient men to fight their guns. They remained at
anchor; but their crews went aboard the barques, so that
the decks of the three men-of-war must have been incon-
veniently crowded. The Spaniards were dead to wind-
wind of the pirates, so that they merely squared their
yards, and ran down the wind "designedly to show their
valour." They had intended to run down the canoas,
and to sail over them, for their captains had orders to

give no quarter to the pirates, but to kill them, every man. "Such bloody commands as these," adds Ringrose piously, "do seldom or never prosper."

It was now a little after sunrise. The wind was light but steady; the sea calm. As the Spaniards drew within range, the pirates rowed up into the wind's eye, and got to windward of them. Their pistols and muskets had not been wetted in the rain, for each buccaneer had provided himself with an oiled cover for his firearms, the mouth of which he stopped with wax whenever it rained. The Spanish ships ran past the three leading canoas, exchanging volleys at long range. They were formed in line of battle ahead, with a ship manned by mulattoes, or "Tawnymores," in the van. This ship ran between the fourth canoa, in which Ringrose was, and the fifth (to leeward of her) commanded by Sawkins. As she ran between the boats she fired two thundering broadsides, one from each battery, which wounded five buccaneers. "But he paid dear for his passage"; because the buccaneers gave her a volley which killed half her sail trimmers, so that she was long in wearing round to repeat her fire. At this moment the two periaguas came into action, and got to windward with the rest of the pirates' fleet.

While Ringrose's company were ramming the bullets down their gun muzzles, the Spanish admiral (in the second ship) engaged, "scarce giving us time to charge." She was a fleet ship, and had a good way on her, and her design was to pass between two canoas, and give to each a roaring hot broadside. As she ran down, so near that the buccaneers could look right into her, one of the pirates fired his musket at her helmsman, and shot him through the heart as he steered. The ship at once "broached-to," and lay with her sails flat aback, stopped dead. The five canoas, and one of the periaguas, got under her stern, and so plied her with shot that her decks were like shambles, running with blood and brains, five minutes after she came to the wind.   Meanwhile Richard Sawkins ran his canoa— which was a mere sieve of cedar wood, owing to the broad- side—alongside the second periagua, and took her steering oar.   He ordered his men to give way heartily, for the third Spanish ship, under old Don Peralta, was now bear- ing down to relieve the admiral.   Before she got near enough to blow the canoas out of water, Captain Sawkins ran her on board, and so swept her decks with shot that she went no farther.   But "between him and Captain Sawkins, the dispute, or fight, was very hot, lying board on board together, and both giving and receiving death unto each other as fast as they could charge."   Indeed, the fight, at this juncture, was extremely fierce.   The two Spanish ships in action were surrounded with smoke and fire, the men " giving and receiving death " most gallantly. The third ship, with her sail trimmers dead, was to leeward, trying to get upon the other tack.

After a time her sailors got her round, and reached to windward, to help the admiral, who was now being sorely battered.   Ringrose, and Captain Springer, a famous pirate, "stood off to meet him," in two canoas, as " he made up directly towards the Admiral."   Don Jacinto, they noticed, as they shoved off from his flagship, was standing on his quarter-deck, waving "with a handker- chief," to the captain of the Tawnymores' ship.   He was signalling him to scatter the canoas astern of the flagship. It was a dangerous moment, and Ringrose plainly saw "how hard it would go with us if we should be beaten from the Admiral's stern."   With the two canoas he ran down to engage, pouring in such fearful volleys of bullets that they covered the Spaniard's decks with corpses and dying men.   "We killed so many of them, that the vessel had scarce men enough left alive, or unwounded, to carry her off. Had he not given us the helm, and made away from us, we had certainly been on board him." Her decks were littered with corpses, and she was literally running blood. The wind was now blowing fresh, and she contrived to put before it, and so ran out of action, a terrible sight for the Panama women.

Having thus put the Tawnymores out of action, Ringrose and Springer hauled to the wind, and "came about again upon the Admiral, and all together gave a loud halloo." The cheer was answered by Sawkins' men, from the periagua, as they fired into the frigate's ports. Ringrose ran alongside the admiral, and crept "so close" under the vessel's stern, "that we wedged up the rudder." The admiral was shot, and killed, a moment later, as he brought aft a few musketeers to fire out of the stern ports. The ship's pilot, or sailing master, was killed by the same volley. As for the crew, the "stout Biscayners," "they were almost quite disabled and disheartened likewise, seeing what a bloody massacre we had made among them with our shot." Two-thirds of the crew were killed, "and many others wounded." The survivors cried out for quarter, which had been offered to them several times before, "and as stoutly denied until then." Captain Coxon thereupon swarmed up her sides, with a gang of pirates, helping up after him the valorous Peter Harris "who had been shot through both his legs, as he boldly adventured up along the side of the ship." The Biscayners were driven from their guns, disarmed, and thrust down on to the ballast, under a guard. All the wounded pirates were helped up to the deck and made comfortable. Then, in all haste, the unhurt men manned two canoas, and rowed off to help Captain Sawkins, "who now had been three times beaten from on board by Peralta."

A very obstinate and bloody fight had been raging round the third man-of-war. Her sides were splintered with musket-balls. She was oozing blood from her scuppers, yet "the old and stout Spaniard" in command, was cheerily giving shot for shot. "Indeed, to give our enemies their due, no men in the world did ever act more bravely than these Spaniards."

Ringrose's canoa was the first to second Captain Sawkins. She ran close in, "under Peralta's side," and poured in a blasting full volley through her after gun-ports. A scrap of blazing wad fell among the red-clay powder jars in the after magazine. Before she could fire a shot in answer, she blew up abaft. Ringrose from the canoa "saw his men blown up, that were abaft the mast, some of them falling on the deck, and others into the sea." But even this disaster did not daunt old Peralta. Like a gallant sea-captain, he slung a bowline round his waist, and went over the side, burnt as he was, to pick up the men who had been blown overboard. The pirates fired at him in the water, but the bullets missed him. He regained his ship, and the fight went on. While the old man was cheering the wounded to their guns, "another jar of powder took fire forward," blowing the gun's crews which were on the fo'c's'le into the sea. The forward half of the ship caught fire, and poured forth a volume of black smoke, in the midst of which Richard Sawkins boarded, and "took the ship." A few minutes later, Basil Ringrose went on board, to give what aid he could to the hurt. "And indeed," he says, "such a miserable sight I never saw in my life, for not one man there was found, but was either killed, desperately wounded, or horribly burnt with powder, insomuch that their black skins [the ship was manned with negroes] were turned white in several places, the powder having torn it from their flesh and bones." But if Peralta's ship was a charnel-house, the admiral's flagship was a reeking slaughter-pen. Of her eighty-six sailors, sixty-one had been killed. Of the remaining twenty-five, "only eight were able to bear arms, all the rest being desperately wounded, and by their wounds totally disabled to make any resistance, or defend themselves. Their blood ran down the decks in whole streams, and scarce one place in the ship was found that was free from blood." The loss on the Tawnymores' ship was never known, but there had been such "bloody massacre" aboard her, that two other barques, in Panama Roads, had been too scared to join battle, though they had got under sail to engage. According to Ringrose, the pirates lost eighteen men killed, and twenty-two men wounded, several of them severely. Sharp, who was not in the fight, gives the numbers as eleven killed, and thirty-four wounded. The battle began "about half an hour after sunrise." The last of the Spanish fire ceased a little before noon.

Having taken the men-of war, Captain Sawkins asked his prisoners how many men were aboard the galleons, in the Perico anchorage. Don Peralta, who was on deck, "much burnt in both his hands," and "sadly scalded," at once replied that "in the biggest alone there were three hundred and fifty men," while the others were manned in proportion to their tonnage. But one of his men "who lay a-dying upon the deck, contradicted him as he was speaking, and told Captain Sawkins there was not one man on board any of those ships that were in view." "This relation" was believed, "as proceeding from a dying man," and a few moments later it was proved to be true. The greatest of the galleons, "the Most Blessed *Trinity*," perhaps the very ship in which Peralta had saved the treasures of the cathedral church, was found to be empty. Her lading of "wine, sugar, and sweetmeats, skins and soap" (or hides and tallow) was still in the hold, but the Spaniards had deserted her, after they had set her on fire, "made a hole in her, and loosened [perhaps cut adrift] her foresail." The pirates quenched the fire, stopped the leak, and placed their wounded men aboard her, "and thus constituted her for the time being our hospital." They lay at anchor, at Perico, for the rest of that day. On the 24th of April they seem to have been joined by a large company of those who had been to leeward at the time of the battle. Reinforced by these, to the strength of nearly 200 men, they weighed their anchors, set two of the prize galleons on fire with their freights of flour and iron, and removed their fleet to the roads of Panama. They anchored near the city, just out of heavy gunshot, in plain view of the citizens. They could see the famous stone walls, which had cost so much gold that the Spanish King, in his palace at Madrid, had asked his minister whether they could be seen from the palace windows. They marked the stately, great churches which were building. They saw the tower of St Anastasius in the distance, white and stately, like a blossom above the greenwood. They may even have seen the terrified people in the streets, following the banners of the church, and the priests in their black robes, to celebrate a solemn Mass and invocation. Very far away, in the green savannahs, they saw the herds of cattle straying between the clumps of trees.

Late that night, long after it was dark, Captain Bartholomew Sharp joined company. He had been to Chepillo to look for them, and had found their fire "not yet out," and a few dead Spaniards, whom the Indians had killed, lying about the embers. He had been much concerned for the safety of the expedition, and was therefore very pleased to find that "through the Divine Assistance" the buccaneers had triumphed. At supper that night he talked with Don Peralta, who told him of some comets, "two strange Comets," which had perplexed the Quito merchants the year before. There was " good

Store of Wine" aboard the *Trinity* galleon, with which all hands "cheered up their Hearts for a While." Then, having set sentinels, they turned in for the night.

The next day they buried Captain Peter Harris, "a brave and stout Soldier, and a valiant Englishman, born in the county of Kent, whose death [from gunshot wounds] we very much lamented." With him they buried another buccaneer who had been hurt in the fight. The other wounded men recovered. They would probably have landed to sack the town on this day, had not a quarrel broken out between some of the company and Captain Coxon. The question had been brought forward, whether the buccaneers should go cruising in the South Sea, in their prizes, or return, overland, to their ships at Golden Island. It was probably suggested, as another alternative, that they should land to sack the town. All the captains with one exception were for staying in the Pacific "to try their Fortunes." Captain Coxon, however, was for returning to Golden Island. He had been dissatisfied ever since the fight at Santa Maria. He had not distinguished himself particularly in the fight off Perico, and no doubt he felt jealous that the honours of that battle should have been won by Sawkins. Sawkins' men taunted him with "backwardness" in that engagement, and "stickled not to defame, or brand him with the note of cowardice." To this he answered that he would be very glad to leave that association, and that he would take one of the prizes, a ship of fifty tons, and a periagua, to carry his men up the Santa Maria River. Those who stayed, he added, might heal his wounded. That night he drew off his company, with several other men, in all about seventy hands. With them he carried "the best of our Doctors and Medicines," and the hearty ill will of the other buccaneers. Old King Golden Cap accompanied these deserters, leaving behind him his son and a nephew, desiring them to be "not less

vigorous" than he had been in harrying the Spanish.
Just before Coxon set sail, he asked Bartholomew Sharp
to accompany him.   But that proven soul "could not hear
of so dirty and inhuman an Action without detestation."
So Coxon sailed without ally, "which will not much
redound to his Honour," leaving all his wounded on the
deck of the captured galleon.   The fleet, it may be added,
had by this time returned to the anchorage at Perico.

They lay there ten days in all, "debating what were
best to be done."   In that time they took a frigate laden
with fowls.   They took the poultry for their own use, and
dismissed some of "the meanest of the prisoners" in the
empty ship.   They then shifted their anchorage to the
island of Taboga, where there were a few houses, which
some drunken pirates set on fire.   While they lay at this
island the merchants of Panama came off to them "and
sold us what commodities we needed, buying also of us
much of the goods we had taken in their own vessels."
The pirates also sold them a number of negroes they had
captured, receiving "two hundred pieces of eight for each
negro we could spare."   "And here we took likewise
several barks that were laden with fowls."   After Coxon's
defection, Richard Sawkins was re-elected admiral, and
continued in that command till his death some days later.

Before they left Taboga, Captain Sharp went cruising
to an island some miles distant to pick up some straggling
drunkards who belonged to his ship.   While he lay at
anchor, in a dead calm, waiting for a breeze to blow, a
great Spanish merchant ship hove in sight, bound from
Lima (or Truxillo) to Panama.   Sharp ran his canoas
alongside, and bade her dowse her colours, at the same
time sending a gang of pirates over her rail, to throw the
crew under hatches.   "He had no Arms to defend himself with, save only Rapiers," so her captain made no battle,
but struck incontinently.   She proved to be a very splendid

prize, for in her hold were nearly 2000 jars of wine and
brandy, 100 jars of good vinegar, and a quantity of powder
and shot, " which came very luckily."   In addition to these
goods there were 51,000 pieces of eight, " 247 pieces of
eight a man," a pile of silver sent to pay the Panama
soldiery ; and a store of sweetmeats, such as Peru is still
famous for.   And there were " other Things," says Sharp,
"that were very grateful to our dis-satisfied Minds."
Some of the wine and brandy were sold to the Panama
merchants a few days later, " to the value of three thousand
Pieces of Eight."   A day or two after this they snapped up
two flour ships, from Paita.   One of these was a pretty
ship of a fine model, of about 100 tons.   Sharp fitted her
for himself, " for I liked her very well."   The other flour
ship was taken very gallantly, under a furious gunfire
from Panama Castle.   The buccaneers rowed in, with
the cannon-balls flying over their heads.   They got
close alongside " under her Guns," and then towed her
out of cannon-shot.

They continued several days at Taboga, waiting for a
Lima treasure ship, aboard which, the Spaniards told
them, were £2500 in silver dollars.   While they waited
for this ship the Governor at Panama wrote to ask them
why they had come into those seas.   Captain Sawkins
answered that they had come to help King Golden Cap,
the King of Darien, the true lord of those lands, and
that, since they had come so far, "there was no reason
but that they should have some satisfaction."   If the
Governor would send them 500 pieces of eight for each
man, and double that sum for each captain, and, further,
undertake " not any farther to annoy the Indians," why,
then, the pirates would leave those seas, "and go away
peaceably.   If the Governor would not agree to these
terms, he might look to suffer."   A day or two later,
Sawkins heard that the Bishop of Panama had been

Bishop at Santa Martha (a little city on the Main), some years before, when he (Sawkins) helped to sack the place. He remembered the cleric favourably, and sent him "two loaves of sugar," as a sort of keepsake, or love-offering. "For a retaliation," the Bishop sent him a gold ring; which was very Christian in the Bishop, who must have lost on the exchange. The bearer of the gold ring, brought also an answer from the Governor, who desired to know who had signed the pirates' commissions. To this message Captain Sawkins sent back for answer: " That as yet all his company were not come together, but that when they were come up, we would come and visit him at Panama, and bring our commissions on the muzzles of our guns, at which time he should read them as plain as the flame of gunpowder could make them."

With this thrasonical challenge the pirates set sail for Otoque, another of the islands in the bay; for Taboga, though it was "an exceeding pleasant island," was by this time bare of meat. Before they left the place a Frenchman deserted from them, and gave a detailed account of their plans to the Spanish Governor. It blew very hard while they were at sea, and two barques parted company in the storm. One of them drove away to the eastward, and overtook John Coxon's company. The other was taken by the Spaniards.

About the 20th or 21st of May, after several days of coasting, the ships dropped anchor on the north coast of the island of Quibo. From here some sixty men, under Captain Sawkins, set sail in Edmund Cook's ship, to attack Pueblo Nuevo, the New Town, situated on the banks of a river. At the river's mouth, which was broad, with sandy beaches, they embarked in canoes, and rowed upstream, under the pilotage of a negro, from dark till dawn. The French deserter had told the Spaniards of the intended attack, so that the canoas found great difficulty in getting upstream. Trees had been felled so as to fall across the river, and Indian spies had been placed here and there along the river-bank to warn the townsmen of the approach of the boats. A mile below the town the river had been made impassable, so here the pirates went ashore to wait till daybreak. When it grew light they marched forward, to attack the strong wooden breastworks which the Spaniards had built. Captain Sawkins was in advance, with about a dozen pirates. Captain Sharp followed at a little distance with some thirty more. As soon as Sawkins saw the stockades he fired his gun, and ran forward gallantly, to take the place by storm, in the face of a fierce fire. " Being a man that nothing upon Earth could terrifie " he actually reached the breastwork, and was shot dead there, as he hacked at the pales. Two other pirates were killed at his side, and five of the brave forlorn were badly hurt. " The remainder drew off, still skirmishing," and contrived to reach the canoas " in pretty good order," though they were followed by Spanish sharpshooters for some distance. Sharp took command of the boats and brought them off safely to the river's mouth, where they took a barque full of maize, before they arrived at their ship.

Sawkins was " as valiant and courageous as any could be," " a valiant and generous-spirited man, and beloved above any other we ever had among us, which he well deserved." His death left the company without a captain, and many of the buccaneers, who had truly loved Richard Sawkins, were averse to serving under another commander. They were particularly averse to serving under Sharp, who took the chief command from the moment of Sawkins' death. At Quibo, where they lay at anchor, " their Mutiny " grew very high, nor did they stick at mere mutiny. They clamoured for a tarpaulin muster, or " full Councel," at which the question of " who should be chief "

might be put to the vote. At the council, Sharp was
elected "by a few hands," but many of the pirates refused
to follow him on the cruise. He swore, indeed, that he
would take them such a voyage as should bring them
£1000 a man; but the oaths of Sharp were not good
security, and the mutiny was not abated. Many of the
buccaneers would have gone home with Coxon had it
not been for Sawkins. These now clamoured to go so
vehemently that Sharp was constrained to give them a
ship with as much provision "as would serve for treble
the number." The mutineers who left on this occasion
were in number sixty-three. Twelve Indians, the last
who remained among the pirates, went with them, to
guide them over the isthmus. 146 men remained with
Sharp. It is probable that many of these would have
returned at this time, had it not been that "the Rains were
now already up, and it would be hard passing so many
Gullies, which of necessity would then be full of water."
Ringrose, Wafer and Dampier remained among the
faithful, but rather on this account, than for any love
they bore their leader. The mutineers had hardly set
sail, before Captain Cook came "a-Board" Sharp's flagship,
finding "himselfe a-grieved." His company had kicked
him out of his ship, swearing that they would not sail
with such a one, so that he had determined "to rule
over such unruly folk no longer." Sharp gave his command to a pirate named Cox, a New Englander, "who
forced kindred, as was thought, upon Captain Sharp, out
of old acquaintance, in this conjuncture of time, only to
advance himself." Cox took with him Don Peralta, the
stout old Andalusian, for the pirates were plying the
captain "of the Money-Ship we took," to induce him to
pilot them to Guayaquil "where we might lay down our
Silver, and lade our vessels with Gold." They feared that
an honest man, such as Peralta, "would hinder the en-

deavours" of this Captain Juan, and corrupt his kindly disposition.

With these mutinies, quarrels, intrigues, and cabals did the buccaneers beguile their time. They stayed at Quibo until 6th June, filling their water casks, quarrelling, cutting wood, and eating turtle and red deer. They also ate huge oysters, so large "that we were forced to cut them into four pieces, each quarter being a large mouthful."

On the 6th of June they set sail for the isle of Gorgona, off what is now Columbia, where they careened the *Trinity*, and took "down our Round House Coach and all the high carved work belonging to the stern of the ship ; for when we took her from the Spaniards she was high as any Third Rate Ship in England." While they were at work upon her, Sharp changed his design of going for Guayaquil, as one of their prisoners, an old Moor, "who had long time sailed among the Spaniards," told him that there was gold at Arica, in such plenty that they would get there "£2000 a man." He did not hurry to leave his careenage, though he must have known that each day he stayed there lessened his chance of booty. It was nearly August when he left Gorgona, and "from this Time forward to the 17th of October there was Nothing occurr'd but bare Sailing." Now and then they ran short of water, or of food. One or two of their men died of fever, or of rum, or of sunstroke. Two or three were killed in capturing a small Spanish ship. The only other events recorded, are the falls of rain, the direction of the wind, the sight of "watersnakes of divers colours," and the joyful meeting with Captain Cox, whom they had lost sight of, while close in shore one evening. They called at "Sir Francis Drake's isle" to strike a few tortoises, and to shoot some goats. Captain Sharp we read, here "showed himself very ingenious" in spearing turtle, "he performing it as well as the tortoise strikers themselves."

It was very hot at this little island.   Many years before Drake had gone ashore there to make a dividend, and had emptied bowls of gold coins into the hats of his men, after the capture of the *Cacafuego*.   Some of the pirates sounded the little anchorage with a greasy lead, in the hopes of bringing up the golden pieces which Drake had been unable to carry home, and had hove into the sea there.   They got no gold, but the sun shone "so hot that it burnt the skin off the necks of our men," as they craned over the rail at their fishery.

At the end of October they landed at the town of Hilo to fill fresh water.   They took the town, and sacked its sugar refineries, which they burnt.   They pillaged its pleasant orange groves, and carried away many sacks of limes and green figs "with many other fruits agreeable to the palate."   Fruit, sugar, and excellent olive oil were the goods which Hilo yielded.   They tried to force the Spaniards to bring them beef, but as the beef did not come, they wrecked the oil and sugar works, and set them blazing, and so marched down to their ships, skirmishing with the Spanish horse as they fell back.   Among the spoil was the carcass of a mule (which made "a very good meal"), and a box of chocolate "so that now we had each morning a dish of that pleasant liquor," such as the grand English ladies drank.

The next town attacked was La Serena, a town five miles from the present Coquimbo.   They took the town, and found a little silver, but the citizens had had time to hide their gold.   The pirates made a great feast of strawberries "as big as walnuts," in the "orchards of fruit" at this place, so that one of their company wrote that "'tis very delightful Living here."   They could not get a ransom for the town, so they set it on fire.   The Spaniards, in revenge, sent out an Indian, on an inflated horse hide, to the pirates' ship the *Trinity*.   This Indian

A pirate's death. The execution of Major Steed Bonnet at Charleston in November 1718. *Johnson.*

thrust some oakum and brimstone between the rudder and the sternpost, and "fired it with a match." The sternpost caught fire and sent up a prodigious black smoke, which warned the pirates that their ship was ablaze. They did not discover the trick for a few minutes, but by good fortune they found it out in time to save the vessel. They landed their prisoners shortly after the fire had been quenched "because we feared lest by the example of this stratagem they should plot our destruction in earnest." Old Don Peralta, who had lately been "very frantic," "through too much hardship and melancholy," was there set on shore, after his long captivity. Don Juan, the captain of the "Money-Ship," was landed with him. Perhaps the two fought together, on the point of honour, as soon as they had returned to swords and civilisation.

From Coquimbo the pirates sailed for Juan Fernandez. On the way thither they buried William Cammock, one of their men, who had drunk too hard at La Serena "which produced in him a calenture or malignant fever, and a hiccough." "In the evening when the pale Magellan Clouds were showing we buried him in the sea, according to the usual custom of mariners, giving him three French vollies for his funeral."

On Christmas Day they were beating up to moorings, with boats ahead, sounding out a channel for the ship. They did not neglect to keep the day holy, for "we gave in the morning early three vollies of shot for solemnization of that great festival." At dusk they anchored "in a stately bay that we found there," a bay of intensely blue water, through which the whiskered seals swam. The pirates filled fresh water, and killed a number of goats, with which the island swarmed. They also captured many goats alive, and tethered them about the decks of the *Trinity*, to the annoyance of all hands, a day or two later, when some flurries of wind drove them to sea, to search out a new anchorage.

Shortly after New Year's Day 1681, "our unhappy Divisions, which had been long on Foot, began now to come to an Head to some Purpose." The men had been working at the caulking of their ship, with design to take her through the Straits of Magellan, and so home to the Indies. Many of the men wished to cruise the South Seas a little longer, while nearly all were averse to plying caulking irons, under a burning sun, for several hours a day. There was also a good deal of bitterness against Captain Sharp, who had made but a poor successor to brave Richard Sawkins. He had brought them none of the gold and silver he had promised them, and few of the men were "satisfied, either with his Courage or Behaviour." On the 6th January a gang of pirates "got privately ashoar together," and held a fo'c's'le council under the greenwood. They "held a Consult," says Sharp, "about turning me presently out, and put another in my Room." John Cox, the "true-hearted dissembling New-England Man," whom Sharp "meerly for old Acquaintance-sake" had promoted to be captain, was "the Main Promoter of their Design." When the consult was over, the pirates came on board, clapped Mr Sharp in irons, put him down on the ballast, and voted an old pirate named John Watling, "a stout seaman," to be captain in his stead. One buccaneer says that "the true occasion of the grudge against Sharp was, that he had got by these adventures almost a thousand pounds, whereas many of our men were not worth a groat," having "lost all their money to their fellow Buccaneers at dice."

Captain Edmund Cook, who had been turned out of his ship by his men, was this day put in irons on the confession of a shameless servant. The curious will find the details of the case on page 121, of the 1684 edition of Ringrose's journal.

John Watling began his captaincy in very godly sort, by ordering his disciples to keep holy the Sabbath day. Sunday, "January the ninth, was the first Sunday that ever we kept by command and common consent, since the loss and death of our valiant Commander Captain Sawkins." Sawkins had been strict in religious matters, and had once thrown the ship's dice overboard "finding them in use on the said day." Since Sawkins' death the company had grown notoriously lax, but it is pleasant to notice how soon they returned to their natural piety, under a godly leader. With Edmund Cook down on the ballast in irons, and William Cook talking of salvation in the galley, and old John Watling expounding the Gospel in the cabin, the galleon, "the Most Holy *Trinity*" must have seemed a foretaste of the New Jerusalem. The fiddler ceased such "prophane strophes" as "Abel Brown," "The Red-haired Man's Wife," and "Valentinian." He tuned his devout strings to songs of Zion. Nay the very boatswain could not pipe the cutter up but to a phrase of the Psalms.

In this blessed state they washed their clothes in the brooks, hunted goats across the island, and burnt and tallowed their ship the *Trinity*. But on the 12th of January, one of their boats, which had been along the coast with some hunters, came rowing furiously into the harbour, "firing of Guns." They had espied three Spanish men-of-war some three or four miles to leeward, beating up to the island under a press of sail. The pirates were in great confusion, for most of them were ashore, "washing their clothes," or felling timber. Those on board, hove up one of their anchors, fired guns to call the rest aboard, hoisted their boats in, and slipped their second cable. They then stood to sea, hauling as close to the wind as she would lie. One of the Mosquito Indians, "one William," was left behind on the island, "at this sudden departure," and remained hidden there, living on fish and fruit, for many weary days. He was not the first man to be marooned there; nor was he to be the last.

The three Spanish men-of-war were ships of good size, mounting some thirty guns among them. As the pirate ship beat out of the harbour, sheeting home her top-gallant-sails, they "put out their bloody flags," which the pirates imitated, "to shew them that we were not as yet daunted." They kept too close together for the pirates to run them aboard, but towards sunset their flagship had drawn ahead of the squadron. The pirates at once tacked about so as to engage her, intending to sweep her decks with bullets, and carry her by boarding. John Watling was not very willing to come to handystrokes, nor were the Spaniards anxious to give him the opportunity. No guns were fired, for the Spanish admiral wore ship, and so sailed away to the island, when he brought his squadron to anchor. The pirates called a council, and decided to give them the slip, having "outbraved them," and done as much as honour called for. They were not very pleased with John Watling, and many were clamouring for the cruise to end. It was decided that they should not attack the Spanish ships, but go off for the Main, to sack the town of Arica, where there was gold enough, so they had heard, to buy them each "a coach and horses." They therefore hauled to the wind again, and stood to the east, in very angry and mutinous spirit, until the 26th of January.

On that day they landed at Yqueque, a mud-flat, or guano island, off a line of yellow sand-hills. They found a few Indian huts there, with scaffolds for the drying of fish, and many split and rotting mackerel waiting to be carried inland. There was a dirty stone chapel in

the place, "stuck full of hides and sealskins." There was
a great surf, green and mighty, bursting about the island
with a continual roaring. There were pelicans fishing
there, and a few Indians curing fish, and an abominable
smell, and a boat, with a cask in her bows, which brought
fresh water thither from thirty miles to the north. The
teeth of the Indians were dyed a bright green by their
chewing of the coca leaf, the drug which made their
"beast-like" lives endurable. There was a silver mine
on the mainland, near this fishing village, but the pirates
did not land to plunder it. They merely took a few
old Indian men, and some Spaniards, and carried them
aboard the *Trinity*, where the godly John Watling examined them.

The next day the examination continued; and the
answers of one of the old men, "a Mestizo Indian," were
judged to be false. "Finding him in many lies, as we
thought, concerning Arica, our commander ordered him
to be shot to death, which was accordingly done." This
cold-blooded murder was committed much against the
will of Captain Sharp, who "opposed it as much as he
could." Indeed, when he found that his protests were
useless, he took a basin of water (of which the ship was
in sore need) and washed his hands, like a modern Pilate.
"Gentlemen," he said, "I am clear of the blood of this
old man; and I will warrant you a hot day for this
piece of cruelty, whenever we come to fight at Arica."
This proved to be "a true and certain prophesy." Sharp
was an astrologer, and a believer in portents; but he
does not tell us whether he had "erected any Figure,"
to discover what was to chance in the Arica raid.

Arica, the most northern port in Chile, has still a
considerable importance. It is a pleasant town, fairly
well watered, and therefore more green and cheerful than

the nitrate ports.   It is built at the foot of a hill (a
famous battlefield) called the Morro.   Low, yellow sand-
hills ring it in, shutting it from the vast blue crags of
the Andes, which rise up, splintered and snowy, to the
east.   The air there is of an intense clearness, and those
who live there can see the Tacna churches, forty miles
away.   It is no longer the port it was, but it does a
fair trade in salt and sulphur, and supplies the nitrate
towns with fruit.   When the pirates landed there it was
a rich and prosperous city.   It had a strong fort, mounting twelve brass guns, defended by four companies of
troops from Lima.   The city had a town guard of 300
soldiers.   There was also an arsenal full of firearms for
the use of householders in the event of an attack.   It
was not exactly a walled town, like new Panama, but
a light wooden palisade ran round it, while other palisades
crossed each street.   These defences had been thrown up
when news had arrived of the pirates being in those seas.
All the "plate, gold and jewels" of the townsfolk had
been carefully hidden, and the place was in such a state
of military vigilance and readiness that the pirates had
no possible chance of taking it, or at least of holding
it.   When the pirates came upon it there were several
ships in the bay, laden with commodities from the south
of Chile.

On the 28th of January, John Watling picked 100
men, and put off for the shore in boats and canoas, to
attack the town.   By the next day they had got close
in shore, under the rocks by the San Vitor River's mouth.
There they lay concealed till the night.   At dawn of the
30th January 1681, "the Martyrdom of our glorious
King Charles the First," they were dipping off some rocks
four miles to the south of Arica.   Here ninety-two of
the buccaneers landed, leaving a small boat guard, with
strict instructions how to act.   They were told that if

the main body "made one smoke from the town," as by firing a heap of powder, one canoa was to put in to Arica ; but that, if two smokes were fired, all the boats were to put in at once. Basil Ringrose was one of those who landed to take part in the fight. Dampier, it is almost certain, remained on board the *Trinity*, becalmed some miles from the shore. Wafer was in the canoas, with the boat guard, preparing salves for those wounded in the fight. The day seems to have been hot and sunny —it could scarcely have been otherwise—but those out at sea, on the galleon, could see the streamers of cloud wreathing about the Andes.

At sunrise the buccaneers got ashore, amongst the rocks, and scrambled up a hill which gave them a sight of the city. From the summit they could look right down upon the streets, little more than a mile from them. It was too early for folk to be stirring, and the streets were deserted, save for the yellow pariahs, and one or two carrion birds. It was so still, in that little town, that the pirates thought they would surprise the place, as Drake had surprised Nombre de Dios. But while they were marching downhill, they saw three horsemen watching them from a lookout place, and presently the horsemen galloped off to raise the inhabitants. As they galloped away, John Watling chose out forty of the ninety-two, to attack the fort or castle which defended the city. This band of forty, among whom were Sharp and Ringrose, carried ten hand-grenades, in addition to their pistols and guns. The fort was on a hill above the town, and thither the storming party marched, while Watling's company pressed on into the streets. The action began a few minutes later with the guns of the fort firing on the storming party. Down in the town, almost at the same moment, the musketry opened in a long roaring roll which never slackened. Ringrose's party waited for no further signal, but at once engaged, running in under the guns and hurling their firepots through the embrasures. The grenades were damp, or badly filled, or had been too long charged. They did not burst or burn as they should have done, while the garrison inside the fort kept up so hot a fire, at close range, that nothing could be done there. The storming party fell back, without loss, and rallied for a fresh attack. They noticed then that Watling's men were getting no farther towards the town. They were halted in line, with their knees on the ground, firing on the breastworks, and receiving a terrible fire from the Spaniards. Five of the fifty-two men were down (three of them killed) and the case was growing serious. The storming party left the fort, and doubled downhill into the firing line, where they poured in volley after blasting volley, killing a Spaniard at each shot, making "a very desperate battle" of it, "our rage increasing with our wounds." No troops could stand such file-firing. The battle became "mere bloody massacre," and the Spaniards were beaten from their posts. Volley after volley shook them, for the pirates "filled every street in the city with dead bodies"; and at last ran in upon them, and clubbed them and cut them down, and penned them in as prisoners. But as the Spaniards under arms were at least twenty times as many as the pirates, there was no taking the city from them. They were beaten from post to post fighting like devils, but the pirates no sooner left a post they had taken, "than they came another way, and manned it again, with new forces and fresh men." The streets were heaped with corpses, yet the Spaniards came on, and came on again, till the sand of the roads was like red mud. At last they were fairly beaten from the chief parts of the town, and numbers of them were penned up as prisoners; more, in fact, than the pirates could guard. The battle paused for a while at this stage, and the pirates took advantage of the lull to get their wounded (perhaps a dozen men), into one of the churches to have their wounds dressed. As the doctors of the party began their work, John Watling sent a message to the fort, charging the garrison to surrender. The soldiers returned no answer, but continued to load their guns, being helped by the armed townsfolk, who now flocked to them in scores. The fort was full of musketeers when the pirates made their second attack a little after noon.

At the second attack, John Watling took 100 of his prisoners, placed them in front of his storming party, and forced them forward, as a screen to his men, when he made his charge. The garrison shot down friend and foe indiscriminately, and repulsed the attack, and repulsed a second attack which followed a few minutes later. There was no taking the fort by storm, and the pirates had no great guns with which to batter it. They found, however, that one of the flat-roofed houses in the town, near the fort's outworks, commanded the interior. "We got upon the top of the house," says Ringrose, "and from there fired down into the fort, killing many of their men and wounding them at our ease and pleasure." While they were doing this, a number of the Lima soldiers joined the citizens, and fell, with great fury, upon the prisoners' guards in the town. They easily beat back the few guards, and retook the city. As soon as they had taken the town, they came swarming out to cut off the pirates from their retreat, and to hem them in between the fort and the sea. They were in such numbers that they were able to surround the pirates, who now began to lose men at every volley, and to look about them a little anxiously as they bit their cartridges. From every street in the town came Spanish musketeers at the double, swarm after

swarm of them, perhaps a couple of thousand.   The
pirates left the fort, and turned to the main army, at the
same time edging away towards the south, to the hospital,
or church, where their wounded men were being dressed.
As they moved away from the battlefield, firing as they
retreated, old John Watling was shot in the liver with
a bullet, and fell dead there, to go buccaneering no more.
A moment later "both our quartermasters" fell, with
half-a-dozen others, including the boatswain.   All this
time the cannon of the fort were pounding over them,
and the round-shot were striking the ground all about,
flinging the sand into their faces.   What with the dust
and the heat and the trouble of helping the many hurt,
their condition was desperate.   "So that now the enemy
rallying against us, and beating us from place to place,
we were in a very distracted condition, and in more likelihood to perish every man than escape the bloodiness of
that day.   Now we found the words of Captain Sharp
to bear a true prophecy, being all very sensible that we
had had a day too hot for us, after that cruel heat in
killing and murdering in cold blood the old Mestizo
Indian whom we had taken prisoner at Yqueque."   In
fact they were beaten and broken, and the fear of death
was on them, and the Spaniards were ringing them round,
and the firing was roaring from every point.   They were
a bloody, dusty, choking gang of desperates, "in great
disorder," black with powder, their tongues hanging out
with thirst.   As they stood grouped together, cursing and
firing, some of them asked Captain Sharp to take command, and get them out of that, seeing that Watling
was dead, and no one there could give an order.   To
this request Sharp at last consented, and a retreat was
begun, under cover of a fighting rear-guard, "and I hope,"
says Sharp, "it will not be esteemed a Vanity in me to
say, that I was mighty Helpful to facilitate this Retreat."

In the midst of a fearful racket of musketry, he fought the pirates through the soldiers to the church where the wounded lay. There was no time, nor was there any conveyance, for the wounded, and they were left lying there, all desperately hurt. The two surgeons could have been saved "but that they had been drinking while we assaulted the fort, and thus would not come with us when they were called." There was no time for a second call, for the Spaniards were closing in on them, and the firing was as fierce as ever. The men were so faint with hunger and thirst, the heat of battle, and the long day's marching, that Sharp feared he would never get them to the boats. A fierce rush of Spaniards beat them away from the hospital, and drove them out of the town "into the Savannas or open fields." The Spaniards gave a cheer and charged in to end the battle, but the pirates were a dogged lot, and not yet at the end of their strength. They got into a clump or cluster, with a few wounded men in the centre, to load the muskets, "resolving to die one by another" rather than to run. They stood firm, cursing and damning the Spaniards, telling them to come on, and calling them a lot of cowards. There were not fifty buccaneers fit to carry a musket, but the forty odd, unhurt men stood steadily, and poured in such withering volleys of shot, with such terrible precision, that the Spanish charge went to pieces. As the charge broke, the pirates plied them again, and made a "bloody massacre" of them, so that they ran to shelter like so many frightened rabbits. The forty-seven had beaten off twenty or thirty times their number, and had won themselves a passage home.

There was no question of trying to retake the town. The men were in such misery that the march back to the boats taxed their strength to the breaking point. They set off over the savannah, in as good order as they could,

with a wounded man, or two, in every rank of them.   As
they set forward, a company of horsemen rode out, and
got upon their flanks "and fired at us all the way, though
they would not come within reach of our guns; for their
own reached farther than ours, and out-shot us more than
one third."   There was great danger of these horsemen
cutting in, and destroying them, on the long open rolls
of savannah, so Sharp gave the word, and the force
shogged westward to the seashore, along which they
trudged to the boats.   The beach to the south of Arica
runs along the coast, in a narrow strip, under cliffs and
rocky ground, for several miles.   The sand is strewn with
boulders, so that the horsemen, though they followed the
pirates, could make no concerted charge upon them.   Some
of them rode ahead of them and got above them on the
cliff tops, from which they rolled down "great stones and
whole rocks to destroy us."   None of these stones did any
harm to the pirates, for the cliffs were so rough and broken
that the skipping boulders always flew wide of the mark.
But though the pirates "escaped their malice for that
time," they were yet to run a terrible danger before getting
clear away to sea.   The Spaniards had been examining,
or torturing, the wounded pirates, and the two drunken
surgeons, left behind in the town.   "These gave them
our signs that we had left to our boats [i.e. revealed the
signals by which the boats were to be called] so that
they immediately blew up two smokes, which were perceived by the canoas."   Had the pirates "not come at
the instant" to the seaside, within hail of the boats, they
would have been gone.   Indeed they were already under
sail, and beating slowly up to the northward, in answer
to the signal.   Thus, by a lucky chance, the whole company escaped destruction.   They lost no time in putting
from the shore, where they had met with "so very bad
Entertainment."   They "got on board about ten a Clock

at night; having been involved in a continual and bloody fight . . . all that day long." Of the ninety-two, who had landed that morning, twenty-eight had been left ashore, either dead, or as prisoners. Of the sixty-four who got to the canoas, eighteen were desperately wounded, and barely able to walk. Most of the others were slightly hurt, while all were too weary to do anything, save sleep or drink. Of the men left behind in the hospital the Spaniards spared the doctors only; "they being able to do them good service in that country." "But as to the wounded men," says Ringrose, "they were all knocked on the head," and so ended their roving, and came to port where drunken doctors could torture them no longer. The Ylo men denied this; and said that the seven pirates who did not die of their wounds were kept as slaves. The Spanish loss is not known, but it was certainly terrible. The Hilo, or Ylo people, some weeks later, said that seventy Spaniards had been killed and about 200 wounded.

All the next day the pirates "plied to and fro in sight of the port," hoping that the Spaniards would man the ships in the bay, and come out to fight. They reinstated Sharp in his command, for they had now "recollected a better Temper," though none of them, it seems, wished for any longer stay in the South Sea. The Arica fight had sickened them of the South Sea, while several of them (including Ringrose) became very ill from the exposure and toil of the battle. They beat to windward, cruising, when they found that the Spaniards would not put to sea to fight them. They met with dirty weather when they had reached the thirtieth parallel, and the foul weather, and their bad fortune made them resolve to leave those seas. At a fo'c's'cle council held on the 3rd of March, they determined to put the helm up, and to return to the North Sea. They were short of water and short of food, "having only one cake of bread a day," or perhaps half-a-pound of "doughboy," for their "whack" or allowance.   After a few days' running before the wind they came to "the port of Guasco," now Huasco, between Coquimbo and Caldera, a little town of sixty or eighty houses, with copper smeltries, a church, a river, and some sheep-runs.   Sixty of the buccaneers went ashore here, that same evening, to get provisions, "and anything else that we could purchase."   They passed the night in the church, or "in a churchyard," and in the morning took "120 sheep and fourscore goats," about 200 bushels of corn "ready ground," some fowls, a fat hog, any quantity of fruit, peas, beans, etc., and a small stock of wine. These goods they conveyed aboard as being "fit for our Turn."   The inhabitants had removed their gold and silver while the ship came to her anchor, "so that our booty here, besides provisions, was inconsiderable."   They found the fat hog "very like our English pork," thereby illustrating the futility of travel; and so sailed away again "to seek greater matters."   Before they left, they contrived to fill their water jars in the river, a piece of work which they found troublesome, owing to the height of the banks.

From Huasco, where the famous white raisins grow, they sailed to Ylo, where they heard of their mates at Arica, and secured some wine, figs, sugar, and molasses, and some "fruits just ripe and fit for eating," including "extraordinary good Oranges of the China sort."   They then coasted slowly northward, till by Saturday, 16th April, they arrived off the island of Plate.   Here their old bickerings broke out again, for many of the pirates were disgusted with Sharp, and eager to go home.   Many of the others had recovered their spirits since the affair at Arica, and wished to stay in the South Seas, to cruise a little longer.   Those who had fought at Arica would not allow Sharp to be deposed a second time, while those who had been shipkeepers on that occasion, were angry that he should have been re-elected. The two parties refused to be reconciled. They quarrelled angrily whenever they came on deck together, and the party spirit ran so high that the company of shipkeepers, the anti-Sharp faction, "the abler and more experienced men," at last refused to cruise any longer under Sharp's command. The fo'c's'le council decided that a poll should be taken, and "that which party soever, upon polling, should be found to have the majority, should keep the ship." The other party was to take the long boat and the canoes. The division was made, and "Captain Sharp's Party carried it." The night was spent in preparing the long boat and the canoes, and the next morning the boats set sail.

CHAPTER XV

ACROSS THE ISTHMUS

The way home—Sufferings and adventures

A T "about Ten a Clock" in the morning of 17th April
1681, the mutineers went over the side into their
"Lanch and Canoas, designing for the River Santa
Maria, in the Gulf of St Michael." "We were in number,"
says Dampier, who was of the party, "44 white Men
who bore Arms, a *Spanish Indian*, who bore Arms also;
and two *Moskito Indians*," who carried pistols and fish
spears. Lionel Wafer "was of Mr Dampier's Side in
that Matter," and acted as surgeon to the forty-seven,
until he met with his accident. They embarked in the
ship's launch or long boat, one canoa "and another Canoa
which had been sawn asunder in the middle, in order to
have made Bumkins, or Vessels for carrying water, if we
had not separated from our Ship." This old canoa they
contrived to patch together. For provisions they brought
with them "so much Flower as we could well carry";
which "Flower" "we" had been industriously grinding
for the last three days. In addition to the "Flower" they
had "rubbed up 20 or 30 pound of Chocolate with Sugar
to sweeten it." And so provided, they hoisted their little
sails and stood in for the shore. "The Sea Breeze came
in strong" before they reached the land, so that they had
to cut up an old dry hide to make a close-fight round
the launch "to keep the Water out." They took a small
timber barque the next morning, and went aboard her,
and sailed her over to Gorgona, where they scrubbed her

An injured Spaniard being shot by one of Captain Edward Low's crew. Low was active in the Caribbean in the early 1720's. His eventual fate is unknown. *Johnson.*

bottom. They learned from their prisoners that the Spaniards were on the alert, eagerly expecting them, and cruising the seas with fast advice boats to get a sight of them. Three warships lay at Panama, ready to hunt them whenever the cruisers brought news of their whereabouts. A day or two later, the pirates saw "two great ships," with many guns in their ports, slowly beating to the southward in search of their company. The heavy rain which was falling kept the small timber barque hidden, while the pirates took the precautions of striking sail, and rowing close in shore. "If they had seen and chased us," the pirates would have landed, trusting to the local Indians to make good their escape over the isthmus.

After twelve days of sailing they anchored about twenty miles from the San Miguel Gulf, in order to clean their arms, and dry their clothes and powder, before proceeding up the river, by the way they had come. The next morning they set sail into the Gulf, and anchored off an island, intending to search the river's mouth for Spaniards before adventuring farther. As they had feared, a large Spanish man-of-war lay anchored at the river's mouth, "close by the shore," with her guns commanding the entrance. Some of her men could be seen upon the beach, by the door of a large tent, made of the ship's lower canvas. "When the Canoas came aboard with this News," says Dampier, "some of our Men were a little dis-heartned ; but it was no more than I ever expected." An hour or two later they took one of the Spaniards from the ship and learned from him that the ship carried twelve great guns, and that three companies of men, with small arms, would join her during the next twenty-four hours. They learned also that the Indians of that district were friendly to the Spaniards. Plainly the pirates were in a dangerous position. "It was not convenient to stay longer there," says Dampier. They got aboard their ship without loss

of time, and ran out of the river " with the Tide of Ebb,"
resolved to get ashore at the first handy creek they
came to.

Early the next morning they ran into " a small Creek
within two Keys, or little Islands, and rowed up to the
Head of the Creek, being about a Mile up, and there we
landed May 1, 1681." The men flung their food and clothes
ashore, and scuttled their little ship, so that she sank at
her moorings. While they packed their "Snap-sacks"
with flour, chocolate, canisters of powder, beads, and
whittles for the Indians, their slaves "struck a plentiful
Dish of Fish" for them, which they presently broiled, and
ate for their breakfasts. Some of the men scouted on
ahead for a mile or two, and then returned with the
news that there were no immediate dangers in front of
them. Some of the pirates were weak and sick, and
" not well able to march." " We," therefore, "gave out,
that if any Man faultred in the Journey over Land he
must expect to be shot to death; for we knew that the
Spaniards would soon be after us, and one Man falling
into their hands might be the ruin of us all, by giving
an account of our strength and condition : yet this would
not deter 'em from going with us."

At three that afternoon they set out into the jungle,
steering a N.E. course " by our Pocket Compasses." The
rain beat upon them all the rest of that day, and all the
night long, a drenching and steady downpour, which
swamped the " small Hutts" they contrived to patch
together. In the morning they struck an old Indian
trail, no broader than a horse-girth, running somewhat
to the east. They followed it through the forest till they
came to an Indian town, where the squaws gave them
some corn-drink or miscelaw, and sold them a few fowls
and " a sort of wild Hogs." They hired a guide at this
village, " to guide us a day's march into the Countrey."

" He was to have for his pains a Hatchet, and his Bargain was to bring us to a certain Indians habitation, who could speak Spanish." They paid faithfully for the food the Indians gave them, and shared " all sorts of our Provisions in common, because none should live better than others," and so stand a better chance of crossing the isthmus. When they started out, after a night's rest, one of the pirates, being already sick of the march, slipped away into the jungle, and was seen no more.

They found the Spanish-speaking Indian in a bad mood. He swore that he knew no road to the North Sea, but that he could take them to Cheapo, or to Santa Maria, "which we knew to be Spanish Garrisons : either of them at least 20 miles out of our way." He was plainly unwilling to have any truck with them, for " his discourse," was in an angry tone, and he " gave very impertinent answers" to the questions put to him. " However we were forced to make a virtue of necessity, and humour him, for it was neither time nor place to be angry with the Indians ; all our lives lying in their hand." The pirates were at their wits' end, for they lay but a few miles from the guard ship, and this surly chief could very well set the Spaniards on them. They tempted him with green and blue beads, with gold and silver, both in the crude and in coin, with beautiful steel axe heads, with machetes, " or long knives " ; " but nothing would work on him." The pirates were beginning to despair, when one of them produced " a Sky-coloured Petticoat," and placed it about the person of the chief's favourite wife. How he had become possessed of such a thing, and whether it came from a Hilo beauty, and whether she gave it as a love token, on the ship's sailing, cannot now be known. It may have been an article brought expressly from Jamaica for the fascination of the Indians. But *honi soit qui mal y pense.* The truth of the matter will never be learned. It is sufficient that the man produced it in the very nick of time, and laid the blue tissue over the copper-coloured lady. She was so much pleased with it "that she immediately began to chatter to her Husband, and soon brought him into a better Humour." He relented at once, and said that he knew the trail to the North Sea, and that he would gladly guide them thither were a cut upon his foot healed. As he could not go himself he persuaded another Indian to guide them " 2 Days march further for another Hatchet." He tried hard to induce the party to stay with him for the rest of the day as the rain was pouring down in torrents. "But our business required more haste, our Enemies lying so near us, for he told us that he could go from his house aboard the Guard-Ship in a Tides time; and this was the 4th day since they saw us. So we marched 3 Miles further and then built Hutts, where we stayed all Night," with the thatch dripping water on to them in a steady trickle.

On taking to the road again, wet and starving as they were, they found themselves in a network of rivers, some thirty of which they had to wade, during the day's march. The heavy rain drenched them as they clambered along across the jungle. They had but a little handful of fire that night, so that they could not dry nor warm themselves. They crouched about the " funk of green-wood," shivering in the smoke, chewing bullets to alleviate their hunger. They slept there in great misery, careless of what happened to them. "The Spaniards were but seldom in our thoughts," says Dampier, for the pirates thought only of guides and food, and feared their own Indian servants more than the enemy. A watch of two pirates kept a guard all that night, with orders to shoot any Indian who showed a sign of treachery. They rose before it was light and pushed on into the woods, biting on the

bullet, or the quid, to help them to forget their hunger.
By ten o'clock they arrived at the house of a brisk young
Indian, who had been a servant to the Bishop of Panama,
the man who gave the gold ring to Sawkins.   Here they
had a feast of yams and sweet potatoes, boiled into a
broth with monkey-meat, a great comfort to those who
were weak and sickly.   They built a great fire in one
of the huts, at which they dried their clothes, now falling
to pieces from the continual soakings.   They also cleaned
their rusty gun-locks, and dried their powder, talking
cheerily together, about the fire, while the rain roared
upon the thatch.   They were close beside the Rio
Congo " and thus far," says Dampier, the most intelligent
man among them, " we might have come in our Canoa,
if I could have persuaded them to it."

As they sat in the hut, in the warmth of the blaze, that
rainy May day, Lionel Wafer met with an accident.   He
was sitting on the ground, beside one of the pirates,
who was drying his powder, little by little, half a pound
at a time, in a great silver dish, part of the plunder of
the cruise.   "A careless Fellow passed by with his Pipe
lighted," and dropped some burning crumb of tobacco
on to the powder, which at once blew up.   It scorched
Wafer's knee very terribly, tearing off the flesh from
the bone, and burning his leg from the knee to the thigh.
Wafer, who was the surgeon of the party, had a bag full
of salves and medicines.   He managed to dress his
wounds, and to pass a fairly comfortable night, "and
being unwilling to be left behind by my Companions,
I made hard shift to jog on, and bear them Company,"
when camp was broken at daybreak.

Lame as he was, he kept up with his mates all that day,
fording rivers "several times," and crossing country which
would tax the strongest man, in good condition.   "The
last time we forded the River, it was so deep, that our

tallest Men stood in the deepest place, and handed the
sick, weak and short Men " ; by which act of comradeship
" we all got over safe." Two of the pirates, " Robert
Spratlin and William Bowman," could get no farther, and
were left behind at the river. Dampier notes that his
" Joint of Bambo, which I stopt at both Ends, closing
it with Wax, so as to keep out any Water," preserved
his " Journal and other Writings from being wet," though
he had often to swim for it.

Drenched and tired, they pitched their huts by the
river-bank, poor Wafer in torment from his knee, and
the rest of them hungry and cold. They had hardly
finished their huts, when the river came down in a great
wall of water, some sudden flood, due to a cloud-burst
higher up. The flood sucked away their huts, and forced
them to run to higher ground. They passed that night
" straggling in the Woods, some under one Tree, some
under another," with the thunder roaring overhead, and
the lightning making a livid brightness all about them.
The rain fell in torrents, and the pirates were far too
wretched to keep watch. " So our Slaves, taking Opportunity, went away in the Night; all but one, who was
hid in some hole, and knew nothing of their design, or
else fell asleep." Among these slaves was a black man,
Lionel Wafer's assistant, who carrried the salves and
medicaments. He took these with him when he slunk
away, nor did he forget the " Chirurgeon's Gun and all
his Money." He left poor Wafer destitute there, in the
forest, " depriv'd of wherewithal to dress my sore."

In the morning, they found that the river had fallen, but
not so much as they had hoped. It was still too deep to
ford, and the current ran very swiftly, but Dampier and
some other swimmers managed to swim across. They
then endeavoured to get a line over, by which to ferry the
men who could not swim, and the arms and powder they

had left on the other bank.   They decided to send a man back with a line, with instructions to pass the goods first, and then the men.   " One George Gayny took the end of a Line and made it fast about his Neck, and left the other end ashore, and one Man stood by the Line, to clear it away to him."   When Gayny was about half way across, the line, which was kinky with the wet, got entangled. The man who was lighting it out checked it a moment to take out the kink, or to clear it.   The check threw Gayny on his back, "and he that had the Line in his hand," instead of slacking away, or hauling in, so as to bring Gayny ashore, "threw it all into the River after him, thinking he might recover himself."   The stream was running down with great fierceness.   Gayny had a bag of 300 dollars on his back, and this bag, with the weight of the line, dragged him under.   He was carried down, and swept out of sight " and never seen more by us."   " This put a period to that contrivance," adds Dampier grimly.

As they had no wish to emulate poor Gayny, they sought about " for a Tree to fell across the River."   They cut it down, as soon as they had found it, " and it reached clean over."   The goods and pirates were then crossed in safety.   All hands soon forgot poor Gayny, for they came across a plantain walk in a clearing, and made a good breakfast, and stripped it of every fruit.   They dismissed their guide here, with the gift of an axe head, and hired an old Indian to guide them farther towards the North Sea.   The next day they reckoned themselves out of danger, and set forth cheerily.

For the last two days Wafer had been in anguish from his burnt knee.   As the pirates made ready to leave their bivouac, on the tenth morning of the march, he declared that he could not " trudge it further through Rivers and Woods," with his knee as it was.   Two other pirates who were broken with the going, declared that they, also, were too tired out to march. There was no talk, among the rest of the band, about shooting the weary ones, according to the order they had made at starting. Instead of "putting them out of their misery," they "took a very kind Leave," giving the broken men such stores as they could spare, and telling them to keep in good heart, and follow on when they had rested.

One of Wafer's comrades on this occasion was "Mr Richard Jopson, who had served an Apprenticeship to a Druggist in London. He was an ingenious Man, and a good Scholar; he had with him a Greek Testament which he frequently read, and would translate *extempore* into *English*, to such of the Company as were dispos'd to hear him." The other weary man was John Hingson, a mariner. They watched their mates march away through the woods, and then turned back, sick at heart, to the shelter of the huts, where the Indians looked at them sulkily, and flung them green plantains, "as you would Bones to a Dog." One of the Indians made a mess of aromatic herbs and dressed Wafer's burn, so that, in three weeks' time, he could walk.

Dampier's party marched on through jungle, wading across rivers, which took them up to the chest, staggering through swamps and bogs, and clambering over rotten tree trunks, and across thorn brakes. They were wet and wretched and half starved, for their general food was macaw berries. Sometimes they killed a monkey, once Dampier killed a turkey, and once they came to a plantain patch where "we fed plentifully on plantains, both ripe and green." Their clothes were rotted into shreds, their boots were fallen to pieces, their feet were blistered and raw, their legs were mere skinless ulcers from the constant soaking. Their faces were swelled and bloody from the bites of mosquitoes and wood-ticks. "Not a Man of us but wisht the Journey at an End." Those who have seen

"Bad Lands," or what is called "timber," or what is called "bush," will know what the party looked like, when, on the twenty-second day, they saw the North Sea. The day after that they reached the Rio Conception, and drifted down to the sea in some canoes, to an Indian village, built on the beach "for the benefit of Trade with the Privateers." About nine miles away, the Indians told them, was a French privateer ship, under one Captain Tristian, lying at La Sounds Key. They stayed a night at the village, and then went aboard the French ship, which was careened in a creek, with a brushwood fire on her side, cleaning away her barnacles for a roving cruise. Here they parted with their Indian guides, not without sorrow, for it is not pleasant to say "So Long" to folk with whom one has struggled, and lived, and suffered. "We were resolved to reward them to their hearts' Content," said Dampier, much as a cowboy, at the end of the trail, will give sugar to his horse, as he bids him good-bye. The pirates spent their silver royally, buying red, blue and green beads, and knives, scissors, and looking-glasses, from the French pirates. They bought up the entire stock of the French ship, but even then they felt that they had not rewarded their guides sufficiently. They therefore subscribed a half-dollar piece each, in coin, as a sort of makeweight. With the toys, and the bags of silver, the delighted Indians passed back to the isthmus, where they told golden stories of the kind whites, so that the Indians of the Main could not do enough for Wafer, and for the four pirates left behind on the march.

Dampier's party had marched in all 110 miles, over the most damnable and heart-breaking country which the mind of man can imagine. They had marched "heavy," with their guns and bags of dollars; and this in the rainy season. They had starved and suffered, and shivered and agonised, yet they had lost but two men, poor Gayny, who was drowned, and (apparently) one who had slipped away on the third day of the march. This man may have been the Spanish Indian. A note in Ringrose's narrative alludes to the capture of one of Dampier's party by the Spanish soldiers, and this may have been the man meant.

Two days later, when the Indian guides had gone, and the privateer was fit for the sea, they set sail for "the rendezvous of the fleet," which had been fixed for Springers' Key "another of the Samballoes Isles." Perhaps the English pirates hove up the anchor, the grand privilege of the guests, aboard ship, to the old anchor tune, with its mournful and lovely refrain—

> " I'll go no more a-roving with you, fair maid."

The old band of never-strikes were outward bound on another foray.

As for Wafer, and his two companions, they stayed with the Indians for some days, living on plantains (given very grudgingly), and wondering whether the Indians would kill them. The natives were kindly, as a rule, to the French and English, but it was now the rainy season, when they liked to stay in their huts, about their fires. The pirates "had in a Manner awed the Indian guides they took . . . and made them go with them very much against their Wills." The Indians had resented this act of the pirates, and as days went by, and the guides did not return, they judged that the white men had killed them. They prepared "a great Pile of Wood to burn us," says Wafer, meaning to avenge their fellows, whom they "had supposed dead." But a friendly old chief dissuaded them from this act, a few hours before the intended execution.

While the three were living thus, in doubt whether they would be speared, or held as slaves, or sold to the Spaniards, the two pirates, Spratlin and Bowman, who had been left behind at the Rio Congo, arrived at the village. They had had a terrible journey together, "among the wild Woods and Rivers," wandering without guides, and living on roots and plantains. On their way, they had come upon George Gayny "lying dead in a Creek where the Eddy had driven him ashore," "with the Rope twisted about him, and his Money at his Neck." They left the body where it lay, with its sack of silver dollars for which the poor man had come so far, and suffered so bitterly. They had no use for dollars at that time "being only in care how to work their way through a wild un-Known Country."

After a time, the Indians helped the five men a two days' march on their journey, and then deserted them, leaving them to find the path by themselves, with no better guide than a pocket compass. While crossing a river by the bole of a fallen tree, the man Bowman "a weakly Man, a Taylor by Trade," slipped into the current, and was carried off, with "400 Pieces of Eight" in his satchel. He was luckier than poor Gayny, for he contrived to get out. In time they reached the North Sea, and came to La Sounds Key, according to the prophecy of an Indian wizard. Here they found Dampier's sloop, and rejoined their comrades, to the great delight of all hands. "Mr Wafer wore a clout about him, and was painted like an Indian," so that "'twas the better Part of an Hour, before one of the Crew cry'd out Here's our Doctor." There was a great feast that night at La Sounds Key, much drinking of rum and firing of small arms, and a grand ringing of bells in honour of the happy return.

In spite of all they could do, poor Mr Jopson, or Cobson, only lived for three or four days after he reached the ship. "His Fatigues, and his Drenching in the Water" had been too much for the poor man. He lay "languishing" in his cot for a few days, babbling of the drugs of Bucklersbury, and thumbing his Greek Testament, and at last passed in his checks, quietly and sadly, and "died there at La Sounds Key." They buried the poor man in the sands, with very genuine sorrow, and then bade the Indians adieu, and gave their dead mate a volley of guns, and so set sail, with the colours at half-mast, for "the more Eastern Isles of the Samballoes."

As for Captain Bartholomew Sharp, in the ship the *Trinity*, he continued to sail the South Seas with the seventy pirates left to him. Some days after Dampier's party sailed, he took a Guayaquil ship, called the *San Pedro*, which he had taken fourteen months before off Panama. Aboard her he found nearly 40,000 pieces of eight, besides silver bars, and ingots of gold. He also took a great ship called the *San Rosario*, the richest ship the buccaneers ever captured. She had many chests of pieces of eight aboard her, and a quantity of wine and brandy. Down in her hold, bar upon bar, " were 700 pigs of plate," rough silver from the mines, not yet fitted for the Lima mint. The pirates thought that this crude silver was tin, and so left it where it lay, in the hold of the *Rosario* "which we turned away loose into the sea," with the stuff aboard her. One pig of the 700 was brought aboard the pirates "to make bullets of." About two-thirds of it was "melted and squandered," but some of it was left long afterwards, when the *Trinity* touched at Antigua. Here they gave what was left to "a Bristol man," probably in exchange for a dram of rum. The Bristol man took it home to England "and sold it thère for £75 sterling." "Thus," said Ringrose, "we parted with the richest booty we got in the whole voyage." Captain Bartholomew Sharp was responsible for the turning adrift of all this silver. Some of the pirates had asked leave to hoist it aboard the *Trinity*. But it chanced that, aboard the *Rosario*, was a Spanish lady, "the beautifullest Creature" that the "Eyes" of Captain Sharp ever beheld. The amorous captain was so inflamed by this beauty that he paid no attention to anything else.

In a very drunken and quarrelsome condition, the pirates worked the *Trinity* round the Horn, and so home to Barbadoes. They did not dare to land there, for one of the King's frigates, H.M.S. *Richmond*, was lying at Bridgetown, and the pirates "feared lest the said frigate should seize us." They bore away to Antigua, where Ringrose, and "thirteen more," shipped themselves for England. They landed at Dartmouth on the 26th of March 1682. A few more of the company went ashore at Antigua, and scattered to different haunts. Sharp and a number of pirates landed at Nevis, from whence they shipped for London. The ship the *Trinity* was left to seven of the gang who had diced away all their money. What became of her is not known.

Sharp and a number of his men were arrested in London, and tried for piracy, but the Spanish Ambassador, who brought the charge, was without evidence and could not obtain convictions. They pleaded that "the Spaniards fired at us first," and that they had acted only in self-defence, so they 'scaped hanging, though Sharp admits that they "were very near it." Three more of the crew were laid by the heels at Jamaica, and one of these was "wheedled into an open confession," and condemned, and hanged. "The other two stood it out, and escaped for want of witnesses."

Of the four men so often quoted in this narrative, only one, so far as we know, died a violent death. This was Basil Ringrose, who was shot at Santa Pecaque a few years later. It is not known how Dampier, Wafer, and Sharp died, but all lived adventurously, and went a-roving, for many years after the *Trinity* dropped her anchor off Antigua.

They were of that old breed of rover whose port lay always a little farther on; a little beyond the sky-line. Their concern was not to preserve life, " but rather to squander it away "; to fling it, like so much oil, into the fire, for the pleasure of going up in a blaze. If they lived riotously let it be urged in their favour that at least they lived. They lived their vision. They were ready to die for what they believed to be worth doing. We think them terrible. Life itself is terrible. But life was not terrible to them; for they were comrades; and comrades and brothers-in-arms are stronger than life. Those who " live at home at ease " may condemn them. They are free to do so. The old buccaneers were happier than they. The buccaneers had comrades, and the strength to live their own lives. They may laugh at those who, lacking that strength, would condemn them with the hate of impotence.

CHAPTER XVI

SHIPS AND RIGS

Galleys—Dromonds—Galliasses—Pinnaces—Pavesses—Top-
arming—Banners—Boats

UNTIL the reign of Henry VIII. the shipping of these
islands was of two kinds. There were longships,
propelled, for the most part, by oars, and used generally
as warships ; and there were roundships, or dromonds,
propelled by sails, and used as a rule for the carriage of
freight. The dromond, in war-time, was sometimes converted into a warship, by the addition of fighting-castles
fore and aft. The longship, in peace time, was no doubt
used as a trader, as far as her shallow draught, and small
beam, allowed.

The longship, or galley, being, essentially, an oar vessel,
had to fulfil certain simple conditions. She had to be
light, or men might not row her. She had to be long, or
she might not carry enough oarsmen to propel her with
sufficient swiftness. Her lightness, and lack of draught,
made it impossible for her to carry much provision ;
while the number of her oars made it necessary for her
to carry a large crew of rowers, in addition to her soldiers
and sail trimmers. It was therefore impossible for such
a ship to keep the seas for any length of time, even had
their build fitted them for the buffetings of the stormy
home waters. For short cruises, coast work, rapid forays,
and "shock tactics," she was admirable ; but she could not
stray far from a friendly port, nor put out in foul weather.
The roundship, dromond, or cargo boat, was often little

more than two beams long, and therefore far too slow to compete with ships of the galley type. She could stand heavy weather better than the galley, and she needed fewer hands, and could carry more provisions, but she was almost useless as a ship of war.

In the reign of Henry VIII. the shipwrights of this country began to build ships which combined something of the strength, and capacity of the dromond, with the length and fineness of the galley. The ships they evolved were mainly dependent upon their sails, but they carried a bank of oars on each side, for use in light weather. The galley, or longship, had carried guns on a platform at the bows, pointing forward. But these new vessels carried guns in broadside, in addition to the bow-chasers. These broadside guns were at first mounted *en barbette*, pointing over the bulwarks. Early in the sixteenth century the port-hole, with a hinged lid, was invented, and the guns were then pointed through the ship's sides. As these ships carried more guns than the galleys, they were built more strongly, lest the shock of the explosions should shake them to pieces. They were strong enough to keep the seas in bad weather, yet they had enough of the galley build to enable them to sail fast when the oars were laid inboard. It is thought that they could have made as much as four or five knots an hour. These ships were known as galliasses,[1] and galleons, according to the proportions between their lengths and beams. The galleons were shorter in proportion to their breadth than the galliasses.[2] There was another kind of vessel, the pinnace, which had an even greater proportionate length than the galliasse. Of the three kinds, the galleon, being the shortest in proportion to her breadth, was the least fitted for oar propulsion.

[1] See Charnock's " Marine Architecture."
[2] See Corbett's " Drake and the Tudor Navy."

and less important of the two. They were set on wooden yards, the foreyard and foretopsail-yard, both of which could be sent on deck in foul weather. The main-mast was stepped a little abaft the beam, and carried three sails, the main-sail, the main topsail, and a third, the main topgallant-sail. This third sail did not set from a yard until many years after its introduction. It began life like a modern "moon-raker," a triangular piece of canvas, setting from the truck, or summit of the topmast, to the yardarm of the main topsail-yard. Up above it, on a bending light pole, fluttered the great colours, a George's cross of scarlet on a ground of white. Abaft the main-mast were the mizzen, carrying one sail, on a lateen yard, one arm of which nearly touched the deck ; and the bona-venture mizzen (which we now call the jigger) rigged in exactly the same way. Right aft, was a banner pole for the display of colours. These masts were stepped, stayed, and supported almost exactly as masts are rigged to-day, though where we use iron, and wire, they used wood and hemp. The shrouds of the fore and main masts led outboard, to "chains" or strong platforms projecting from the ship's sides. These "chains" were clamped to the ship's sides with rigid links of iron. The shrouds of the after masts were generally set up within the bulwarks. On each mast, just above the lower yard, yet below the masthead, was a fighting-top built of elm wood and gilded over. It was a little platform, resting on battens, and in ancient times it was circular, with a diameter of perhaps six or seven feet. It had a parapet round it, inclining outboard, perhaps four feet in height. It was entered by a lubber's hole in the flooring, through which the shrouds passed. In each top was an arm chest containing Spanish darts, crossbows, longbows, arrows, bolts, and perhaps granadoes. When the ship went into battle a few picked marksmen were stationed in the tops with orders to search the enemy's decks with their missiles, particularly the afterparts, where the helmsman stood.   In later days the tops were armed with light guns, of the sorts known as slings and fowlers ; but top-fighting with firearms was dangerous, as the gunners carried lighted matches, and there was always a risk of sparks, from the match, or from the wads, setting fire to the sails.   The running rigging was arranged much as running rigging is arranged to-day, though its quality, in those times, was probably worse than nowadays.   The rope appears to have been very fickle stuff which carried away under slight provocation. The blocks were bad, for the sheaves were made of some comparatively soft wood, which swelled, when wet, and jammed.   Lignum vitæ was not used for block-sheaves until after the Dutch War in Cromwell's time.   Iron blocks were in use in the time of Henry VIII. but only as fair-leads for chain topsail sheets, and as snatches for the boarding of the " takkes."   The shrouds and stays, were of hawser stuff, extremely thick nine-stranded hemp ; and all those parts exposed to chafing (as from a sail, or a rope) were either served, or neatly covered up with matting.   The matting was made by the sailors, of rope, or white line, plaited curiously.   When in its place it was neatly painted, or tarred, much as one may see it in Norwegian ships at the present day.   The yardarms, and possibly the chains, were at one time fitted with heavy steel sickles, projecting outboard, which were kept sharp, so that, when running alongside an enemy, they might cut her rigging to pieces.   These sickles were known as sheer-hooks.   They were probably of little use, for they became obsolete before the end of the reign of Queen Elizabeth.

Most of the sails used in these old ships were woven in Portsmouth on hand-looms.   The canvas was probably of good quality, as good perhaps as the modern stout No. 1, for hand-woven stuff is always tighter, tougher, better put together, than that woven by the big steam-loom. It was at one time the custom to decorate the sail, with a design of coloured cloth, cut out, as one cuts out a paper pattern, and stitched upon its face with sail twine. In the royal ships this design was of lions rampant, cut out of scarlet say. The custom of carrying such coloured canvas appears to have died out by the end of the sixteenth century. Perhaps flag signalling had come into vogue making it necessary to abandon anything that might tend to confuse the colours. About the same time we abandoned the custom of making our ships gay with little flags, of red and white linen, in guidons like those on a trooper's lance. All through the Tudor reigns our ships carried them, but for some reason the practice was allowed to die out. A last relic of it still flutters on blue water in the little ribbons of the wind-vane, on the weather side the poop, aboard sailing ships.

The great ship carried three boats, which were stowed on chocks in the waist, just forward of the main-mast, one inside the other when not in use. The boats were, the long boat, a large, roomy boat with a movable mast; the cock, cog or cok boat, sometimes called the galley-watt; and the whale, or jolly boat, a sort of small balenger, with an iron-plated bow, which rowed fourteen oars. It was the custom to tow one or more of these boats astern, when at sea, except in foul weather, much as one may see a brig, or a topsail schooner, to-day, with a dinghy dragging astern. The boat's coxswain stayed in her as she towed, making her clean, fending her off, and looking out for any unfortunate who chanced to fall overboard.

Authorities.—W. Charnock: "History of Marine Architecture." Julian Corbett: "Drake and the Tudor Navy." A. Jal: "Archeologie Navale"; "Glossaire Nautique." Sir W. Monson: "Naval Tracts." Sir H. Nicholas: "History of the Royal Navy." M. Oppenheim: "History of the Administration of the Royal Navy"; "Naval Inventories of the Reign of Henry VII."

CHAPTER XVII

GUNS AND GUNNERS

Breech-loaders—Cartridges—Powder—The gunner's art

CANNON were in use in Europe, it is thought, in the eleventh century; for the art of making gunpowder came westward, from China, much earlier than people have supposed. It is certain that gunpowder was used "in missiles," before it was used to propel them. The earliest cannon were generally of forged iron built in strips secured by iron rings. They were loaded by movable chambers which fitted into the breech, and they were known as "crakys of war." We find them on English ships at the end of the fourteenth century, in two kinds, the one a cannon proper, the other an early version of the harquebus-a-croc. The cannon was a mere iron tube, of immense strength, bound with heavy iron rings. The rings were shrunken on to the tube in the ordinary way. The tube, when ready, was bolted down to a heavy squared beam of timber on the ship's deck. It was loaded by the insertion of the "gonne-chambre," an iron pan, containing the charge, which fitted into, and closed the breech. This gonne-chambre was wedged in firmly by a chock of elm wood beaten in with a mallet. Another block of wood, fixed in the deck behind it, kept it from flying out with any violence when the shot was fired. Cannon of this sort formed the main armament of ships until after the reign of Henry the Eighth. They fired stone cannon-balls, "pellettes of lead, and dyce of iron." Each gun had some half-dozen chambers, so that the firing from them may have been rapid, perhaps three rounds a minute. The powder was not kept loose in tubs, near the guns, but neatly folded in conical cartridges, made of canvas or paper (or flannel) which practice prevailed for many years. All ships of war carried "pycks for hewing stone-shott," though after 1490, "the iron shott callyd bowletts," and their leaden brothers, came into general use. The guns we have described, were generally two or four pounders, using from half-a-pound, to a pound and a quarter, of powder, at each discharge. The carriage, or bed, on which they lay, was usually fitted with wheels at the rear end only.

The other early sea-cannon, which we have mentioned, were also breech-loading. They were mounted on a sort of iron wheel, at the summit of a stout wooden staff, fixed in the deck, or in the rails of the poop and forecastle. They were of small size, and revolved in strong iron pivot rings, so that the man firing them might turn them in any direction he wished. They were of especial service in sweeping the waist, the open spar-deck, between the breaks of poop and forecastle, when boarders were on board. They threw "base and bar-shot to murder near at hand"; but their usual ball was of stone, and for this reason they were called petrieroes, and petrieroes-a-braga. The harquebus-a-croc, a weapon almost exactly similar, threw small cross-bar shot "to cut Sails and Rigging." In Elizabethan times it was carried in the tops of fighting ships, and on the rails and gunwales of merchantmen,

In the reign of Henry VIII., a ship called the *Mary Rose*, of 500 tons, took part in the battle with the French, in St Helens Roads, off Brading. It was a sultry summer day, almost windless, when the action began, and the *Mary Rose* suffered much (being unable to stir) from the gun-fire of the French galleys. At noon, when a breeze sprang up, and the galleys drew off, the *Mary Rose* sent her men to dinner. Her lower ports, which were cut too low down, were open, and the wind heeled her over, so that the sea rushed in to them. She sank in deep water, in a few moments, carrying with her her captain, and all the gay company on board. In 1836 some divers recovered a few of her cannon, of the kinds we have described, some of brass, some of iron. The iron guns had been painted red and black. Those of brass, in all probability, had been burnished, like so much gold. These relics may be seen by the curious, at Woolwich, in the Museum of Ordnance, to which they were presented by their salver.

In the reign of Elizabeth, cannon were much less primitive, for a great advance took place directly men learned the art of casting heavy guns. Until 1543, they had forged them; a painful process, necessarily limited to small pieces. After that year they cast them round a core, and by 1588 they had evolved certain general types of ordnance which remained in use, in the British Navy, almost unchanged, until after the Crimean War. The Elizabethan breech-loaders, and their methods, have now been described, but a few words may be added with reference to the muzzle-loaders. The charge for these was contained in cartridges, covered with canvas, or "paper royall" (*i.e.* parchment), though the parchment used to foul the gun at each discharge. Burning scraps of it remained in the bore, so that, before reloading, the weapon had to be "wormed," or scraped out, with an instrument like an edged corkscrew. A tampion, or wad, of oakum or the like, was rammed down between the cartridge and the ball, and a second wad kept the ball in place. When the gun was loaded the gunner filled the touch-hole with his priming powder, from a horn he carried in his belt, after thrusting a sharp wire, called the priming-iron, down the touch-hole, through the cart-ridge, so that the priming powder might have direct access to the powder of the charge. He then sprinkled a little train of powder along the gun, from the touch-hole to the base-ring, for if he applied the match directly to the touch-hole the force of the explosion was liable to blow his linstock from his hand. In any case the "huff" or "spit" of fire, from the touch-hole, burned little holes, like pock-marks, in the beams overhead. The match was applied smartly, with a sharp drawing back of the hand, the gunner stepping quickly aside to avoid the recoil. He stepped back, and stood, on the side of the gun oppo-site to that on which the cartridges were stored, so that there might be no chance of a spark from his match setting fire to the ammunition. Spare match, newly soaked in saltpetre water, lay coiled in a little tub beside the gun. The cartridges, contained in latten buckets, were placed in a barrel by the gun and covered over with a skin of leather. The heavy shot were arranged in shot racks, known as "gardens," and these were ready to the gunner's hand, with "cheeses" of tampions or wads. The wads were made of soft wood, oakum, hay, straw, or "other such like." The sponges and rammers were hooked to the beams above the gun ready for use. The rammers were of hard wood, shod with brass, "to save the Head from cleaving." The sponges were of soft fast wood, " As Aspe, Birch, Willow, or such like," and had heads covered with "rough Sheepes skinne wooll," nailed to the staff with "Copper nayles." " Ladels," or powder shovels, for the loading of guns, were seldom used at sea.

The guns were elevated or depressed by means of handspikes and quoins. Quoins were blocks of wood, square, and wedge-shaped, with ring-hooks screwed in them for the greater ease of handling Two of the gun's crew raised the base of the cannon upon their handspikes, using the "steps" of the gun carriage as their fulcra. A third slid a quoin along the "bed" of the carriage, under the gun, to support it at the required height. The recoil of the gun on firing, was often very violent, but it was limited by the stout rope called the breeching, which ran round the base of the gun, from each side of the port-hole, and kept it from running back more than its own length. When it had recoiled it was in the position for sponging and loading, being kept from running out again, with the roll of the ship, by a train, or preventer tackle, hooked to a ring-bolt in amidships. In action, particularly in violent action, the guns became very hot, and "kicked" dangerously. Often they recoiled with such force as to overturn, or to snap the breeching, or to leap up to strike the upper beams. Brass guns were more skittish than iron, but all guns needed a rest of two or three hours, if possible, after continual firing for more than eight hours at a time. To cool a gun in action, to keep it from bursting, or becoming red-hot, John Roberts advises sponging "with spunges wet in ley and water, or water and vinegar, or with the coolest fresh or salt water, bathing and washing her both within and without." This process "if the Service is hot, as it was with us at Bargen" should be repeated, "every eighth or tenth shot." The powder in use for cannon was called Ordnance or Corne-powder. It was made in the following proportion. To every five pounds of refined saltpetre, one pound of good willow, or alder, charcoal, and one pound of fine yellow sulphur. The ingredients were braised together in a mortar, moistened with water distilled of orange rinds, or aqua-vitæ, and finally dried and sifted. It was a bright, "tawny blewish colour" when well made. Fine powder, for muskets or priming seems to have had a greater proportion of saltpetre.

The Naval Tracts of Sir W. Monson, contain a list of the sorts of cannon mounted in ships of the time of Queen Elizabeth. It is not exhaustive, but as Robert Norton and Sir Jonas Moore give similar lists, the curious may check the one with the other.

	Bore	Weight of Cannon	Weight of Shot	Weight of Powder	Point Blank Range	Random		Length in Feet
	ins.	lb.	lb.	lb.	paces	paces		
Cannon Royal or Double Cannon .	8½	8000	66	30	800	1930	M.L.	12
Cannon or Whole Cannon .	8	6000	60	27	770	2000	,,	11
Cannon Serpentine	7	5500	53½	25	200	2000	,,	10
Bastard Cannon .	7	4500	41½	20	180	1800	,,	10
Demi-Cannon .	6½-7	4000	33½	18	170	1700	,,	10
Cannon Petro or Cannon Perier .	6	4000	24½	14	160	1600	,,	4
Culverin . .	5-5½	4500	17½	12	200	2500	,,	13
Basilisk . .	5	4000	15	10	230	3000	,,	4
Demi-Culverin .	4	3400	9½	8	200	2500	,,	11
Bastard Culverin .	4	3000	7	5¾	170	1700	,,	11
Saker . . .	3½	1400	5½	5½	170	1700	,, 9 or	10
Minion . . .	3½	1000	4	4	170	1700	,,	8
Falcon . . .	2½	660	3	3	150	1500	,,	7
Falconet . .	2	500	1½	1¼	150	1500	,,	6½
Serpentine . .	1½	400	¾	¾	140	1400	,,	4½
Rabinet . .	1	300	½	½	120	1000	,,	2½

To these may be added bases, port pieces, stock fowlers, slings, half slings, and three-quarter slings, breech-loading guns ranging from five and a half to one-inch bore.

Other firearms in use in our ships at sea were the matchlock musket, firing a heavy double bullet, and the harquabuse[1] or arquebus, which fired a single bullet. The musket was a heavy weapon, and needed a rest, a forked staff, to support the barrel while the soldier aimed. This staff the musketeer lashed to his wrist, with a cord, so that he might drag it after him from place to place. The musket was fired with a match, which the soldier lit from a cumbrous pocket fire-carrier.

[1] or caliver.

The harquabuse was a lighter gun, which was fired without a rest, either by a wheel-lock (in which a cog-wheel, running on pyrites, caused sparks to ignite the powder), or by the match and touch-hole. Hand firearms were then common enough, and came to us from Italy, shortly after 1540. They were called Daggs. They were wheel-locks, wild in firing, short, heavy, and beautifully wrought. Sometimes they carried more than one barrel, and in some cases they were made revolving. They were most useful in a hand-to-hand encounter, as with footpads, or boarders; but they were useless at more than ten paces. A variation from them was the hand-cannon or blunder-buss, with a bell-muzzle, which threw rough slugs or nails. In Elizabethan ships the musketeers sometimes fired short, heavy, long-headed, pointed iron arrows from their muskets, a missile which flew very straight, and penetrated good steel armour. They had also an infinity of subtle fireworks, granadoes and the like, with which to set their opponents on fire. These they fired from the bombard pieces, or threw from the tops, or cage-works. Crossbows and longbows went to sea, with good store of Spanish bolts and arrows, until the end of Elizabeth's reign, though they were, perhaps, little used after 1590. The gunner had charge of them, and as, in a way, the gunner was a sort of second captain, sometimes taking command of the ship, we cannot do better than to quote from certain old books concerning his duties on board. Mr W. Bourne, the son of an eminent mathematician, has left a curious little book on "The Arte of Shooting in Great Ordnance," first published in London, in 1587, the year before the Armada. Its author, W. Bourne, was at one time a gunner of the bulwark at Gravesend. The art of shooting in great guns did not improve very much during the century following; nor did the guns change materially. The breech-loading, quick-firing guns fell out of use as the musket became more handy; but otherwise the province of the gunner changed hardly at all. It is not too much to say that gunners of Nelson's time, might have studied some of Bourne's book with profit.

"As for gunners that do serve by the Sea, [they] must observe this order following. First that they do foresee that all their great Ordnannce be fast breeched, and foresee that all their geare be handsome and in a readinesse. & Furthermore that they be very circumspect about their Pouder in the time of service, and especially beware of their lint stockes & candels for feare of their Pouder, & their fireworks, & their Ducum [or priming powder], which is very daungerous, and much to be feared. Then furthermore, that you do keep your peeces as neer as you can, dry within, and also that you keep their tutch-holes cleane, without any kind of drosse falling into them."

The gunners were also to know the "perfect dispart" of their pieces: that is they were to make a calculation which would enable them in sighting, to bring "the hollow of the peece," not the outer muzzle rim, "right against the marke." In the case of a breech-loader this could not be done by art, with any great exactness, "but any reasonable man (when he doth see the peece and the Chamber) may easily know what he must doe, as touching those matters." In fighting at sea, in any-thing like a storm, with green seas running, so that "the Shippes do both heave and set" the gunner was to choose a gun abaft the main-mast, on the lower orlop, "if the shippe may keepe the porte open," as in that part of the vessel the motion would be least apparent.

"Then if you doe make a shotte at another Shippe, you must be sure to have a good helme-man, that can stirre [steer] steady, taking some marke of a Cloude that is above by the Horizon, or by the shadowe of the Sunne, or by your standing still, take some marke of the other shippe through some hole, or any such other like. Then he that giveth levell [takes aim] must observe this: first consider what disparte his piece must have, then lay the peece directly with that parte of the Shippe that he doth meane to shoote at: then if the Shippe bee under the lee side of your Shippe, shoote your peece in the comming downe of the Gayle, and the beginning of the other Ship to rise upon the Sea, as near as you can, for this cause, for when the other shippe is aloft upon the Sea, and shee under your Lee, the Gayle maketh her for to head, and then it is likest to do much good."

The helmsman also was to have an eye to the enemy, to luff when she luffed, and "putte roomer," or sail large, when he saw her helmsman put the helm up. If the enemy made signs that she was about to lay the ship aboard, either by loosing more sail, or altering her course, the gunner had to remember certain things.

"If the one doe meane to lay the other aboorde, then they do call up their company either for to enter or to defend: and first, if that they doe meane for to enter . . . then marke where that you doe see anye Scottles for to come uppe at, as they will stande neere thereaboutes, to the intente for to be readie, for to come uppe under the Scottles: there give levell with your Fowlers, or Slinges, or Bases, for there you shall be sure to do moste good, then further more, if you doe meane for to enter him, then give level with your fowlers and Port peeces, where you doe see his chiefest fight of his Shippe is, and especially be sure to have them charged, and to shoote them off at the first boording of the Shippes, for then you shall be sure to speede. And furthermore, mark where his men have most recourse, then discharge your Fowlers and Bases. And furthermore for the annoyance of your enemie, if that at the boording that the Shippes lye therefore you may take away their steeradge

with one of your great peeces, that is to shoote at his
Rother, and furthermore at his mayne maste and so
foorth."

The ordering of cannon on board a ship was a matter
which demanded a nice care. The gunner had to see
that the carriages were so made as to allow the guns
to lie in the middle of the port. The carriage wheels,
or trocks, were not to be too high, for if they were too
high they hindered the mariners, when they ran the
cannon out in action (*Norton, Moore, Bourne, Monson*).
Moreover, if the wheels were very large, and the ship
were heeled over, the wheel rims would grind the ship's
side continually, unless large skids were fitted to them.
And if the wheels were large they gave a greater fierceness to the impetus of the recoil, when the piece was
fired. The ports were to be rather "deepe uppe and
downe" than broad in the traverse, and it was very
necessary that the lower port-sill should not be too
far from the deck, "for then the carriage muste bee
made verye hygh, and that is verye evill" (*Bourne*). The
short cannon were placed low down, at the ship's side,
because short cannon were more easily run in, and secured,
when the ports were closed, owing to the ship's heeling,
or the rising of the sea. A short gun, projecting its
muzzle through the port, was also less likely to catch
the outboard tackling of the sails, such as "Sheetes and
Tackes, or the Bolynes." And for these reasons any very
long guns were placed astern, or far forward, as bow, or
stern chasers. It was very necessary that the guns
placed at the stern should be long guns, for the tall
poops of the galleons overhung the sea considerably. If
the gun, fired below the overhang, did not project beyond
the woodwork, it was liable to "blowe up the Counter
of the Shyppes Sterne," to the great detriment of gilt
and paint. Some ships cut their stern ports down to

the deck, and continued the deck outboard, by a projecting platform. The guns were run out on to this
platform, so that the muzzles cleared the overhang.
These platforms were the originals of the quarter-
galleries, in which, some centuries later, the gold-laced
admirals took the air (*Bourne*).

Sir Jonas Moore, who published a translation of
Moretti's book on artillery, in 1683, added to his chapters
some matter relating to sea-gunners, from the French
of Denis Furnier.

"The Gunner, whom they call in the *Straights Captain*,
Master-Canoneer, and in *Bretagne* and *Spain*, and in
other places *Connestable*, is one of the principal Officers
in the Ship; it is he alone with the Captain who can
command the Gunners. He ought to be a man of
courage, experience, and vigilant, who knows the goodness of a Peece of Ordnance, the force of Powder, and
who also knows how to mount a Peece of Ordnance
upon its carriage, and to furnish it with Bolts, Plates,
Hooks, Capsquares [to fit over the Trunnions on which
the gun rested] Axletrees and Trucks, and that may
not reverse too much; to order well its Cordage as
Breeching [which stopped the recoil] and Tackling [by
which it was run out or in]; to plant the Cannon to
purpose in the middle of its Port; to know how to
unclow[1] it [cast it loose for action], make ready his
Cartridges, and to have them ready to pass from hand
to hand through the Hatches, and to employ his most
careful men in that affair; that he have care of all, that
he be ready everywhere to assist where necessity shall
be; and take care that all be made to purpose.

"He and his Companions [the gunner's mates] ought

[1] This word unclow may be a misprint for uncloy. To uncloy was to get rid
of the spike, or soft metal nail, thrust into a piece's touch-hole by an enemy.
It was done by oiling the spike all over, so as to make it "glib," and then
blowing it out, from within, by a train of powder.

Another female pirate, Anne Bonney, who was tried and convicted with Mary Read. The death sentence was never carried out, though her ultimate fate is unknown. *Johnson.*

with their dark Lanthornes continually to see if the Guns play, and if the Rings in Ships do not shake." (That is, a strict watch was to be kept, at night, when at sea in stormy weather, to see that the cannon did not work or break loose, and that the ring-bolts remained firm in their places.)

"If there be necessity of more Cordage, and to see that the Beds and Coins be firm and in good order; when the Ship comes to Anker, he furnisheth Cordage, and takes care that all his Companions take their turn [stand their watch] and quarters, that continually every evening they renew their priming Powder [a horn of fine dry powder poured into the touch-holes of loaded cannon, to communicate the fire to the charge], and all are obliged to visit their Cannon Powder every eight dayes, to see if it hath not receiv'd wet, although they be well stopped a top with Cork and Tallow; to see that the Powder-Room be kept neat and clean, and the Cartridges ranged in good order, each nature or Calibre by itself, and marked above in great Letters the weight of the Powder and nature of the Peece to which it belongs, and to put the same mark over the Port-hole of the Peece; that the Linstocks [*or forked staves of wood, about two and a half feet long, on which the match was carried*] be ready, and furnished with Match [*or cotton thread, boiled in ashes-lye and powder, and kept smouldering, with a red end, when in use*], and to have alwaies one lighted, and where the Cannoneer makes his Quarter to have two one above another below [*this last passage is a little obscure, but we take it to mean that at night, when the gunner slept in his cabin, a lighted match was to be beside him, but that in the gun-decks below and above his cabin (which was in the half-deck) lit matches were to be kept ready for immediate use, by those who kept watch*], that his Granadoes [*black clay, or thick glass bottles, filled with priming powder, and fired by a length of tow, well soaked in saltpetre water*] and Firepots [*balls of hard tar, sulphur-meal and rosin, kneaded together and fired by a priming of bruised powder*] be in readiness, and 3 or 400 Cartridges ready fill'd, Extrees [?] and Trucks [*wheels*] to turn often over the Powder Barrels that the Powder do not spoil ; to have a care of Rings [*ring-bolts*] and of the Ports [he here means port-lids] that they have their Pins and small Rings."

Sir William Monson adds that the gunner was to acquaint himself with the capacities of every known sort of firearm, likely to be used at sea. He also gives some professional hints for the guidance of gunners. He tells us (and Sir Richard Hawkins confirms him) that no sea-cannon ought to be more than seven or eight feet long ; that they ought not to be taper-bored, nor honey-combed within the bore, and that English ordnance, the best in Europe, was sold in his day for twelve pounds a ton.

In Boteler's time the gunner commanded a gang, or crew, who ate and slept in the gun-room, which seems in those days to have been the magazine. He had to keep a careful account of the expenditure of his munitions, and had orders "not to make any shot without the Knowledge and order of the captain."

Authorities.—N. Boteler : " Six Dialogues." W. Bourne : " The Art of Shooting in Great Ordnance " ; " Regiment for the Sea " ; " Mariner's Guide." Sir W. Monson : " Naval Tracts." Sir Jonas Moore. R. Norton : " The Gunner." John Roberts : " Complete Cannoneer."

CHAPTER XVIII

THE SHIP'S COMPANY

Captain—Master—Lieutenant—Warrant officers—Duties and privileges

BY comparing Sir Richard Hawkins' "Observations" and Sir W. Monson's "Tracts" with Nicolas Boteler's "Dialogical Discourses," we find that the duties of ship's officers changed hardly at all from the time of the Armada to the death of James I. Indeed they changed hardly at all until the coming of the steamship. In modern sailing ships the duties of some of the supernumeraries are almost exactly as they were three centuries ago.

The captain was the supreme head of the ship, empowered to displace any inferior officer except the master (*Monson*). He was not always competent to navigate (*ibid.*), but as a rule he had sufficient science to check the master's calculations. He was expected to choose his own lieutenant (*ibid.*), to keep a muster-book, and a careful account of the petty officer's stores (*Monson and Sir Richard Hawkins*), and to punish any offences committed by his subordinates.

A lieutenant seems to have been unknown in ships of war until the early seventeenth century. He ranked above the master, and acted as the captain's proxy, or ambassador, "upon any occasion of Service" (*Monson*). In battle he commanded on the forecastle, and in the forward half of the ship. He was restrained from meddling with the master's duties, lest "Mischiefs and factions" should ensue. Boteler adds that a lieutenant ought not to be "too fierce in his Way at first . . . but to carry himself with Moderation and Respect to the Master Gunner, Boatswain, and the other Officers."

The master was the ship's navigator, responsible for the performance of "the ordinary Labours in the ship." He took the height of the sun or stars "with his Astrolabe, Backstaff or Jacob's-staff" (*Boteler*). He saw that the watches were kept at work, and had authority to punish misdemeanants (*Monson*). Before he could hope for employment he had to go before the authorities at Trinity House, to show his "sufficiency" in the sea arts (*Monson*).

The pilot, or coaster, was junior to the master; but when he was bringing the vessel into port, or over sands, or out of danger, the master had no authority to interfere with him (*Monson*). He was sometimes a permanent official, acting as junior navigator when the ship was out of soundings (*Hawkins*), but more generally he was employed temporarily, as at present, to bring a ship into or out of port (*Monson* and *Boteler*).

The ship's company was drilled by a sort of junior lieutenant (*Boteler*), known as the corporal, who was something between a master-at-arms and a captain of marines. He had charge of the small arms, and had to see to it that the bandoliers for the musketmen were always filled with dry cartridges, and that the muskets and "matches" were kept neat and ready for use in the armoury (*Monson*). He drilled the men in the use of their small arms, and also acted as muster master at the setting and relieving of the watch.

The gunner, whose duties we have described at length, was privileged to alter the ship's course in action, and may even have taken command during a chase, or running fight. He was assisted by his mates, who commanded the various batteries while in action, and aimed and fired according to his directions.

The boatswain, the chief seaman of the crew, was generally an old sailor who had been much at sea, and knew the whole art of seamanship. He had charge of all the sea-stores, and " all the Ropes belonging to the Rigging [more especially the fore-rigging], all her Cables, and Anchors; all her Sayls, all her Flags, Colours, and Pendants;[1] and so to stand answerable for them " (*Boteler*). He was captain of the long boat, which was stowed on the booms or spare spars between the fore and main masts. He had to keep her guns clean, her oars, mast, sails, stores, and water ready for use, and was at all times to command and steer her when she left the ship (*Hawkins*). He carried a silver whistle, or call, about his neck, which he piped in various measures before repeating the master's orders (*Monson*). The whistle had a ball at one end, and was made curved, like a letter S laid sideways. The boatswain, when he had summoned all hands to their duty, was expected to see that they worked well. He kept them quiet, and " at peace one with another," probably by knocking together the heads of those disposed to quarrel. Lastly, he was the ship's executioner, his mates acting as assistants, and at his hands, under the supervision of the marshal, the crew received their " red-checked shirts," and such bilboed solitude as the captain might direct.

The coxswain was the commander of the captain's row barge which he had to keep clean, freshly painted and gilded, and fitted with the red and white flag—" and when either the Captain or any Person of Fashion is to use the Boat, or be carryed too and again from the Ship, he is to have the Boat trimmed with her Cushions and Carpet and himself is to be ready to steer her out of her Stern [in the narrow space behind the back board of the stern-sheets] and with his Whistle to chear up

[1] He had to hang out the ship's colours on going into action (*Monson*).

and direct his Gang of Rowers, and to keep them together when they are to wait : and this is the lowest Officer in a Ship, that is allowed to carry a Whistle" (*Boteler*). The coxswain had to stay in his barge when she towed astern at sea, and his office, therefore, was often very wretched, from the cold and wet. He had to see that his boat's crew were at all times clean in their persons, and dressed alike, in as fine a livery as could be managed (*Monson*). He was to choose them from the best men in the ship, from the "able and handsome men" (*Monson*). He had to instruct them to row together, and to accustom the port oarsmen to pull starboard from time to time. He also kept his command well caulked, and saw the chocks and skids secure when his boat was hoisted to the deck.

The quartermasters and their mates had charge of the hold (*Monson*), and kept a sort of check upon the steward in his "delivery of the Victuals to the Cook, and in his pumping and drawing of the Beer" (*Boteler*). In far later times they seem to have been a rating of elderly and sober seamen who took the helm, two and two together, in addition to their other duties. In the Elizabethan ship they superintended the stowage of the ballast, and were in charge below, over the ballast shifters, when the ships were laid on their sides to be scraped and tallowed. They also had to keep a variety of fish hooks ready, in order to catch any fish, such as sharks or bonitos.

The purser was expected to be "an able Clerk" (*Monson*) for he had to keep an account of all provisions received from the victualler. He kept the ship's muster-book, with some account of every man borne upon it. He made out passes, or pay-tickets for discharged men (*ibid.*), and, according to *Boteler*, he was able "to purse up roundly for himself" by dishonest dealing. The purser (*Boteler* says the cook) received 6d. a month from every seaman, for "Wooden Dishes, Cans, Candles, Lanthorns, and Candlesticks for the Hold" (*Monson*). It was also his office to superintend the steward, in the serving out of the provisions and other necessaries to the crew.

The steward was the purser's deputy (*Monson*). He had to receive "the full Mass of Victual of all kinds," and see it well stowed in the hold, the heavy things below, the light things up above (*Boteler*). He had charge of all the candles, of which those old dark ships used a prodigious number. He kept the ship's biscuits or bread, in the bread-room, a sort of dark cabin below the gun-deck. He lived a life of comparative retirement, for there was a "several part in the Hold, which is called the Steward's room, where also he Sleeps and Eats" (*Boteler*). He weighed out the provisions for the crew, "to the several Messes in the Ship," and was cursed, no doubt, by every mariner, for a cheating rogue in league with the purser. Though Hawkins tells us that it was his duty "with discretion and good tearmes to give satisfaction to all."

The cook did his office in a cook-room, or galley, placed in the forecastle or "in the Hatchway upon the first Orlope" (*Boteler*). The floor of the galley was not at that time paved with brick or stone, as in later days, and now. It was therefore very liable to take fire, especially in foul weather, when the red embers were shaken from the ash-box of the range. It was the cook's duty to take the provisions from the steward, both flesh and fish, and to cook them, by boiling, until they were taken from him (*Monson*). It was the cook's duty to steep the salt meat in water for some days before using, as the meat was thus rendered tender and fit for human food (*Smith*). He had the rich perquisite of the ship's fat, which went into his slush tubs, to bring him money from the candle-makers. The firewood he used was generally green, if not wet, so that when he lit his fire of a morning, he fumigated the fo'c's'le with bitter smoke. It was his duty to pour water on his fire as soon as the guns were cast loose for battle. Every day, for the saving of firewood, and for safety, he had to extinguish his fire directly the dinner had been cooked, nor was he allowed to relight it, "but in case of necessity, as . . . when the Cockswain's Gang came wet aboard" (*Monson*). He would allow his cronies in the forenoons to dry their wet gear at his fire, and perhaps allow them, in exchange for a bite or sup, to cook any fish they caught, or heat a can of drink.

Another supernumerary was the joiner, a rating only carried in the seventeenth century on great ships with much fancy work about the poop. He it was who repaired the gilt carvings in the stern-works, and made the bulkheads for the admiral's cabin. He was a decorator and beautifier, not unlike the modern painter, but he was to be ready at all times to knock up lockers for the crew, to make boxes and chests for the gunner, and bulkheads, of thin wood, to replace those broken by the seas. As a rule the work of the joiner was done by the carpenter, a much more important person, who commanded some ten or twelve junior workmen. The carpenter was trusted with the pumps, both hand and chain, and with the repairing of the woodwork throughout the vessel. He had to be super-excellent in his profession, for a wooden ship was certain to tax his powers. She was always out of repair, always leaking, always springing her spars. In the summer months, if she were not being battered by the sea, she was getting her timber split by cannon-shot. In the winter months, when laid up and dismantled in the dockyard, she was certain to need new planks, beams, inner fittings and spars (*Hawkins*). The carpenter had to do everything for her, often with grossly insufficient means, and it was of paramount importance that his work-room in the orlop should be fitted with an excellent tool chest. He had to provide the "spare Pieces of Timber wherewith to make Fishes, for to strengthen and succour the Masts." He had to superintend the purchase of a number of spare yards, already tapered, and bound with iron, to replace those that "should chance to be broken." He was to see these lashed to the ship's sides, within board, or stopped in the rigging (*Monson* and *Boteler*). He had to have all manner of gudgeons for the rudder, every sort of nuts or washers for the pumps, and an infinity of oakum, sheet lead, soft wood, spare canvas, tallow, and the like, with which to stop leaks, or to caulk the seams. In his stores he took large quantities of lime, horse hair, alum, and thin felt with which to wash and sheathe the ship's bottom planking (*Monson*). The alum was often dissolved in water, and splashed over spars and sails, before a battle, as it was supposed to render them non-inflammable. It was his duty, moreover, to locate leaks, either by observing the indraught (which was a tedious way), or by placing his ear to a little earthen pot inverted against one of the planks in the hold. This little pot caused him to hear the water as it gurgled in, and by moving it to and fro he could locate the hole with considerable certainty (*Boteler*). He had to rig the pumps for the sailors, and to report to the captain the depth of water the ship made daily. The pumps were of two kinds, one exactly like that in use on shore, the other, of the same principle, though more powerful. The second kind was called the chain-pump, because "these Pumps have a Chain of Burs going in a Wheel." They were worked with long handles, called brakes (because they broke sailor's hearts), and some ten men might pump at one spell. The water was discharged on to the deck, which was slightly rounded, so that it ran to the ship's side, into a graved channel called the trough,

or scuppers, from which it fell overboard through the
scupper-holes, bored through the ship's side. These
scupper-holes were bored by the carpenter. They slanted
obliquely downwards and were closed outside by a hinged
flap of leather, which opened to allow water to escape, and
closed to prevent water from entering (*Maynwaring*).
Each deck had a number of scupper-holes, but they
were all of small size. There was nothing to take the
place of the big swinging-ports fitted to modern iron
sailing ships, to allow the green seas to run overboard.

The cooper was another important supernumerary. He
had to oversee the stowing of all the casks, and to make,
or repair, or rehoop, such casks as had to be made or
repaired. He had to have a special eye to the great water
casks, that they did not leak ; binding them securely with
iron hoops, and stowing them with dunnage, so that they
might not shift. He was put in charge of watering parties,
to see the casks filled at the springs, to fit them, when
full, with their bungs, and to superintend their embarka-
tion and stowage (*Monson* and *Boteler*).

The trumpeter was an attendant upon the captain,
and had to sound his silver trumpet when that great man
entered or left the ship (*Monson*). " Also when you hale
a ship, when you charge, board, or enter her ; and the
Poop is his place to stand or sit upon." If the ship carried
a "noise," that is a band, "they are to attend him, if there
be not, every one he doth teach to bear a part, the Captain
is to encourage him, by increasing his Shares, or pay, and
give the Master Trumpeter a reward." When a prince,
or an admiral, came on board, the trumpeter put on a
tabard, of brilliant colours, and hung his silver instrument
with a heavy cloth of the same. He was to blow a blast
from the time the visitor was sighted until his barge came
within 100 fathoms of the ship. " At what time the
Trumpets are to cease, and all such as carry Whistles are

to Whistle his Welcome three several times." As the gilt
and gorgeous row boat drew alongside, the trumpets
sounded a point of welcome, and had then to stand about
the cabin door, playing their best, while the great man ate
his sweetmeats. As he rowed away again, the trumpeter,
standing on the poop, blew out " A loath to depart," a sort
of ancient "good-bye, fare you well," such as sailors sing
nowadays as they get their anchors for home. In battle
the trumpeter stood upon the poop, dressed in his glory,
blowing brave blasts to hearten up the gunners. In hail-
ing a friendly ship, in any meeting on the seas, it was
customary to "salute with Whistles and Trumpets, and
the Ship's Company give a general shout on both sides."
When the anchor was weighed, the trumpeter sounded
a merry music, to cheer the workers. At dinner each
night he played in the great cabin, while the captain
drank his wine. At the setting and discharging of the
watch he had to sound a solemn point, for which duty he
received an extra can of beer (*Monson* and *Boteler*).

The crew, or mariners, were divided into able seamen,
ordinary seamen, grummets, or cabin-boys, ship-boys and
swabbers. Swabbers were the weakest men of the crew ;
men, who were useless aloft, or at the guns, and therefore
set to menial and dirty duties. They were the ship's
scavengers, and had much uncleanly business to see to.
Linschoten, describing a Portuguese ship's company,
dismisses them with three contemptuous words, " the
swabers pump"; but alas, that was but the first duty of
your true swabber. Boteler, writing in the reign of James
I., gives him more than half-a-page, as follows :—

"The Office of the Swabber is to see the Ship Kept
neat and clean, and that as well in the great Cabbin as
everywhere else betwixt the Decks ; to which end he is,
at the least once or twice a week, if not every day, to
cause the Ship to be well washed within Board and

without above Water, and especially about the Gun-
walls [Gunwales or gunnels, over which the guns once
pointed] and the Chains and for prevention of Infection,
to burn sometimes Pitch, or the like wholsom perfumes,
between the Decks : He is also to have a regard to every
private Man's Sleeping-place ; (to clean the cabins of the
petty officers in the nether orlop), and to admonish them
all in general [it being dangerous perhaps, in a poor
swabber, to admonish in particular] to be cleanly and
handsom, and to complain to the Captain, of all such
as will be any way nastie and offensive that way. Surely,
if this Swabber doth thoroughly take care to discharge
this his charge I easily believe that he may have his
hands full, and especially if there chance to be any number
of Landmen aboard."

Under the swabber there was a temporary rate known
as the liar. He had to keep the ship clean "without
board," in the head, chains, and elsewhere. He held his
place but for a week. " He that is first taken with a Lie
upon a *Monday* morning, is proclaimed at the Main-Mast
with a general Crie, *a Liar, a Liar, a Liar*, and for that
week he is under the Swabber" (*Monson*).

The able seamen, or oldest and most experienced hands,
did duty about the decks and guns, in the setting up and
preservation of the rigging, and in the trimming of the
braces, sheets, and bowlines. The ordinary seamen,
younkers, grummets, and ship-boys, did the work aloft,
furled and loosed the sails, and did the ordinary, never-
ceasing work of sailors. They stood "watch and watch"
unless the weather made it necessary for all to be on
deck, and frequently they passed four hours of each day
in pumping the leakage from the well. They wore no
uniform, but perhaps some captains gave a certain uni-
formity to the clothes of their crews by taking slop
chests to sea, and selling clothes of similar patterns to

the seamen. In the navy, where the crews were pressed, the clothes worn must have been of every known cut and fashion, though no doubt all the pressed men contrived to get tarred canvas coats before they had been many days aboard.

The bodies and souls of the seamen were looked after ; a chaplain being carried for the one, and a chirurgeon, or doctor, for the other. The chaplain had to read prayers twice or thrice daily, to the whole ship's company, who stood or knelt reverently as he read. He had to lead in the nightly psalms, to reprove all evil-doers, and to exhort the men to their duty. Especially was he to repress all blasphemy and swearing. He was to celebrate the Holy Communion whenever it was most convenient. He was to preach on Sunday, to visit the sick ; and, in battle, to console the wounded. Admirals, and peers in command of ships, had the privilege of bringing to sea their own private chaplains.

The chirurgeon had to bring on board his own instruments and medicines, and to keep them ready to hand in his cabin beneath the gun-deck, out of all possible reach of shot. He was expected to know his business, and to know the remedies for those ailments peculiar to the lands for which the ship intended. He had to produce a certificate from "able men of his profession," to show that he was fit to be employed. An assistant, or servant, was allowed him, and neither he, nor his servant did any duty outside the chirurgeon's province (*Monson*).

CHAPTER XIX

THE CHOOSING OF WATCHES

The petty tally—Food—Work—Punishments

AS soon as an ancient ship of war was fitted for the sea, with her guns on board, and mounted, her sails bent, her stores and powder in the hold, her water filled, her ballast trimmed, and the hands aboard, some "steep-tubs" were placed in the chains for the steeping of the salt provisions, "till the salt be out though not the saltness." The anchor was then weighed to a note of music. The "weeping Rachells and mournefull Niobes" were set packing ashore. The colours were run up and a gun fired. The foresail was loosed. The cable rubbed down as it came aboard (so that it might not be faked into the tiers wet or dirty). The boat was hoisted inboard. The master "took his departure," by observing the bearing of some particular point of land, as the Mew Stone, the Start, the Lizard, etc. Every man was bidden to "say his private prayer for a bonne voyage." The anchor was catted and fished. Sails were set and trimmed. Ropes were coiled down clear for running, and the course laid by the master.

The captain or master then ordered the boatswain "to call up the company," just as all hands are mustered on modern sailing ships at the beginning of a voyage. The master "being Chief of the Starboard Watch" would then look over the mariners for a likely man. Having made his choice he bade the man selected go over to the starboard side, while the commander of the port-watch made his choice. When all the men had been chosen, and the crew "divided into two parts," then each man was bidden to choose "his Mate, Consort or Comrade." The bedding arrangements of these old ships were very primitive. The officers had their bunks or hammocks in their cabins, but the men seem to have slept wherever and however they could. Some, no doubt had hammocks, but the greater number lay in their cloaks between the guns, on mattresses if they had them. A man shared his bed and bedding (if he had any) with his "Mate, Consort, or Comrade," so that the one bed and bedding served for the pair. One of the two friends was always on deck while the other slept. In some ships at the present time the forecastles are fitted with bunks for only half the number of seamen carried, so that the practice is not yet dead. The boatswain, with all "the Younkers or Common Sailors" then went forward of the main-mast to take up their quarters between decks. The captain, master's mates, gunners, carpenters, quarter-masters, etc., lodged abaft the main-mast "in their severall Cabbins." The next thing to be done was the arrange-ment of the ship's company into messes, "four to a mess," after which the custom was to "give every messe a quarter Can of beere and a bisket of bread to stay their stomacks till the kettle be boiled." In the first dog-watch, from 4 to 6 P.M., all hands went to prayers about the main-mast, and from their devotions to supper. At 6 P.M. the com-pany met again to sing a psalm, and say their prayers, before the setting of the night watch ; this psalm singing being the prototype of the modern sea-concert, or sing-song. At 8 P.M. the first night watch began, lasting until midnight, during which four hours half the ship's com-pany were free to sleep. At midnight the sleepers were called on deck, to relieve the watch. The watches were changed as soon as the muster had been called and a psalm sung, and a prayer offered. They alternated thus throughout the twenty-four hours, each watch having four hours below, after four hours on deck, unless "some flaw of winde come, some storm or gust, or some accident that requires the help of all hands." In these cases the whole ship's company remained on deck until the work was done, or until the master discharged the watch below.[1] The decks were washed down by the swabbers every morning, before the company went to breakfast. After breakfast the men went about their ordinary duties, cleaning the ship, mending rigging, or working at the thousand odd jobs the sailing of a ship entails. The tops were always manned by lookouts, who received some small reward if they spied a prize. The guns were sometimes exercised, and all hands trained to general quarters.

A few captains made an effort to provide for the comfort of their men by laying in a supply of "bedding, linnen, arms [2] and apparel." In some cases they also provided what was called the petty tally, or store of medical comforts. "The Sea-man's Grammar" of Captain John Smith, from which we have been quoting, tells us that the petty tally contained :

"Fine wheat flower close and well-packed, Rice, Currants, Sugar, Prunes, Cynamon, Ginger, Pepper, Cloves, Green Ginger, Oil, Butter, Holland cheese or old Cheese, Wine-Vinegar, Canarie-Sack, Aqua-vitæ, the best Wines, the best Waters, the juyce of Limons for the scurvy, white Bisket, Oatmeal, Gammons of Bacons, dried Neats tongues, Beef packed up in Vineger, Legs of Mutton minced and stewed, and close packed up, with tried Sewet or Butter in earthen Pots. To entertain Strangers Marmalade, Suckets, Almonds, Comfits and such like."

"Some," says the author of this savoury list, "will say

[1] See "The Sea-man's Grammar," by Captain John Smith.
[2] The men were expected to bring their own swords and knives.

drink for human beings until the beer was spent. The salt meat was as bad as the beer, or worse. Often enough the casks were filled with lumps of bone and fat which were quite uneatable, and often the meat was so lean, old, dry and shrivelled that it was valueless as food. The victuallers often killed their animals in the heat of the summer, when the meat would not take salt, so that many casks must have been unfit for food after lying for a week in store. Anti-scorbutics were supplied, or not supplied, at the discretion of the captains. It appears that the sailors disliked innovations in their food, and rejected the substitution of beans, flour "and those white Meats as they are called" for the heavy, and innutritious pork and beef. Sailors were always great sticklers for their "Pound and Pint," and Boteler tells us that in the early seventeenth century "the common Sea-men with us, are so besotted on their Beef and Pork, as they had rather adventure on all the Calentures, and Scarbots [scurvy] in the World, than to be weaned from their Customary Diet, or so much as to lose the least Bit of it."

The salt-fish ration was probably rather better than the meat, but the cheese was nearly always very bad, and of an abominable odour. The butter was no better than the cheese. It was probably like so much train-oil. The bread or biscuit which was stowed in bags in the bread-room in the hold, soon lost its hardness at sea, becoming soft and wormy, so that the sailors had to eat it in the dark. The biscuits, or cakes of bread, seem to have been current coin with many of the West Indian natives. In those ships where flour was carried, in lieu of biscuit, as sometimes happened in cases of emergency, the men received a ration of doughboy, a sort of dumpling of wetted flour boiled with pork fat. This was esteemed a rare delicacy either eaten plain or with butter.

This diet was too lacking in variety, and too destitute of anti-scorbutics to support the mariners in health. The ships in themselves were insanitary, and the crews suffered very much from what they called calentures, (or fevers such as typhus and typhoid), and the scurvy. The scurvy was perhaps the more common ailment, as indeed it is to-day. It is now little dreaded, for its nature is understood, and guarded against. In the sixteenth, seventeenth, and eighteenth centuries, it killed its thousands, owing to the ignorance and indifference of responsible parties, and to other causes such as the construction of the ships and the length of the voyages. A salt diet, without fresh vegetables, and without variety, is a predisposing cause of scurvy. Exposure to cold and wet, and living in dirty surroundings are also predisposing causes. The old wooden ships were seldom very clean, and never dry, and when once the scurvy took hold it generally raged until the ship reached port, where fresh provisions could be purchased. A wooden ship was never quite dry, in any weather, for the upper-deck planks, and the timbers of her topsides, could never be so strictly caulked that no water could leak in. The sea-water splashed in through the scuppers and through the ports, or leaked in, a little at a time, through the seams. In bad weather the lower gun-decks (or all decks below the spar-deck) were more or less awash, from seas that had washed down the hatchways. The upper-deck seams let in the rain, and when once the lower-decks were wet it was very difficult to dry them. It was impossible to close the gun-deck ports so as to make them watertight, for the water would find cracks to come in at, even though the edges of the lids were caulked with oakum, and the orifices further barred by deadlights or wooden shutters. Many of the sailors, as we have seen, were without a change of clothes, and with no proper sleeping-place, save the wet deck and the wet jackets that they worked in.   It often happened that the gun-ports would be closed for several weeks together, during which time the gun-decks became filthy and musty, while the sailors contracted all manner of cramps and catarrhs.   In addition to the wet, and the discomfort of such a life, there was also the work, often extremely laborious, incidental to heavy weather at sea.   What with the ceaseless handling of sails and ropes, in frost and snow and soaking sea-water; and the continual pumping out of the leaks the rotten seams admitted, the sailor had little leisure in which to sleep, or to dry himself.   When he left the deck he had only the dark, wet berth-deck to retire to, a place of bleakness and misery, where he might share a sopping blanket, if he had one, with the corpse of a drowned rat and the flotsam from the different messes.   There was no getting dry nor warm, though the berth-deck might be extremely close and stuffy from lack of ventilation.   The cook-room, or galley fire would not be lighted, and there would be no comforting food or drink, nothing but raw meat and biscuit, and a sup of sour beer.   It was not more unpleasant perhaps than life at sea is to-day, but it was certainly more dangerous.[1]   When at last the storm abated and the sea went down, the ports were opened and the decks cleaned.   The sailors held a general washing-day, scrubbing the mouldy clothes that had been soaked so long, and hanging them to dry about the rigging.   Wind-sails or canvas ventilators were rigged, to admit air to the lowest recesses of the hold.   The decks were scrubbed down with a mixture of vinegar and sand, and then sluiced with salt water, scraped with metal scrapers, and dried with swabs and small portable firepots.   Vinegar was carried about the decks in large iron pots, and converted into vapour by the insertion of

[1] The mortality among the sailors was very great.

red-hot metal bars.   The swabbers brought pans of burning pitch or brimstone into every corner, so that the
smoke might penetrate everywhere.   But even then the
decks were not wholesome.   There were spaces under
the guns which no art could dry, and subtle leaks in
the topsides that none could stop.   The hold accumulated
filth, for in many ships the ship's refuse was swept on
to the ballast, where it bred pestilence, typhus fever and
the like.   The bilge-water reeked and rotted in the bilges,
filling the whole ship with its indescribable stench.
Beetles, rats and cockroaches bred and multiplied in
the crannies, until (as in Captain Cook's case two centuries
later), they made life miserable for all on board.   These
wooden ships were very gloomy abodes, and would have
been so no doubt even had they been dry and warm.
They were dark, and the lower-deck, where most of the
men messed, was worse lit than the decks above it, for
being near to the water-line the ports could seldom be
opened.   Only in very fair weather could the sailors have
light and sun below decks.   As a rule they ate and slept
in a murky, stuffy atmosphere, badly lighted by candles
in heavy horn lanthorns.   The gloom of the ships must
have weighed heavily upon many of the men, and the
depression no doubt predisposed them to scurvy, making
them less attentive to bodily cleanliness, and less ready to
combat the disease when it attacked them.   Perhaps some
early sea-captains tried to make the between decks less
gloomy by whitewashing the beams, bulkheads and ship's
sides.   In the eighteenth century this seems to have been
practised with success, though perhaps the captains who
tried it were more careful of their hands in other ways, and
the benefit may have been derived from other causes.

Discipline was maintained by some harsh punishments,
designed to "tame the most rude and savage people in
the world."   Punishment was inflicted at the discretion

of the captain, directly after the hearing of the case, but the case was generally tried the day after the commission of the offence, so that no man should be condemned in hot blood. The most common punishment was that of flogging, the men being stripped to the waist, tied to the main-mast or to a capstan bar, and flogged upon the bare back with a whip or a "cherriliccum." The boatswain had power to beat the laggards and the ship's boys with a cane, or with a piece of knotted rope. A common punishment was to put the offender on half his allowance, or to stop his meat, or his allowance of wine or spirits. For more heinous offences there was the very barbarous punishment of keel-hauling, by which the victim was dragged from the main yardarm right under the keel of the ship, across the barnacles, to the yard-arm on the farther side. Those who suffered this punishment were liable to be cut very shrewdly by the points of the encrusted shells. Ducking from the main yardarm was inflicted for stubbornness, laziness, going on shore without leave, or sleeping while on watch. The malefactor was brought to the gangway, and a rope fastened under his arms and about his middle. He was then hoisted rapidly up to the main yardarm, "from whence he is violently let fall into the Sea, some times twice, some times three severall times, one after another" (*Boteler*). This punishment, and keel-hauling, were made more terrible by the discharge of a great gun over the malefactor's head as he struck the water, "which proveth much offensive to him" (*ibid.*). If a man killed another he was fastened to the corpse and flung overboard (*Laws of Oleron*). For drawing a weapon in a quarrel, or in mutiny, the offender lost his right hand (*ibid.*). Theft was generally punished with flogging, but in serious cases the thief was forced to run the gauntlet, between two rows of sailors all armed with thin knotted cords. Ducking from the bowsprit end, towing in a rope astern, and marooning, were also practised as punishments for the pilferer. For sleeping on watch there was a graduated scale. First offenders were soused with a bucket of water. For the second offence they were tied up by the wrists, and water was poured down their sleeves. For the third offence they were tied to the mast, with bags of bullets, or gun-chambers tied about their arms and necks, until they were exhausted, or "till their back be ready to break" (*Monson*). If they still offended in this kind they were taken and tied to the bowsprit end, with rations of beer and bread, and left there with leave to starve or fall into the sea. Destruction or theft of ships' property was punished by death. Petty insurrections, such as complaints of the quality or quantity of the food, etc., were punished by the bilboes. The bilboes were iron bars fixed to the deck a little abaft the main-mast. The prisoner sat upon the deck under a sentry, and his legs and hands were shackled to the bars with irons of a weight proportioned to the crime. It was a rule that none should speak to a man in the bilboes. For blasphemy and swearing there was "an excellent good way"[1] of forcing the sinner to hold a marline-spike in his mouth, until his tongue was bloody (*Teonge*). Dirty speech was punished in a similar way, and sometimes the offending tongue was scrubbed with sand and canvas. We read of two sailors who stole a piece of beef aboard H.M.S. *Assistance* in the year 1676.[2] Their hands were tied behind them, and the beef was hung about their necks, "and the rest of the seamen cam one by one, and rubd them over the mouth with the raw beife; and in this posture they stood two howers." Other punishments were "shooting to death," and hanging at the yardarm.

[1] *Circa* 1670.
[2] The punishment would have been no less severe a century earlier.

" And the Knaveries of the Ship-boys are payd by the
Boat-Swain with the Rod; and commonly this execution
is done upon the Munday Mornings ; and is so frequently
in use, that some meer Seamen believe in earnest, that
they shall not have a fair Wind, unless the poor Boys
be duely brought to the Chest, that is, whipped, every
Munday Morning " (*Boteler*).

Some of these punishments may appear unduly harsh ;
but on the whole they were no more cruel than the
punishments usually inflicted ashore. Indeed, if anything they were rather more merciful.

CHAPTER XX

IN ACTION

IN engaging an enemy's ship at sea the custom was to display the colours from the poop, and to hang streamers or pennons from the yardarms.[1] The spritsail would then be furled, and the spritsail-yard brought alongship. The lower yards were slung with chain, and the important ropes, sheets and braces,[2] etc., were doubled. The bulkheads and wooden cabin walls were knocked away, or fortified with hammocks or bedding, to minimise the risk of splinters. The guns were cast loose and loaded. The powder or cartridge was brought up in "budge barrels," covered with leather, from the magazine, and stowed well away from the guns, either in amidships, or on that side of the ship not directly engaged. Tubs of water were placed between the guns with blankets soaking in them for the smothering of any fire that might be caused. Other tubs were filled with "vinegar water or what we have" for the sponging of the guns. The hatches leading to the hold were taken up, so that no man should desert his post during the engagement. The light sails were furled, and in some cases sent down on deck. The magazines were opened, and hung about with wet blankets to prevent sparks from entering. Shot was sent to the shot-lockers on deck. Sand was sprinkled on the planking to give a greater firmness to the foothold of the men at the guns. The gunner and his mates went round the batteries to make sure that all was ready. The caps, or leaden plates,

---

[1] Monson.   [2] *Ibid.*

were taken from the touch-holes, and the priming powder was poured down upon the cartridge within the gun. The carpenter made ready sheets of lead, and plugs of oakum, for the stopping of shot-holes.[1] The cook-room fire was extinguished. The sails were splashed with a solution of alum. The people went to eat and drink at their quarters. Extra tiller ropes, of raw hide, were rove abaft. The trumpeters put on their[2] tabards, "of the Admiral's colours," and blew points of war as they sailed into action. A writer of the early seventeenth century[3] has left the following spirited account of a sea-fight:—

"A sail, how bears she or stands shee, to winde-ward or lee-ward? set him by the Compasse; he stands right ahead, or on the weather-Bowe, or lee-Bowe, let fly your colours if you have a consort, else not. Out with all your sails, a steady man to the helme, sit close to keep her steady, give him chase or fetch him up; he holds his own, no, we gather on him. Captain, out goes his flag and pendants, also his waste-clothes and top-armings, which is a long red cloth about three quarters of a yard broad, edged on each side with Calico, or white linnen cloth, that goeth round about the ship on the outsides of all her upper works fore and aft, and before the cubbridge-heads, also about the fore and maine tops, as well for the countenance and grace of the ship, as to cover the men for being seen, he furles and slinges his maine yarde, in goes his spret-saile. Thus they use to strip themselves into their short sailes, or fighting sailes, which is only the fore sail, the main and fore topsails, because the rest should notb e fired nor spoiled; besides they would be troublesome to handle, hinder our fights and the using our armes; he makes ready his close fights fore and aft.

"Master, how stands the chase? Right on head I say;

---

[1] Monson.   [2] *Ibid.*   [3] Captain John Smith.

Well we shall reatch him by and by; what's all ready?
Yea, yea, every man to his charge, dowse your topsaile to
salute him for the Sea, hale him with a noise of trumpets;
Whence is your ship? Of Spaine; Whence is yours? Of
England. Are you a Merchant, or a Man of War? We
are of the Sea. He waves us to Lee-ward with his drawne
Sword, cals amaine for the King of Spaine and springs
his loufe. Give him a chase piece with your broadside,
and run a good berth ahead of him; Done, done. We
have the winde of him, and he tackes about, tacke you
aboute also and keep your loufe [keep close to the wind]
be yare at the helme, edge in with him, give him a volley
of small shot, also your prow and broadside as before, and
keep your loufe; He payes us shot for shot; Well, we
shall requite him; What, are you ready again? Yea, yea.
Try him once more, as before; Done, Done; Keep your
loufe and charge your ordnance again; Is all ready?
Yea, yea, edge in with him again, begin with your bowe
pieces, proceed with your broadside, and let her fall off
with the winde, to give her also your full chase, your
weather broadside, and bring her round that the stern
may also discharge, and your tackes close aboord again;
Done, done, the wind veeres, the Sea goes too high to
boord her, and we are shot thorow and thorow, and
betwene winde and water. Try the pump, bear up the
helme; Master let us breathe and refresh a little, and
sling a man overboard [*i.e.* lower a man over the side] to
stop the leakes; that is, to trusse him up aboute the
middle in a piece of canvas, and a rope to keep him from
sinking, and his armes at liberty, with a malet in the one
hand, and a plug lapped in Okum, and well tarred in a
tarpawling clowt in the other, which he will quickly beat
into the hole or holes the bullets made; What cheere
mates? is all well? All well, all well, all well. Then
make ready to bear up with him again, and with all your

great and small shot charge him, and in the smoke boord him thwart the hawse, on the bowe, midships, or rather than faile, on the quarter [where the high poop made it difficult to climb on board] or make fast your graplings [iron hooks] if you can to his close fights and shear off [so as to tear them to pieces]. Captain, we are fowl on each other, and the Ship is on fire, cut anything to get clear and smother the fire with wet clothes. In such a case they will presently be such friends, as to helpe one the other all they can to get clear, lest they should both burn together and sink ; and if they be generous, the fire quenched, drink kindely one to another ; heave their cans overboord, and then begin again as before.

"Well, Master, the day is spent, the night drawes on, let us consult. Chirurgion, look to the wounded, and winde up the slain, with each a weight or bullet at their heades and feet to make them sinke, and give them three Gunnes for their funerals. Swabber, make clean the ship [sprinkle it with hot vinegar to avoid the smell of blood]; Purser, record their Names ; Watch, be vigilant to keep your berth to windeward that we lose him not in the night; Gunners, spunge your Ordnance ; Sowldiers, scowre your pieces ; Carpenters about your leakes ; Boatswaine and the rest repair your sails and shrouds ; and Cooke, you observe your directions against the morning watch ; Boy, Holla, Master, Holla, is the Kettle boiled ? Yea, yea ; Boat-swaine, call up the men to prayer and breakfast [We may suppose the dawn has broken].

"Boy, fetch my cellar of bottels [case of spirits], a health to you all fore and aft, courage my hearts for a fresh charge ; Gunners beat open the ports, and out with your lower tire [lower tier of guns] and bring me from the weather side to the lee, so many pieces as we have ports to bear upon him. Master lay him aboord loufe for loufe ; mid Ships men, see the tops and yards well manned, with stones, fire pots and brass bailes, to throw amongst them before we enter, or if we be put off, charge them with all your great and small shot, in the smoke let us enter them in the shrouds, and every squadron at his best advantage; so sound Drums and Trumpets, and Saint George for England.

"They hang out a flag of truce, hale him a main, abase, or take in his flag [to hale one to amaine, a main or a-mayn, was to bid him surrender; to abase was to lower the colours or the topsails], strike their sails, and come aboord with their Captaine, Purser, and Gunner, with their commission, cocket, or bills of loading. Out goes the boat, they are launched from the ship's side, entertaine them with a generall cry God save the Captain and all the company with the Trumpets sounding, examine them in particular, and then conclude your conditions, with feasting, freedom or punishment as you find occasion; but alwayes have as much care to their wounded as your own, and if there be either young women or aged men, use them nobly, which is ever the nature of a generous disposition. To conclude, if you surprise him, or enter perforce, you may stow the men, rifle, pillage, or sack, and cry a prise."

Down below in the gun-decks during an action, the batteries became so full of the smoke of black powder that the men could hardly see what they were doing. The darkness prevented them from seeing the very dangerous recoiling of the guns, and many were killed by them. It was impossible to judge how a gun carriage would recoil, for it never recoiled twice in the same manner, and though the men at the side tackles did their best to reduce the shock they could not prevent it altogether. It was the custom to close the gun-ports after each discharge, as the musketeers aboard the enemy could otherwise fire through them as the men reloaded. The guns were not fired in a volley, as no ship could have stood the tremendous shock occasioned by the simultaneous discharge of all her guns. They were fired in succession, beginning from the bows. In heavy weather the lower tiers of guns were not cast loose, for the rolling made them difficult to control, and the sea came washing through the ports and into the muzzles of the guns, knocking down the men and drenching the powder. It sometimes happened that the shot, and cartridge, were rolled clean out of the guns. In sponging and ramming the men were bidden to keep the sponge or rammer on that side of them opposite to the side exposed to the enemy so that if a shot should strike it, it would not force it into the body of the holder. A man was told off to bring cartridges and shot to each gun or division of guns and he was strictly forbidden to supply any other gun or guns during the action. The wounded were to be helped below by men told off especially for the purpose. Once below, in the cockpit, they were laid on a sail, and the doctor or his mates attended to them in turn. In no case was a man attended out of his turn. This system seems equitable, and the sailors were insistent that it should be observed ; but many poor fellows bled to death, from shattered arteries, etc., while waiting till the doctor should be ready. The chaplain attended in the cockpit to comfort the dying, and administer the rites of the Church. When a vessel was taken, her crew were stripped by those in want of clothes. The prisoners were handcuffed, or chained together, and placed in the hold, on the ballast. The ship's company then set to work to repair damages, clean and secure the guns, return powder, etc., to the armoury, and magazines, and to give thanks for their preservation round the main-mast.

INDEX

VI Zachy

1 S Juan de Porto Rico

Cabo del Enganõ

I Turtuga

t Eyland Tur
int Groot

E   S

Calie de Samana

Schotse Bay

Porto Plata

I Belle

ff de la 3

Islas Turques

Auaune

Pas kaart
Van de Noord Kust van
ESPANIOLA
met d Eylanden daar Beneorden.
Door Vooght Geometra
t AMSTERDAM by
JOHANNES VAN KEULEN
Boek en Zee Kaart verkoper aande Niewe-brugh
Inde Gekroonde Loptman
Met Privilegie voor 15 Iaren

Duytsche Mylen 15 in een Graadt

Spaanische Mylen 17 1/2 in een Graadt

Chart of the West Indies. Van Keulen's : The Gre